LEAVING CERTIFIC

Geography Revision

Patrick O'Dwyer

Gill & Macmillan

Gill & Macmillan

Hume Avenue

Park West

Dublin 12

with associated companies throughout the world

www.gillmacmillan.ie

978 07171 4683 3

Design by Liz White Designs

Artwork and print origination by MPS Limited, a Macmillan Company

Maps and photographs reproduced by kind permission of Ordnance Survey Ireland. © Ordnance Survey Ireland and Government of Ireland.

The paper used in this book is made from the wood pulp of managed forests. For every tree felled, at least one tree is planted, thereby renewing natural resources.

For permission to reproduce photographs, the author and publisher gratefully acknowledge the following:

© Alamy: 8, 21, 29, 34, 39T, 62, 96, 100, 108, 111, 125, 147, 152, 161, 182, 197, 204, 206T, 206B, 207, 210B, 211, 221, 224, 226, 243, 247, 266, 274, 282, 283T, 283B, 284T, 284B, 295; © Collins: 202; © Corbis: 24, 288; © Getty Images: 14, 59, 103, 106, 118, 129, 130, 134, 138, 141, 175, 186, 233, 236, 293; © Imagefile: 39B, 210T; © Inpho: 286; © Kevin Dwyer: 72, 73; © Ordnance Survey: 71T, 71B; © Peter Barrow: 185; © Photocall Ireland!: 165; Courtesy of Pfizer: 170.

The authors and publisher have made every effort to trace all copyright holders, but if any has been inadvertently overlooked we would be pleased to make the necessary arrangement at the first opportunity.

CONTENTS

Introduction..v

Exam breakdown v

The Geography exam booklet vi

What are SRPs? vii

Structure of the exam paper and questions vii

Preparing for the exam vii

What to do in the exam vii

SECTION 1: Core Units..1

Core Unit 1: Patterns and Processes in the Physical Environment..2

1. The Tectonic Cycle 2

2. The Rock Cycle 16

3. Weathering Processes 23

4. Landforms Influenced by the Tectonic Cycle 26

5. Landforms Influenced by Rock Type.......................................34

6. Landforms Influenced by Surface Processes..........................41

7. People's Interaction with Surface Processes...........................59

8. The Process of Isostasy, Adjustment to Base Level and Landforms...64

9. Ordnance Survey Maps, Photographs, Graphs and Charts 67

Core Unit 2: Regional Geography 91

10. Types and Definitions of Regions...91

11. The Dynamics of Regions: Contrasting Regions in Ireland and Europe 97

12. The Dynamics of Regions: A Subcontinental Region (India or the American Southwest) 121

13. The Complexity of Regions 1...139

14. The Complexity of Regions 2...147

**SECTION 2: Electives (Choose *either* Elective 1
or Elective 2)**...**155**

Elective 1: Patterns and Processes in Economic Activities **156**

15. Patterns in Economic Development 156
16. Changing Patterns in Economic Development 159
17. Globalisation 164
18. Ireland and the European Union 173
19. The Environmental Impact of Economic Development 179

Or

**Elective 2: Patterns and Processes in the Human
Environment** **191**

20. Population 191
21. Overpopulation 197
22. Migration 200
23. Settlement 208
24. Land Use 216
25. Urban Problems 221

**SECTION 3: Options (HIGHER LEVEL STUDENTS ONLY)
Choose ONE option only** **227**

Option 1: Global Interdependence **228**

26. Models of Development 229
27. The Impact of the Global Economy 232
28. Linking Economic Growth with Human Development 240
29. Sustainable Development – The Way Forward 250

Option 2: Geoecology **255**

30. The Development of Soils 256
31. Factors that Affect Soil Characteristics 260
32. Biomes 270
33. How People's Activities have Altered Biomes 278

Option 3: Culture and Identity **280**

34. Populations: Physical and Cultural Factors 281
35. Language and Religion as Cultural Indicators 290
36. Nationality and Nation States 296

Introduction

The purpose of this book is to help you recall the key points from your class textbook on the main areas of the course and to offer you some sample answers that are focused on the exam marking scheme. Practical skills, such as exam tips, key points and map work are also covered to maximise your choices and improve your performance in the examination.

There are some choices of topics: these are marked 'OR' to suit the main textbooks used in different schools.

 Note: Material that is to be studied only by those taking Higher level is indicated in the text.

Exam breakdown

CORE
ALL STUDENTS MUST COVER
Core Units 1 and 2 (pages 1–154)

ELECTIVES
ALL STUDENTS MUST COVER *ONE ELECTIVE*
Either
Elective 1: Chapters 15–19 inclusive (pages 156–190)
Or
Elective 2: Chapters 20–25 (pages 191–226)

OPTIONS
HIGHER LEVEL STUDENTS ONLY
must cover *one* option
Either
Option 1: Chapters 26–29 (pages 228–254)
Or
Option 2: Chapters 30–33 (pages 255–279)
Or
Option 3: Chapters 34–36 (pages 280–300)

The Geography exam booklet

All students must do the short-answer questions.

 Higher level students must do **four** other questions:

- one multi-part question from Physical Geography
- one multi-part question from Regional Geography
- one multi-part Elective question
- one Option question.

Each question is worth 80 marks.

Ordinary level students must do **three** other questions:

- one multi-part question from Physical Geography
- one multi-part question from Regional Geography
- one multi-part Elective question.

Each question is worth 100 marks.

Allow 10 minutes to read the paper carefully and another 10 minutes at the end to check over your script. This will give higher level students **30 minutes** for each full question and ordinary level students **40 minutes** for each full question. Careful timing of your answers during the exam will help you gain maximum marks.

Structure of core and elective questions

These are all multi-part questions and they all have **three parts**.

- Part A is a skills-based question, e.g. sketch maps, map-reading, charts, skills.
- Parts B and C test syllabus-based material and skills.

Ordinary level marks are generally:

Part A – 30 marks

Part B – 40 marks

Part C – 30 marks.

Give *at least* 8 significant relevant points (SRPs) for parts B and C and name examples.

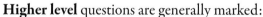 **Higher level** questions are generally marked:

- Part A – 20 marks
- Part B – 30 marks
- Part C – 30 marks.

Think in terms of 12 to 15 SRPs for parts B and C.

For both ordinary and higher level, write your SRPs in paragraph format. Bullet points may lose you marks for lack of cohesion.

The **Option answer** must be in **essay format**. You should divide this answer into sections using **three or four headings**. For each heading write a well-developed paragraph (*not* bullet points) that has at least eight SRPs. Cohesion is vital. Focus on your headings and stay with the topic.

What are SRPs?

SRPs are **significant relevant points**. They are statements of factual information. **Each SRP is worth 2 marks.**

An SRP may be:

- A fully explained statement or short paragraph.
- A statistic with some associated explanation.
- A relevant diagram or chart.
- Extra labels on the diagram that are not already mentioned in your answer.
- A full explanation of a geographical term.

Structure of the exam paper and questions

All students must do the following:

Question Structure	Marks	Timing for Higher Level
12 short-answer questions on Core Units 1, 2 and Elective (only 10 required). Do all 12 questions.	Higher level: 80 marks Ordinary level: 100 marks	30 minutes – 12 × 2.5 minutes 40 minutes – 12 × 3.25 minutes
One question from **each** of the following multi-part questions: • Core 1 **Physical** Section • Core 2 **Regional** Section • **Elective** Section	Higher level: 3 × 80 = 240 marks Ordinary level: 3 × 100 = 300 marks	3 × 30 minutes, each 30 minutes divided into 6 + 12 + 12 minutes (for a 30-mark question) or 16 minutes (for a 40-mark question)
Option section Do **ONE** question from **ONE** of the following: • Global Interdependence • Geoecology • Culture and Identity	80 marks	30 minutes

Higher level students do one **additional** Option question.

Preparing for the exam

- Make sure you have all your equipment with you: pens, pencils, rubber, ruler, etc.
- Get to bed early and get up early.
- Have a good healthy breakfast.

What to do in the exam

1. **Carefully** read each question.
2. **Make sure** you can attempt **all** parts of the questions you have chosen to do. Don't rush in only to find you can do only two parts.
3. Watch the **timing** for each answer.

4. Don't waste time using lots of colour in sketch maps. Colour is helpful but not essential.

5. **Make notes** on the paper near the question to structure your answer and recall key words.

6. Write notes on the topics you have chosen as soon as you think of them. It's so easy to forget things under pressure in the exam.

7. Spend only a limited time on sketch maps. Write/mark **only** what is asked of you. Get the shape of the sketch map correct.

8. Do the Option question/question you know best first.

SECTION 1
Core Units

CORE UNIT 1
Patterns and Processes
in the Physical Environment

CORE UNIT 2
Regional Geography

All students must study
both of these units (pages 1–154).

1 The Tectonic Cycle

aims You need to know about:
- the structure of the earth
- plate tectonics (in detail).

key point

The earth is made up of layers: the **crust**, the **mantle** and the **core**.

The crust is broken into **plates**. These plates move. They **separate**, **collide** and **slide past** each other.

The plates are carried about by **convection currents** in the mantle.

The crust

The crust is composed of the continents, the ocean floors and the rigid upper mantle. This is called the **lithosphere** and all its rocks are solid.

The continents are formed mostly of light, granite-like rocks. They are 45 km thick on average, and up to 70 km thick under the mountain ranges.

The ocean floors are formed mostly of **basalt**, which is heavy. They have an average thickness of 8 km, but may be as thin as 3 km in places.

The mantle

- The **upper mantle** is solid rock.
- The **middle and lower mantle** consists of plastic-like rock that moves to form convection currents. The plates of the lithosphere move about on these slow-moving currents. The rock in the lower mantle is in a semi-liquid state because its temperature is very high.

key point

The lithosphere is formed of the crust and upper mantle.

The core

The core is made up of **nickel and iron**. It is the hottest part of the earth: temperatures are greater than 4000°C.

Crust
- earth's outer skin
- consists of solid rock
- about 45–70 km thick under the continents
- only about 3–20 km thick under the oceans

Outer Core
- liquid, or molten, state
- consists mainly of iron

Inner core
- extremely hot
- solid
- consists of iron and nickel
- temperatures > 4000°C

Mantle
- consists of rock in a molten or semi-molten state
- this moves in convection currents that carry the plates

A section through the earth

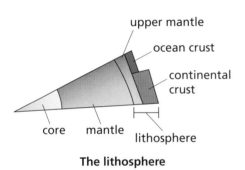

upper mantle
ocean crust
continental crust
core   mantle   lithosphere

The lithosphere

key point

- Forces within the earth are called **endogenic forces**. *Examples:* convection currents, subducting plates.
- They create, change and destroy landforms on and within the earth's surface.

WHAT WAS PANGAEA?
- All continents were joined together to form a single continent called Pangaea.
- It was surrounded by a single ocean called **Panthalassa**.

Proofs of seafloor spreading

- Mid-ocean ridges form at the boundaries of construction.
- New rock forms at mid-ocean ridges.
- The oldest rock is closest to the continents.

exam focus

Make sure you know these basic facts about plate tectonics theory.

Proofs of continental drift

- Matching rocks found on continents that are thousands of miles apart.
- Matching fossils found in precise locations where the continents were once joined together.
- Edges of continents along the continental shelves fit together like a jigsaw.

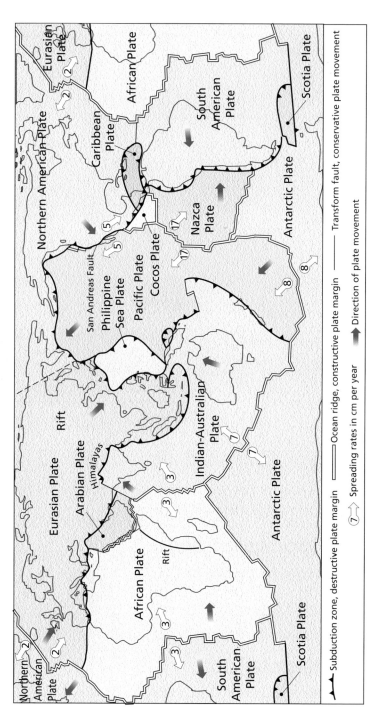

Plates of the earth's crust

Subduction zone, destructive plate margin —— Ocean ridge, constructive plate margin —— Transform fault, conservative plate movement

Spreading rates in cm per year ➡ Direction of plate movement

Plate boundaries

There are three types of plate boundary: **divergent or constructive, convergent or destructive** and **transform or passive**.

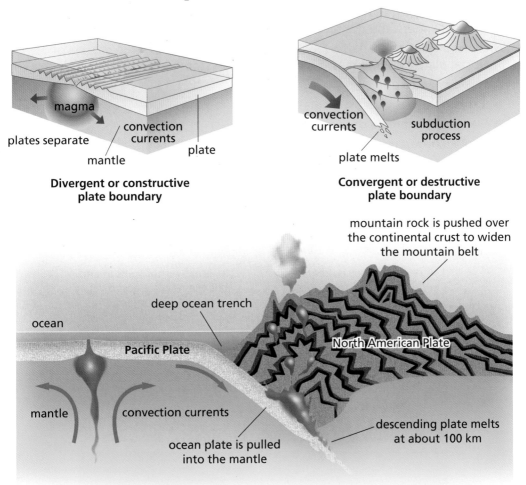

Divergent or constructive plate boundary

Convergent or destructive plate boundary

Convergent or destructive plate boundary

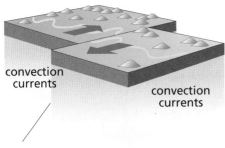

plates slide past each other along the transform fault

Transform or passive plate boundary

SAMPLE EXAM QUESTIONS

A similar answer may be given to many different questions on plate tectonics.

Questions:

1. Explain, with reference to examples you have studied, how plate tectonics helps us understand the forces at work along crustal plate boundaries.   (2009)
2. Explain – with the aid of a labelled diagram or diagrams – the process of crustal plate movement as it is currently understood.   (2006 sample paper)

What you need to do:

- Explain the basic theory of plate tectonics.
- Name one example of each boundary.
- Explain how crust is created at boundaries of construction.
- Explain how crust is destroyed at boundaries of destruction.
- Draw a diagram or diagrams.
- Write (in paragraphs) at least 12 to 15 SRPs in total.

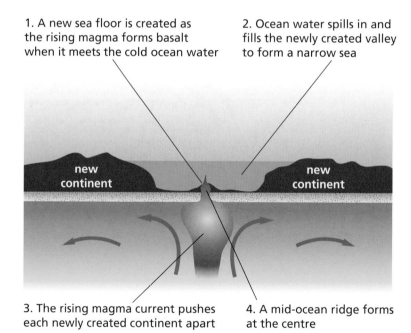

1. A new sea floor is created as the rising magma forms basalt when it meets the cold ocean water

2. Ocean water spills in and fills the newly created valley to form a narrow sea

new continent

new continent

3. The rising magma current pushes each newly created continent apart

4. A mid-ocean ridge forms at the centre

A mid-ocean ridge is a boundary of construction associated with seafloor spreading

Plate tectonics states that the earth's crust is divided into plates and these plates move, driven by convection currents of semi-molten rock within the mantle.

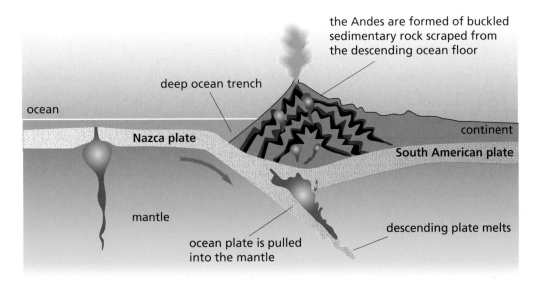

the Andes are formed of buckled sedimentary rock scraped from the descending ocean floor

deep ocean trench

ocean

Nazca plate

continent

South American plate

mantle

ocean plate is pulled into the mantle

descending plate melts

Subduction – a boundary of destruction associated with *continental drift*

These currents carry the plates of the earth's crust in a **piggy-back motion**.

At divergent or constructive boundaries the plates move apart and at convergent or destructive boundaries the plates collide.

Seafloor spreading

- The **rifting** of a continent occurs when a continent is pulled apart and new narrow seas form. *Example:* the **Red Sea**.
- These new seafloors become boundaries of construction along their centres.
- New rock is formed from magma where the plates separate.
- It cools instantly on contact with the cold seawater and forms basalt rock. This widens the sea.
- The new rock is carried away from the ridge by **convection currents**. **Transform boundaries or faults** help this sideways movement to fit the shape of the earth.

key point

This answer also explains how fold mountains form.

Continental drift

- Continents are pushed across the globe by expanding ocean floors and convection currents to locations where they collide with other continents. *Example:* along the **Peru Trench**.
- These form **boundaries of destruction** where ocean floors, such as the **Nazca plate**, are sucked into the mantle and are destroyed by the process of subduction.

exam focus

You can refer to the causes of earthquakes at plate boundaries (see page 13) to extend an answer on continental drift.

- As the ocean plates sink into the mantle they heat up and eventually **melt at a depth of 100 km** to form magma.
- The sinking plates are **saturated with seawater**, which helps melt the rock.
- Sediments on the ocean floor are **scraped off** the descending plate and are crushed and buckled upwards against the continent to form **fold mountains** of sedimentary rock. *Example:* the **Andes**.
- The **magma** from the melted plates **rises up through the folded rock** to create batholiths and volcanoes. *Example:* **Cotopaxi**.
- The **batholiths** form **granite rock** within mountains and the volcanoes form basalt and lava at the surface.

Summary: Plate Boundaries

Type	Example	Process
Divergent or Constructive	Mid-Atlantic Ridge	• Separation • American and Eurasian plates move apart • New rock formed
Convergent or Destructive	Nazca/South American plates	• Collision • Fold mountains formed • Volcanoes, earthquakes
Transform or Passive	Pacific/North American plates	• Sliding past each other • Earthquakes along the San Andreas Fault in California

Volcanoes

key point

Most volcanoes occur at subduction zones where plates collide.

Some volcanoes also occur at hot spots.

Volcanoes at hot spots throw pyroclasts into the air

The best way to revise volcanoes is by using past questions and sample answers.

SAMPLE EXAM QUESTION AND ANSWER

Question: Discuss how plate tectonics has increased our understanding of the global distribution of volcanoes. (2008; 30 marks)

Note: draw a **simple** diagram or diagrams with a few label sentences/SRPs.

Marking scheme:

- Two global examples – 2 marks each.
- Plate tectonics examined – 13 SRPs @ 2 marks each.

Answer: Most volcanoes form at boundaries of destruction.

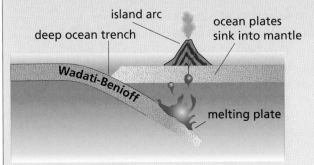

island arc

deep ocean trench

ocean plates sink into mantle

Wadati-Benioff

melting plate

Ocean–ocean boundary: Western Pacific

You should:

- write at least 15 SRPs (2 marks each)
- name two plates that collide to cause subduction
- name a volcano.

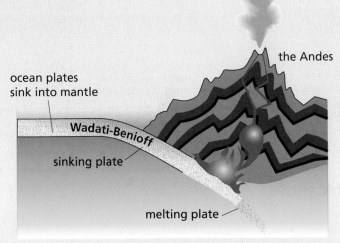

the Andes

ocean plates sink into mantle

Wadati-Benioff

sinking plate

melting plate

Ocean–continent boundary: Eastern Pacific

- The earth's crust is divided into plates and these plates move due to seafloor spreading and continental drift.
- Convection currents carry the plates of the earth's crust in a piggy-back motion.
- The plates collide at boundaries of collision or destruction.
- **Most volcanoes form at two types of destructive plate boundaries: (a) where an ocean plate collides with a continental plate; and (b) where two ocean plates collide.**
- As plates approach each other, the intervening ocean floor plate is subducted into the mantle. As it descends, it melts at a depth of about 100 km.
- The continental plate scrapes layers of sediment from the descending ocean floor and they are forced upwards, buckled and compressed into fold mountains.
- The melting descending plate creates magma that rises through the folded rock above.
- Small amounts of this magma rise and collect into huge masses of magma called batholiths.
- These batholiths are the source of magma, which creates volcanoes at the surface in fold mountains such as Cotopaxi in the Andes.
- Most volcanoes are located around the western edge of the Pacific Ocean where ocean plates collide. They form part of the Pacific Ring of Fire.
- The sinking plates melt forming magma.
- Eventually, the compressed gases and liquid magma are blasted through the ocean floor and build up volcanic cones, such as those in the Philippines and Japan.

Some volcanoes occur at **hot spots**. These are areas where large batholiths are close to the surface at locations away from plate boundaries. *Examples:* Yellowstone National Park, USA.

A question on hot spots may appear in short-answer questions.

- **Black smokers are chimney-like openings at mid-ocean ridges.**
- **Very hot water containing dissolved minerals gushes from these openings.**
- **Hot spots are localised areas of volcanic activity that may be far from plate boundaries.**

Effects of volcanoes

Positive

- Lava soils are rich in iron, which is good for coffee production.
- Geothermal energy can be generated from hot rock and geysers.

- Mineral ores and veins are important resources.
- New land is created on volcanic islands.
- Tourists visit volcanic regions. *Examples:* Iceland; Mount Etna, Sicily.

Negative

- People can be killed by **nuées ardentes** (clouds of poisonous gases and ash).
- Lava flows destroy houses and towns.
- Eruptions force people to evacuate their homes.

Earthquakes

- Earthquakes usually occur at plate boundaries as a result of plate tectonic processes.
- There are three types of earthquake: shallow-focus, intermediate-focus and deep-focus.
- Some earthquakes, like those in Ireland, occur on old faultlines.

Causes of earthquakes

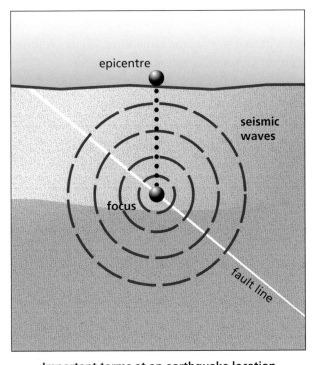

epicentre

seismic waves

focus

fault line

Important terms at an earthquake location

Make sure you know: where and why earthquakes occur; the damage they cause; how they are detected.

Tectonic plates

Strain builds up in tectonic plates as they get stuck when they try to move past, apart or under each other. This strain suddenly releases and readjusts itself. This readjustment is felt on the surface as an earthquake.

The Ice Age

Thousands of metres of ice pressed down the land surface. When the ice sheets melted at the end of the Ice Age, the land gradually bounced back to its original level. This change still causes earthquakes from time to time.

Ancient faults

Plates move along ancient faults that lie buried deep beneath the earth's surface.

Rising magma

Magma rushes towards the surface through the vent pipe just before a volcanic eruption. This movement creates numerous small earthquakes.

The measurement and effects of earthquakes

- A **seismologist** is a person who studies earthquakes.
- A **seismograph** is an instrument that records and measures earthquakes.
- The **focus** is the spot at the origin of an earthquake.
- The **epicentre** is a spot on the earth's surface directly above the focus.
- **Seismic waves** radiate from the epicentre.
- There are two types of seismic (earthquake) waves: **body waves** and **surface waves**.
- Surface waves make the ground move in two ways at the same time: (a) in a rolling motion like waves on the sea; and (b) in a snake-like sideways movement.
- Buildings roll and twist at the same time.
- The **Richter scale** indicates the size or magnitude of an earthquake.
- An earthquake measuring 7 on the Richter scale is ten times more powerful than one measuring 6 and 100 times more powerful than one measuring 5.
- The **Mercalli scale** measures earthquake damage on a 12-point scale: 1 = no damage; 12 = total destruction.

SAMPLE QUESTION AND ANSWER

Question: Discuss how plate tectonics has increased our understanding of the global distribution of earthquakes.

Answer:
Most earthquakes occur along major plate boundaries (faultlines).

exam focus

- For every 30-mark question, write at least 15 SRPs @ 2 marks each.
- Draw a simple diagram with a couple of labels as SRPs.
- Give examples.

- Earthquakes occur along all major plate boundaries: these boundaries are called faultlines. Most earthquakes occur along the Pacific Ring of Fire around the Pacific Ocean.

- As the plates collide, the heavier ocean plate **subducts** beneath the lighter continental plate.

- All earthquakes at these boundaries of destruction occur along the line of the descending plate. This is called the **Wadati-Benioff Zone**.

Draw this diagram

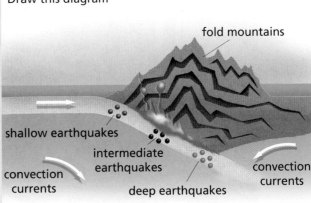

Earthquakes occur along the Wadati-Benioff Zone

- Three categories of earthquake occur along this zone: **shallow-focus** **earthquakes**; **intermediate earthquakes**; and **deep earthquakes**.
  - **Shallow-focus earthquakes** occur near the surface.
  - **Intermediate earthquakes** occur where the descending plate melts to form magma.
  - **Deep earthquakes** occur when chemical and mineral changes occur within the rocks of the descending plate.

- Plate edges at all boundaries tend to grind against each other as they slide past. Sometimes the plates get jammed, for example along the **San Andreas Fault** in California.

- This causes the rock within the plates to stretch but it will eventually break and the plates snap back to a spot where there is no stress. This process is called 'elastic rebound'.

- This movement releases seismic waves, or shock waves, to radiate through the earth from the focus, so creating an earthquake.

Read more at: http://en.wikipedia.org/wiki/Great_Hanshin_earthquake

Learn some facts about two recent earthquakes in contrasting regions, e.g. Sumatra/Indonesia, Kobe in Japan or Kashmir in Pakistan.

Case study: Indonesian/Sumatra–Andaman earthquake (2004)

Tsunamis are caused by earthquakes on the ocean floor

Cause

- The 2004 Indian Ocean earthquake was an undersea megathrust earthquake that occurred on 26 December 2004 in the Indian Ocean off the western coast of northern Sumatra.
- It happened at a subduction zone where the Indian plate sinks under the Eurasian plate.
- An estimated 1600 km of the jammed plates/faultline slipped in two stages, each stage causing a continuous slip along the faultline and massive earthquakes at a depth of 30 km beneath the sea bed.
- The largest of these earthquakes or aftershocks measured 9.1 on the Richter scale – the second largest earthquake ever recorded on a seismograph.
- The earthquake was the biggest in the Indian Ocean for 700 years.
- The Indian plate, which is a heavy ocean plate of basalt, dips under the lighter continental Eurasian plate and jams as it sinks into the mantle.
- Stress builds up in the jammed plates until the plate slips or the rock breaks. In this case the rock was strong and great stress had built up in the rocks before they snapped.

- The snapping or release of the stressed plates raised the seafloor several metres, so displacing huge volumes of water and causing massive tsunamis up to 30 metres high in places.

Consequences

- The shift of the crust and the massive release of energy slightly altered the Earth's rotation. This could have some minor effects on climate.
- Giant waves, called **tsunamis**, were created. These devastated the Indian Ocean coastal areas, especially the Indonesian and Thailand coasts.
- More than 230,000 people were killed and over 1 million displaced.
- Coastal villages and towns and some regions, such as Aceh in Sumatra, were completely devastated by the tsunamis.

Read more at: http://en.wikipedia.org/wiki/Indian_Ocean_earthquake

How to reduce the effects of earthquakes

- Enforce strict building regulations in earthquake-prone regions.
- Install earthquake-proof technology in new tall buildings.
- Practise emergency earthquake drills and regional emergency plan procedures.
- Develop tsunami warning stations for all countries throughout the Pacific and Indian Ocean regions.

Predicting volcanic eruptions and earthquakes

- **Scientific instruments** (e.g. strain meters, lasers) are placed in susceptible regions.
- **Seismic gaps** are places that have not had an earthquake for a long time but are bordered by areas of recent earthquake activity. Seismic gaps are the most likely spots for future earthquakes.
- A **dating pattern** of past earthquakes and volcanoes can help to predict the likelihood of new ones.
- Observations of **animal behaviour** – animals are sensitive to tremors.

Plate boundaries:
   Questions 2B, SEC Sample Exam Paper 2006; 2B, 2007; 2B, 2009.
Volcanoes:
Questions 2C, SEC Sample Exam Paper 2006; 3C, 2006; 2B, 2008.

2 The Rock Cycle

 What you need to know:

- Rocks are classified into groups, according to how they were formed. These groups are: **igneous, sedimentary** and **metamorphic.**
- Some are formed, changed and destroyed by forces within the earth (**endogenic** forces).
- Weathering and erosion (**exogenic** forces) destroy rocks, and their sediments form new rock on the surface.
- All these forces create the rock cycle.

- Learn how rocks are formed, modified, destroyed and reformed as part of the rock cycle.
- You should also know about the impact of human interaction with the rock cycle.

The rock cycle

1. The first rocks were igneous rocks, which formed from magma.
2. All rocks are broken down by weathering and erosion.
3. Their sediments are deposited, compressed and hardened to form sedimentary rocks.
4. Some sedimentary, igneous and metamorphic rocks are heated by other hot igneous rocks and changed to new rocks. These new changed rocks are metamorphic rocks.
5. So some metamorphic rocks can be changed to new metamorphic rocks.
6. Igneous rocks can be changed to metamorphic rocks and sedimentary rocks can be changed to metamorphic rocks.
7. Rocks are destroyed and melt to form magma at subduction zones

Write out a detailed account of this rock cycle, starting with igneous rocks. Make sure you have at least 15 SRPs (each worth two marks in the exam).

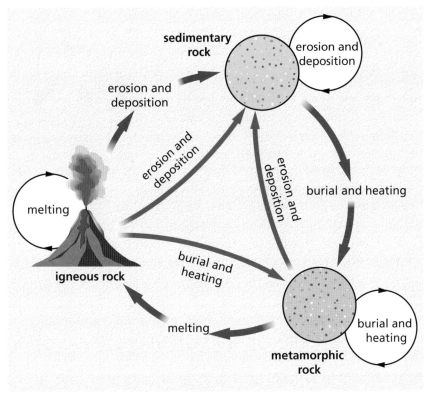

The rock cycle

Types of rock

Igneous rocks

- Igneous rocks form from **magma** when it cools and hardens.
- **Plutonic** rock cools slowly within the earth. *Example:* granite.
- **Volcanic** rock cools on the earth's surface. *Examples:* basalt and lava.

Rock type	Origin	Location
Granite	*Plutonic:* ● Magma in batholiths ● Large crystals	Wicklow Donegal Connemara
Basalt	*Volcanic:* ● Lava cooled quickly ● Tiny crystals	Giant's Causeway, Antrim

SAMPLE EXAM QUESTION AND ANSWER

Question:

Explain how igneous rocks form.

Answer:

- Most igneous rocks form from hot molten magma that comes from the mantle.
- Most magma forms at **subduction zones** when ocean plates sink into the mantle.
- Some magma forms when other igneous, sedimentary or metamorphic rocks melt.

> - Give at least 15 SRPs for a 30-mark question.
> - Use Irish examples.

- This magma rises and gathers in great masses to form **batholiths** within fold mountains. *Example:* Wicklow.
- The magma in batholiths **cools very slowly** and forms granite.
- Granite is a **plutonic** rock because it formed within the earth's crust.
- Granite has **large crystals** – mica, feldspar and quartz.
- Some magma finds its way to the surface through a vent. At the surface this magma is called **lava**.
- Lava cools quickly and forms **small crystals**, so lava is a volcanic rock.
- Some magma is blasted into the air and forms **volcanic ash**.
- The ash and lava form **volcanic cones**.
- Some lumps of magma harden quickly in the air to form **volcanic bombs**.
- Some lava pours out through **fissures** (cracks/tears) onto the surface to form **basalt**. *Example:* Antrim.

Sedimentary rocks

Sedimentary rocks form from cemented deposits of rock particles.

Rock type	Origin	Location
Limestone	Coral and shells in warm tropical seas	● Burren, Co. Clare ● Central Plain
Sandstone	Deposited rock particles, mostly quartz	● Galtees ● All mountains in Munster
Shale	Clay particles	● Wicklow ● South Co. Clare

'Describe how one rock type is formed and how it produces a distinctive landscape' is a question that appears regularly. (See page 35 for how to answer this question using limestone as an example.)

How sedimentary rocks form

SAMPLE EXAM QUESTION AND ANSWER

Question:

Examine, with reference to Ireland, the formation of sedimentary rocks.

(2009; 30 marks)

Marking:

- Name two sedimentary rocks – 2
  + 2 marks.
- Name two associated Irish locations – 2
  + 2 marks.
- Examination: 11 SRPs.

Describe how two sedimentary rocks form and name one Irish location for each.

Answer:

How sandstone formed:

- Sandstone was formed from grains of **quartz**, during the **Devonian period** (400–350 million years ago).
- Ireland was located at **20°S**, about where the **Kalahari Desert** is today.
- The region had occasional heavy downpours that eroded the Caledonian mountains and washed their sand and gravel particles in **flash floods** to lowland areas.
- The sandstone formed from sandy delta deposits, river channel and floodplain deposits, beach sand and sand dunes.
- Large deposits of gravel (stream pebbles) formed **conglomerate** rock.
- Each flood deposit is separated from the next by a hairline crack called a **bedding plane**.
- All these sands and gravels were compressed by overlying layers and were cemented by **iron oxide**.
- The iron oxide turned the sandstones a **red** colour, so all these deposits are called **old red sandstone**.
- The mountains of Munster, e.g. the **Galtees**, are formed of old red sandstone.

How limestone formed:

See page 35.

Metamorphic rock

- Metamorphic rock is formed from other rocks that were heated and changed.
- Heat caused by nearby magma or very hot ground water or both changed some rock to metamorphic rock.

- The closer the rock to the magma, the greater was the change. For example, when shale touched off magma it was turned to schist. With a little distance from the magma the shale changed to slate. With greater distance the shale may have been unchanged.
- If sandstone touched off magma it changed to quartzite.
- If limestone touched off magma it changed to marble.
- Impurities in the limestone created marble of varying colour, e.g. Connemara marble is green.

Rock type	Origin	Location
Marble	Heated limestone	● Connemara ● Kilkenny
Slate	Heated shale	● Wicklow ● Valentia Island
Quartzite	Heated sandstone	● Donegal

North American active and trailing plate margins

- America's west coast is **tectonically active** and has **new igneous rocks.**
- America's east coast is **not tectonically active** and has **new coastal sediments and rock.** This is America's trailing plate margin.

People's interaction with the rock cycle

You need to study **only one** of the following:
- mining
- extraction of building materials (quarrying)
- oil and gas exploration
- geothermal energy.

Extraction of building materials (quarrying)

Irish example: Roadstone quarry, Ballyneety, Co. Limerick.

Quarrying is the process of blasting rock from quarry faces (man-made cliff faces) or excavating it from the ground and preparing it for the construction industry.

**Quarrying is carried out in many locations throughout Ireland.
Roadstone, for example, has many quarries making rock aggregates.**

Sands and gravels
- Excavated from ridges (**eskers**), and other deposits of sands and gravels that were laid down by rivers that flowed at the end of the Ice Age.
- Sand is generally **mixed with cement** to make mortar and concrete.
- Gravel is used as filling in housing, for surfacing paths, and as subsurface material in road construction.

Limestone and sandstone
Parallel lines of holes are drilled along the top of a quarry face. Explosive charges are placed in these drill-holes. Controlled explosions release thousands of tonnes of limestone or sandstone rock that fall to the base of the quarry face. Loads of this shattered rock are removed by dumper truck to crushers. They are then broken down into smaller particles of stone of various sizes called aggregates. The angular nature and hardness of these particles allows them to be used:
- to make concrete and concrete products, such as concrete blocks and roofing tiles
- for road surfacing
- as filling for passages and driveways.
Powdered limestone – lime – is used as a fertiliser.

Gypsum
- Quarried at Kingscourt, Co. Cavan.
- Used to make plaster slabs for house construction.
- Has both insulating and fireproofing characteristics.

Marble

- Quarried in Connemara and Kilkenny.
- In industry, the term *marble* refers to any polished rock.
- Pure marble forms from metamorphosed limestone.
- Also quarried at Carrara, Tuscany. In its purest form it is white. It is used for flooring, wall tiles and fireplaces. Marble from these quarries was used by Renaissance sculptors such as Michelangelo.

The rock cycle:

Questions 1C, 2006; 3C, SEC Sample Exam Paper 2006; 2C, 2007; 2B and 2C, 2009.

3 Weathering Processes

Weathering is the breaking down of rocks that lie on or near the earth's surface. There are two types of weathering: **mechanical** and **chemical**.

Mechanical weathering

Joint formation (jointing)

The removal, by erosion, of surface rock reduces the weight on deeply buried rocks. Joints develop and this breaks rock into large and small rectangular blocks.

Sheeting/exfoliation

Sheeting and exfoliation occur due to stresses and strains that act within rock. Granite was formed deep within fold mountains, under extreme pressure from great forces that squeezed it from all sides. Later, after overlying rock layers and pressures were removed by erosion, the rock expands and the granite batholiths split into onion-like sheets when exposed at the surface. This is called **sheeting** or **exfoliation**.

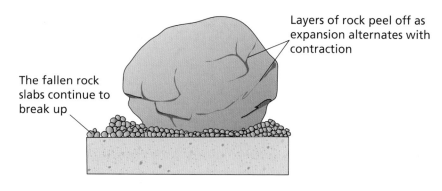

Layers of rock peel off as expansion alternates with contraction

The fallen rock slabs continue to break up

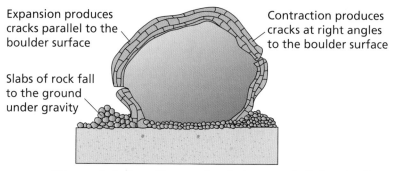

Expansion produces cracks parallel to the boulder surface

Contraction produces cracks at right angles to the boulder surface

Slabs of rock fall to the ground under gravity

When exfoliation affects rocks, their outer shells break off

Exfoliation of granite is also called sheeting

Freeze-thaw

When water freezes in cracks or joints in bedrock it widens the cracks and so helps to break up rock.

Trapped water freezes during winter at night on high mountains

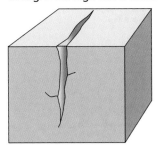

Surface water fills cracks in rocks

Ice expands by about 9 per cent and lengthens joints

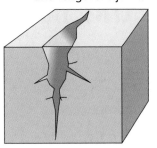

Freeze-thaw action shatters rocks

Plant roots

Plant roots penetrate joints, cracks and crevices, widening them as the roots thicken with age.

Surface flaking

Water soaks into rock in buildings, walls and bedrock. As the rock dries, mineral crystals grow. These mineral crystals push out surface rock grains to cause flaking.

Chemical weathering

Chemical weathering is most active in hot, wet regions. Types of chemical weathering include **carbonation, oxidation, hydration** and **hydrolysis**.

Carbonation

Rainwater is weak carbonic acid. As it trickles through rock joints it changes the limestone to calcium and bicarbonate minerals. These are soluble in water and are washed away in solution. (For more detail on carbonation, see page 35–36.)

Oxidation

This is the rusting of minerals. It is particularly effective in rocks that contain iron. Most iron in rocks is in the form of a bonding/cementing agent. Iron reacts with water to become iron oxide. Because oxides are soluble in water the iron oxide is washed away in solution and the rock crumbles.

Hydration

Some minerals absorb water. This creates stresses in rock and over time the rock shatters.

Hydrolysis

This affects granite. Water bonds with micas and feldspar to form clay minerals. These become oxidised and lose their bonding effect; the remaining minerals are separated and the rock crumbles.

Landforms Influenced by the Tectonic Cycle

> **aims** You need to know about volcanic and plutonic landforms.

Volcanic and plutonic landforms

Rifting and subduction form **volcanic** and **plutonic** landforms.

- **Volcanic landforms** form on the earth's surface. They include volcanic cones, basalt plateaus and fumaroles.
- **Plutonic landforms** form beneath the earth's surface, within the crust. They include batholiths, dykes, sills, laccoliths and lopoliths.

Volcanic landforms

SAMPLE EXAM QUESTION AND ANSWER

Question: Describe the processes that have led to the formation of any two volcanic landforms. (2006; 30 marks)

Answer:

1. Basalt plateau

Irish example – Antrim Plateau.

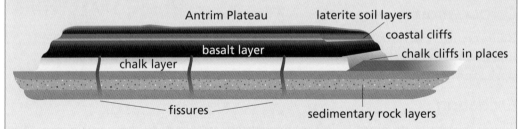

The basalt plateau in Antrim is a volcanic landform

- About 65 million years ago a new hot spot caused **rifting** and the American and Eurasian continents began to split apart.
- The Mid-Atlantic Ridge extended northwards over what is now the Norwegian Sea.
- The crust was stretched and cracks or **fissures** appeared on the surface.
- Hot lava poured out through the these fissures from the batholith underneath. There were many successive lava flows and each flow cooled quickly to form basalt.

- Because the lava flows were 5–40 metres thick, they formed five-sided basalt columns such as those at the **Giant's Causeway**.
- Basalt is a fine-grained volcanic rock with tiny crystals that are not visible to the eye.
- Eventually the basalt layers built up to form a flat-topped plateau.

2. Volcanic cone
Example: Cotopaxi (the Andes) or Mount Etna (Sicily).

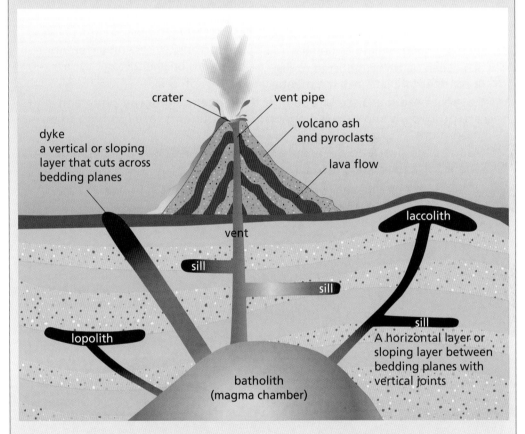

A volcanic cone is a volcanic landform. Some plutonic landforms form part of a volcano. Can you name them?

- Magma gathers in a **batholith** within fold mountains when an ocean plate sinks beneath another plate.
- The magma contains **compressed gases** that are under extreme pressure. This magma finds its way to the surface through weaknesses in the folded rock.
- As magma rises, the gases expand and create huge pressure that forces the magma upwards. Eventually it reaches the surface through an opening called the vent.
- An explosion blasts ash and molten rock high into the air; this then falls back to the surface and gathers around the **vent**.
- Lava flows pour out through an opening at the top called the **crater**.
- Alternate layers of ash and lava build up a cone-shaped mountain around the vent.

Plutonic landforms

SAMPLE EXAM QUESTION AND ANSWER

Question: Describe the process that has led to the development of any one plutonic landform.

Answer:

A batholith

Irish example: the Wicklow batholith.

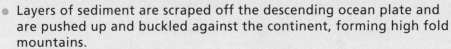

- A batholith forms in fold mountains where two plates collide at a destructive plate boundary.

> Most of these bullet points can be used to answer several different questions on the tectonic cycle.

- An ocean plate is subducted under a continental plate into the mantle.
- Layers of sediment are scraped off the descending ocean plate and are pushed up and buckled against the continent, forming high fold mountains.
- As the plate sinks into the mantle it gets hotter and melts at a depth of about 100 km, forming magma.
- Magma rises up through the folded rock layers above because it is less dense (lighter) than surrounding rock.

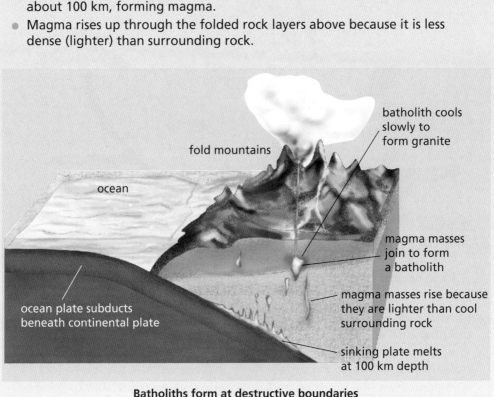

Labels:
- fold mountains
- batholith cools slowly to form granite
- ocean
- magma masses join to form a batholith
- magma masses rise because they are lighter than cool surrounding rock
- ocean plate subducts beneath continental plate
- sinking plate melts at 100 km depth

Batholiths form at destructive boundaries

**Half Dome is an exposed batholith in Yosemite
National Park, California**

- The presence of gas bubbles makes the magma more buoyant, so it rises easily.
- As the magma melts its way upwards, much of the surrounding rock melts into the magma, making it rich in silica (up to 70 per cent).
- The magma gathers within the fold mountain into one large mass to form a batholith that may be many kilometres wide.
- The magma cools slowly and forms large crystals of mica, feldspars and quartz.
- The cooling magma heats the surrounding rocks and metamorphoses them. Sandstone changes to quartzite, limestone changes to marble and shale changes to schist and slate.
- Over millions of years the overlying rock is eroded away and the granite batholith is exposed at the surface.
- The granite weathers by shedding thin layers or shells of rock in a process called sheeting or exfoliation.
- Distinctive exfoliation granite domes develop. *Example:* Half Dome in Yosemite National Park, California
- Tors form on granite hilltops and create a distinctive landscape. *Example:* Dartmoor, England.

Landforms of sedimentary rock

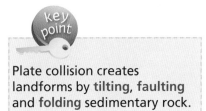

key point

Plate collision creates landforms by **tilting, faulting** and **folding** sedimentary rock.

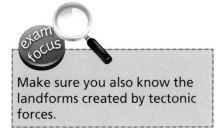

exam focus

Make sure you also know the landforms created by tectonic forces.

Tilting

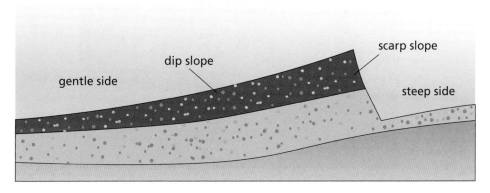

gentle side

dip slope

scarp slope

steep side

An escarpment has one gentle side and one steep side

Escarpment
One side is steep and the other has a gentle slope. *Examples:* the Dartry-Cuileagh uplands and the Brecon Beacons in Wales.

Faulting

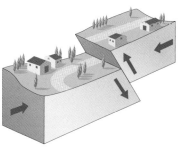

Reverse fault

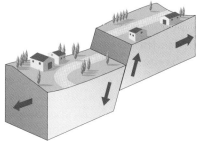

Normal fault

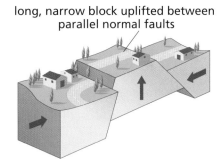

Block mountain (horst) – compression

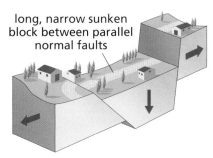

Rift valley (graben) – tension

Block mountain (horst – compression/squeezing laterally); rift valley (graben – tension/stretching laterally)

Folding

Compression buckles and shortens rock layers.

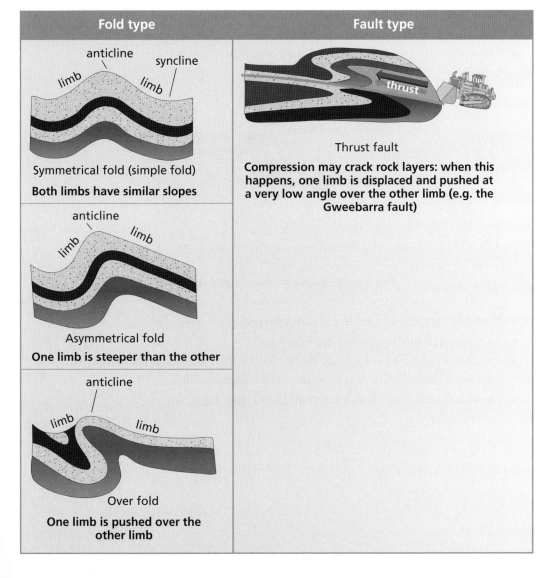

Fold type	Fault type
Symmetrical fold (simple fold) — Both limbs have similar slopes	**Thrust fault** — Compression may crack rock layers: when this happens, one limb is displaced and pushed at a very low angle over the other limb (e.g. the Gweebarra fault)
Asymmetrical fold — One limb is steeper than the other	
Over fold — One limb is pushed over the other limb	

Ridges and valleys in Munster

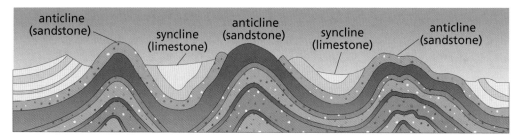

Munster's ridges and valleys were folded during the Armorican foldings

- Forces of compression folded the land in Munster into a series of anticlines and synclines.
- This occurred during the **Armorican (Variscan) foldings**.
- Today the ridges are of sandstone and the valleys of limestone.
- These ridges and valleys run **west to east** across Munster.
- Each rock layer is separated from the next by a **bedding plane**.
- Where folding was severe, an **overthrust fold** was formed.

The Paris Basin

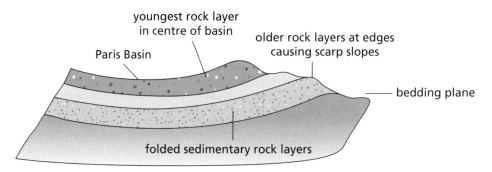

The Paris Basin is a saucer-shaped structure

- Forces of compression folded the rock layers.
- This occurred during the **Alpine foldings**.
- The centre sagged after folding, so the basin is dish-shaped, level at its centre, and with steep slopes called **scarps** at its eastern edges.
- The oldest rock layers are exposed on the eastern scarp slopes.

Doming

The Weald, southern England

A dome was created here by folding. Weathering and erosion of the youngest rocks have exposed the older rocks in the centre.

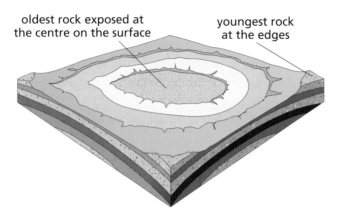

A dome landform in the Weald, southern England

Questions 3C, 2006; 2B, 2006; 2B, 2007; 3B, 2007; 1B, 2008; 1C, 2009.

5 Landforms Influenced by Rock Type

aims You need to know about:

- the formation of rock types, e.g. limestone
- how limestone weathers to form a distinctive **karst** landscape
- how limestone bedrock produces specific surface and underground landforms
- how granite weathers to produce a distinctive **rounded** landscape with **tors** on top.

exam focus

You should know how at least one major rock type is formed; how this rock type weathers to form a distinctive landscape, with an Irish example.

Landforms of limestone rock

Limestone pavement displays grikes and clints that allow water to drain through freely from the surface

SAMPLE EXAM QUESTION AND ANSWER

Question:

With reference to any **one** rock type, explain how it was formed **and** how it can produce a distinctive landscape. (2006; 30 marks)

Answer:

How limestone and karst landscape formed. Example: the Burren in Co. Clare.

How limestone forms

- Limestone is formed from the mineral calcium carbonate or calcite. Its chemical formula is $CaCO_3$.

exam focus

- name a rock type – 2 marks
- name a distinctive landscape, e.g. karst landscape – 2 marks
- describe its formation – 14–16 marks

- It is found throughout the Central Plain and the Burren in Co. Clare in Ireland.
- Limestone formed when low-lying regions of the continents were submerged beneath shallow seas in the tropics about 350–300 million years ago.
- Limestone formed from calcium carbonate from seawater that collected around tiny sand grains floating or rolling back and forth in shallow lagoons near the tropics.
- Limestone also formed from **billions of shells and skeletons** of organisms such as coral and seashells that lived in warm seas near the Equator.
- These organisms made calcium carbonate by extracting it from seawater to grow protective shells and skeletons.

The Burren, Co. Clare

The Burren in north-west Co. Clare

- Later, other sediments such as sand were washed into the sea and they covered the limestone with layers of sandstone.
- The seabed eventually stopped sinking and began to rise. With erosion, the limestone that was once deeply buried was eventually exposed at the surface, where we find it today.
- There is less pressure at the surface so the limestone developed obvious horizontal bedding planes and vertical cracks called joints.

How does limestone develop a distinctive landscape?
Carbonation

- **Karst** only develops where limestone rock is exposed at the surface. The **Burren** in Co. Clare is a karst landscape.
- Because limestone is formed of only one mineral (calcite), it weathers evenly, forming a **level landscape**.

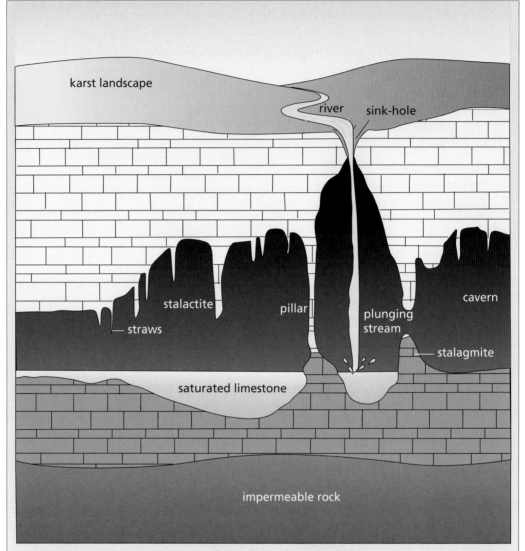

Limestone features in a karst landscape

- Rainwater is a weak acid, carbonic acid, which forms when carbon dioxide joins with moisture in the air. Once it falls on limestone it forms a chemical reaction, called carbonation that dissolves the rock.
- This type of reaction is visible when hydrochloric acid is dropped on limestone. The acid releases carbon dioxide from the rock and the gas bubbles or fizzes as it is released.
- Rainwater trickles through the vertical **joints** and horizontal **bedding planes** in the limestone and widens them through solution.
- The joints at the surface widen to form **grikes**: the remaining rock between the grikes forms **clints**. Together they form **limestone pavement**.
- Underground, the rainwater continues to dissolve the limestone, forming narrow **passages that form the routes of underground streams**.

- The beds of surface streams regularly collapse into these passages, creating **sinkholes** or **swallow holes**. Poulnagolm in the Burren is an example.
- These sinkholes create **dry valleys** downstream from the sinkhole as surface water no longer flows through them.
- Large **caverns** are formed when limestone bedrock lies below the water table and large masses of it are washed away in solution.
- **Stalactites**, **stalagmites** and **columns** form from dripping water when calcite is deposited on cavern surfaces.

In **Ordinary level** papers, some questions ask for two surface or two underground landforms in a limestone region. **Always give Irish examples.**
Higher level papers may ask for just one landform, so describe it with 15 SRPs.

Some other limestone landforms

Sinkholes

Examples: Poulnabunny, Co. Mayo; the Cradle Hole in the Cuilcagh Uplands, Co. Fermanagh.

- Rainwater is a weak acid, **carbonic acid**, which forms when rain absorbs carbon dioxide in the atmosphere.
- The parallel vertical joints allow the rainwater to trickle through the rock.
- When underground, the flowing **ground water dissolves** the limestone and **sediment erodes** the rock through abrasion along these lines of weakness. These processes create underground **passages** that begin under the river bed.
- The joints and bedding planes divide limestone into blocks. Some blocks fall from the ceiling of these passages, eventually leading to a collapse of the rock on the river bed above.
- This creates an **opening from the passage to the surface**, through which the river plunges vertically downwards.
- This opening, which swallows up the river, is called a **sinkhole**.
- The remaining river valley downstream of the sinkhole becomes dry and so is called a **dry valley**.

Caverns

Examples: Marble Arch Cave, Co. Fermanagh; Mammoth Cave, Kentucky, USA.

- Limestone is composed of calcium carbonate which is soluble in water.
- Most caverns form in the **zone of saturation**.

- The flowing ground water dissolves away the limestone.
- This process creates huge cavities that become enlarged by other processes over time: **sediment** in flowing ground water erodes the rock by **abrasion; collapsing limestone blocks** from the ceilings of small caverns increase the height of the cavern.
- **Melt-water** from melting ice sheets and glaciers at the end of the last Ice Age released vast amounts of melt-water that carried sand, rocks and boulders into these underground channels through sinkholes and enlarged them into enormous caverns.
- Many of these caverns are dry because of a fall in the water table or tectonic uplift.

Stalactites and stalagmites

Examples: Marble Arch Caves, Co. Fermanagh; Mitchelstown Caves, Co. Tipperary.

Ground water in limestone regions is saturated in dissolved **calcium atoms** and **bicarbonate atoms**. Ground water is also **supersaturated in carbon dioxide**. Calcite is deposited where the water drops from cracks in cave roofs. Initially, calcite gathers around the outside of the drip, forming a delicate hollow stalactite, called a **soda straw**; but eventually the hollow fills up or gets blocked with grit, and water seeps around the hanging stem to form a more massive, solid **stalactite**.

Where the drip hits the floor, it splashes, and the resulting calcite builds up to form an upward-pointing cone called a **stalagmite**.

If this process continues over a very long time the stalagmites and stalactites join to form limestone **columns**.

Granite landscapes

The weathering of granite – Unloading, hydration and gravity

- Granite forms under extreme pressure deep within fold mountains. It contains three minerals: mica, feldspar and quartz. It forms from a magma batholith that gathered from melted ocean plates.
- Weathering and erosion removes the surrounding mountain rock. Eventually the granite reaches the surface. This reduces the weight of overlying rock and so expands in a process called **unloading**. Unloading creates joints/cracks in the granite. Ground water and rainwater seep into the joints. Two new processes then weather the rock:
- **Hydration** allows micas and feldspars to absorb water. This creates stresses within the rock and helps to break it up.
- **Hydrolysis** occurs when ground water, which is acidic, reacts with the feldspars in granite. Some atoms in the feldspar dissolve in the ground water, while others join with new atoms to form entirely new minerals to create clay. So the rock crumbles apart.
- **Gravity** moves the weathered particles downslope.

Granite tors

Example: Dartmoor, south-west England.

Tors are like blocks of granite stacked on each other. The cracks that divide them are called joints.

Tors are found on the **summits of granite hills and mountains.** They are blocks of granite that have their joints widened. The joints open for two reasons:

1. Pressure is released because the granite is no longer deep within a mountain where pressure is severe. This released pressure allows the rock to expand, creating the joints.
2. Weathering of the feldspar and mica minerals along the joints widens them even more so the granite splits into stacked blocks. *Example:* Wicklow Mountains.

Quartzite peaks

Example: Sugarloaf peaks, Co. Wicklow.

Croagh Patrick in Co. Mayo is formed from quartzite. It is pointed because of freeze-thaw action.

Pointed mountain peaks of quartzite rock are found close to granite landscapes. The granite batholith **metamorphosed** nearby **sandstone** layers and changed them to quartzite. When quartzite weathers on mountain tops, the freeze-thaw process sharpens the peak and scree gathers at its base.

Questions 3B, SEC Sample Exam Paper 2006; 1B, 2006; 1C, 2007; 2C, 3B, 2008.

6 Landforms Influenced by Surface Processes

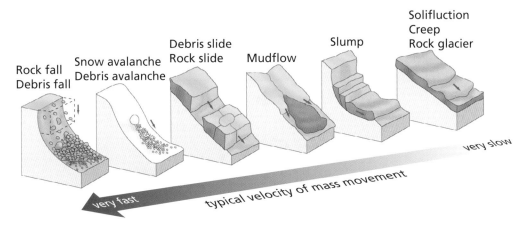

Processes of mass movement

Slow movements

Soil creep

This is the movement of soil particles downslope. It occurs due to the influences of:

- **gravity** – pulls soil particles downslope
- **solifluction** – some soil particles swell as a result of absorbing ground water. This swelling pushes neighbouring particles away from each other.
- **frost heave** – ice crystals form under stones and move them to the surface.

Fast movements

Gravity

This pulls large rocks, boulders and soil downslope to create rock falls and landslides.

Earth flows

These occur when soil is saturated with water on gentle slopes.

Lahars or mud flows

Lahars occur when enormous amounts of soil, rock, trees and other debris move rapidly downslope. They are triggered when volcanic eruptions on ice-capped volcanic mountains cause large masses of ice to melt.

Slumping

This happens when cliff edges collapse; as they slip downwards there is a rotational movement of the falling material.

Glacial processes

Plucking

Water from melting ice trickles into cracks at the base of a glacier and then freezes. The glacier becomes attached to the rock under it. When the ice moves, rock particles are plucked from the ground.

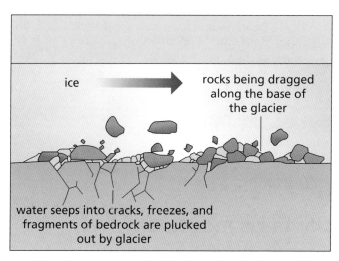

Rock fragments and bedrock are plucked out and somewhat rounded by movement of a glacier

Abrasion

The glacier moves these plucked rocks, which erode the base and sides of valleys, making them deeper.

It also involves the scouring of lowland areas, leading to the removal of soil in some regions.

Basal slip
The sliding movement of a glacier over its rock floor.

Freeze–thaw
During the day melt-water seeps into cracks in rock; at night the water freezes and expands, breaking up the rock.

River processes

- **Hydraulic action** – rocks are broken up by the force of moving water.
- **Corrasion or abrasion** – a river's load erodes the banks and bed of the river.
- **Cavitation** – bubbles of air collapse and form tiny shock waves against the outer bank of a river.
- **Deposition** – eroded material is dropped on the bed or flood plain of a river when the slope, the speed or the volume of a river is reduced.
- **Attrition** – fragments of stone are rounded and made smaller by hitting off each other.
- **Slumping** – rotational movement of a collapsing river bank as it is undermined by a river.

Coastal processes

- **Abrasion** – boulders, pebbles and sand are pounded by the waves against the coastline.
- **Hydraulic action** – the direct impact of strong waves on a coast.
- **Compression** – air is squeezed in cracks and caves, breaking up the rock.
- **Attrition** – fragments of stone are rounded and made smaller by hitting off each other.
- **Longshore drift** – a zigzag movement of material along a shore. It builds up bars, spits and lagoons and leads to the development of salt marshes.

Surface processes, patterns and landforms

Study only **one** of the following in detail:
- Mass movement processes, patterns and landforms: pages 44–46.
- Glacial processes, patterns and landforms: pages 46–49.
- River processes, patterns and landforms: pages 50–55.
- Coastal processes, patterns and landforms: pages 56–58.

Mass movement processes, patterns and landforms

Factors that influence mass movement

- Steepness of slope: the steeper the slope, the faster the movement.
- Type of material: loose material slips faster than compacted material.
- Water content: the higher the water content, the faster the movement.
- Vegetation cover: plant roots help to bind surface material to reduce movement.
- Earth movements: earthquakes shake and loosen material to aid movement.

Processes of mass movement

Soil creep

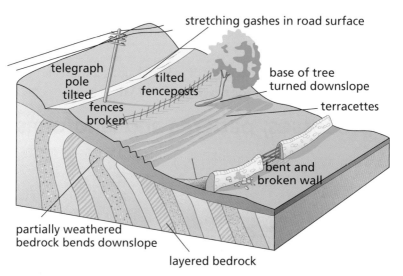

The effects of soil creep

This is the movement of soil particles downslope. It occurs because of the influences of:

- **gravity** – pulls soil particles downslope
- **solifluction** – some soil particles swell when they absorb ground water. This swelling causes neighbouring particles to move away from each other
- **frost heave** – the movement of soil particles by ice crystals that form under stones and move the soil particles to the surface.

Gravity
This pulls large rocks, boulders and soil downslope to create rock falls and landslides.

Earth flows
These occur when soil is saturated with water on gentle slopes.

Lahars or mud flows
Lahars occur when enormous amounts of soil, rock, trees and other debris move rapidly downslope. They are triggered when large masses of ice melt as a result of volcanic eruptions on ice-capped volcanic mountains.

Landforms of mass movement

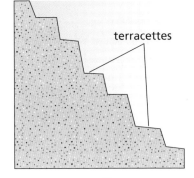

Terracettes
These are parallel ridges of soil on a steep slope, much like long steps of a flight of stairs. They form because of:

1. Wet–dry periods: moisture increases the weight and volume of soil, causing expansion and the movement of the soil downhill under the pull of gravity. When the soil dries it contracts.
2. Freeze–thaw: when a soil freezes, its water particles expand and push up the soil at right angles to the slope. When the soil thaws, the material slips downslope under the pull of gravity. This is the slowest form of mass movement.

Terracettes are like steps on a steep slope

Sloping cliffs due to slumping
Slumping is caused by undermining of a slope. When this happens, areas such as coastal cliffs and river cliffs collapse and slip and as they do there is a rotational movement of the falling material. *Example:* chalk cliffs at Garron Point, Co. Antrim.

Flows
Flows are moving masses of soil, stones, mud and water.

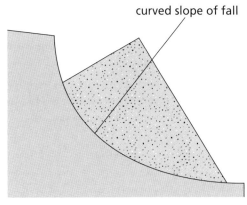

curved slope of fall

Slumping occurs when steep slopes are undercut

Bog bursts

Blanket bogs that cover hill and mountain tops may flow after spells of continuous heavy rain. *Example:* Derrybrien, Co. Galway.

Lahars

A lahar is a particular type of mud flow that occurs when hot lava or hot ash from a vent falls on great deposits of snow or ice on a high, snow-capped volcanic peak. The water from the melted snow or ice saturates the ground, which then rushes downhill rooting up soil, trees and other material on its journey.

Landslides and rock falls

Landslides

These occur when loose soil, stones and clay become loose and fall downhill owing to the pull of gravity. Water may or may not be an influencing factor. Landslides leave a **concave scar** on the slope where the material originated, and a **convex mound** of material where it ended.

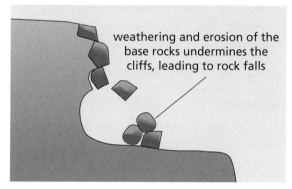

weathering and erosion of the base rocks undermines the cliffs, leading to rock falls

Rock falls

Rock falls occur when loose boulders are set free on a slope and roll downhill. They may become loose for a number of reasons, including earthquakes or the erosion of surrounding soil or stones. Weathering and erosion of base rocks undermines cliffs, creating rock falls.

Weathering and erosion of base rocks undermines cliffs, creating rock falls

Glacial processes, patterns and landforms

Causes of Ice Ages

Ice Ages occur because of three factors that happen to occur at the same time. These are:

- changes in the tilt of the earth's axis – every 41,000 years
- the orbit of the earth changing from a circular path to a more elliptical one – every 100,000 years
- the tendency of the earth to 'wobble' – every 23,000 years.

DEFINITIONS

Arête: a knife-edged ridge created where two cirques form side by side.

Crevasse: a long, narrow, deep crack in the surface of a glacier.

Erratic: a large boulder that was carried a long distance from its place of origin.

Fjord: a glaciated valley that has been drowned by sea water.

Glaciated valley: a steep-sided and flat-floored valley (U-shaped) formed by the action of a glacier.

Glacier: a very slow moving river of ice.

Outwash plain: a large, gently sloping area of sand and gravel that was deposited by streams flowing from the front of an ice-sheet.

Overflow channel: a V-shaped valley cut by water that flowed from an ice-dammed lake.

Pyramidal peak: a peak pointed by frost action formed when there were three or more cirques back to back (e.g. Carrauntoohil, Co. Kerry).

Landforms of glacial action

Landform: U-shaped glaciated valley

Highland erosional landform

Example: Gap of Dunloe, Co. Kerry.

Formation

- Ice moved downslope under **gravity** through river valleys from snowfields and cirques high in the mountains.
- Melt-water seeped between the base of the ice and the bedrock.
- This allowed glaciers to slide downslope in a process called **basal sliding**.
- This melt-water regularly froze when the ice stopped moving. **Freeze-thaw** then occurred.
- When the glacier moved again it **plucked** large boulders and rocks from the bedrock surface.
- Rocks fell to the glacier surface gathered along the valley sides to form lateral moraines.
- These originated from freeze-thaw action above

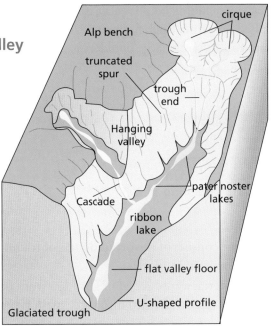

A glaciated valley or trough. These are the characteristic features of a glaciated valley.

Processes involved: plucking, abrasion, gravity, basal sliding.

the glacier and gravity dragged them downslope. The ice used them to erode and deepen the valley by **abrasion**.

- The process of abrasion created **truncated spurs** on the valley sides by eroding the fronts of interlocking spurs.
- **Erosion** and **plucking** created long, deep hollows that later filled with water to form **ribbon lakes** on the valley floor.
- **Hanging valleys** formed where smaller glaciers entered the main valley.
- These end abruptly on the sides of the main valley, often causing waterfalls to form. *Example:* Torc waterfall in Killarney.
- Some deep glaciated valleys in coastal areas were drowned by the sea. These inlets are called **fjords**.

Landform: Moraine

Upland and lowland depositional landforms
Example: Cumeenduff Glen, Co. Kerry.

All rock material transported by a glacier, including boulder clay, is called **moraine**. Rock fragments range in size from large boulders to particles of dust.

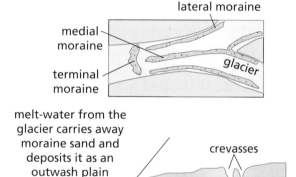

Processes involved: transportation, deposition, ablation (melting of ice).

The main types of moraine

Formation

Moraine consists of **unsorted debris** of rounded and angular boulders, stones, soil and sand deposited by glaciers.

This material was **plucked** or **abraded** from the landscape over which the glaciers passed. It may be divided into three main types:

- **Lateral moraine** formed **long sloping ridges** of material deposited **along valley sides**.
- **Medial moraine** is an uneven, long ridge of similarly unsorted material that runs along the centre of valleys.
- **Terminal moraine** formed **crescent-shaped ridges** of unsorted debris across valleys and plains where glaciers or ice sheets stopped and melted for a long time. They represent the **furthest advance** of the ice.

Landform: Esker

Lowland depositional landform

Examples: Eiscir Riada, near Clonmacnoise, Co. Westmeath.

> **key point**
>
> Processes involved: transportation, deposition, ice action.

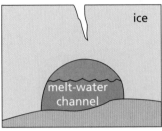

1. As ice melts, melt-water channels form under the ice.

2. Sand, gravel and boulders are deposited, depending on the speed of melt-water flow.

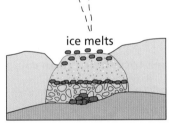

3. Melt-water channel fills with deposits as the ice melts.

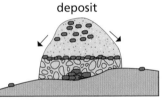

4. After all the ice has disappeared, esker slopes slump and stabilise, leaving a ridge of sand, gravel and boulders.

Formation of an esker

Formation

- Melting ice sheets produced vast amounts of melt-water, some of which flowed through tunnels under the ice.
- The **fast flow** of the water allowed it to pick up **large quantities of sediment** from the ground moraine beneath the glacier.
- It washed and cleaned the sediment and carried it along, some in **suspension**, some by **saltation** and more by **traction**.
- The silt and clay particles were carried far from their source to lakes or the sea.
- But the **sand and gravel particles** were laid down in **alternate sorted layers** on the beds of these enclosed rivers and streams.
- Layers of fine sediment, such as **fine sand**, were deposited during times of **low water**. **Gravels** were laid down during periods of **rapid ice melt**, such as in summer.
- These sub-glacial rivers formed a **winding course** across level plains beneath the ice, just as rivers do when they **meander** in their late stage of development.
- So their deposits today form winding ridges of sand and gravel across lowland regions.

OR

River processes, patterns and landforms

River patterns

A **basin** is the area drained by a river. The pattern of drainage in a basin may be:

- **dendritic** – the tributaries form a pattern like the branches of a tree

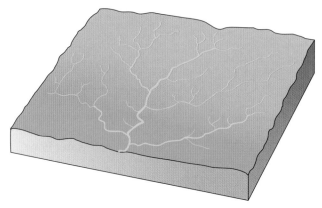

Dendritic drainage is tree-shaped

- **trellised** – tributaries run parallel to each other towards the main course and meet the main river at right angles

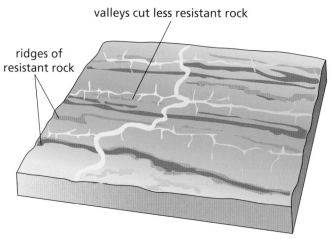

Trellised drainage shows tributaries that meet the main river at right angles

- **radial** – streams flow downhill, radiating from a central hilltop or mountain top.

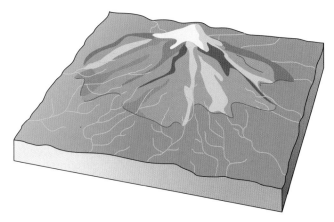

In radial drainage, rivers radiate outwards from a central area

---

DEFINITIONS

Basin: the entire area drained by a river and its tributaries.

Confluence: the place where rivers join.

Estuary: that part of a river's course that is tidal.

Mouth: the place where a river enters a sea or lake.

Source: the place where a river begins.

Tributary: a river that joins a larger river.

Watershed: the high ground that separates one river basin from another.

Landforms of river action

SAMPLE EXAM QUESTION

Question:

With the aid of a labelled diagram, examine the processes that have led to the formation of any one Irish landform of your choice.

Note: you may be asked for *two* landforms.

You should:

- Know at least two landforms from rivers and explain the processes.
- Write 15 SRPs (2 marks each) if you are asked for *one* landform, and eight SRPs for each landform if you are asked for *two*.
- Include a simple sketch with three labels/SRPs.
- Give an Irish example of each landform.

Landform: V-shaped valley

Landform of erosion, upper course
Examples: upper Liffey valley, upper Blackwater valley.

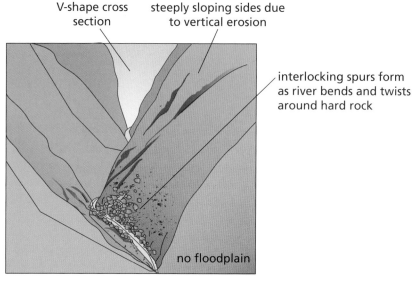

V-shape cross section

steeply sloping sides due to vertical erosion

interlocking spurs form as river bends and twists around hard rock

no floodplain

V-shaped valleys are found in the upper stage of a river's course

Formation

- Water flows quickly on steep slopes so it rushes down slope and winds and twists its way around obstacles.
- The force of the rushing water, called **hydraulic action**, causes vertical erosion of the channel.
- Through **abrasion**, the load of the river also **erodes vertically** so that eventually a V-shaped valley is formed.
- The water **erodes laterally** (sideways) where the channel bends and twists around obstacles.
- The current erodes most strongly on the outside of the bends, causing **undercutting** and **slumping** of the bank.
- The sediment is constantly removed by hydraulic action.
- The bends and twists become more pronounced, creating **interlocking spurs**.
- **Gravity** and rainfall on the valley sides supplies the channel with sediment, which is removed, making the valley deeper.
- Bands of hard rock may lie across the path of the stream. Waterfalls form at these locations by eroding the soft rock downstream of the hard rock.
- **Plunge pools** form at the base of the waterfalls due to abrasion and hydraulic action.
- As a waterfall retreats upstream it leaves a steep-sided channel called a **gorge** below the falls.

- **Potholes** form by abrasion where **eddies** (swirling pools) occur.
- The pebbles and sediment are rounded by attrition as they are moved downstream.

Landform: Waterfall
Landform of erosion; upper course
Examples: Asleagh Falls on the Erriff River; Torc Waterfall in Killarney.

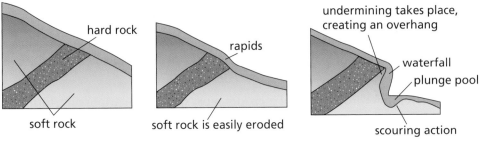

The formation of a waterfall

Formation

- A waterfall usually occurs in the upper course of a river.
- It forms where a layer of **hard rock** that lies across the riverbed is **horizontal** or **tilted upward**.
- Due to the **uneven hardness** of the bedrock there is **differential erosion**. The softer rock is eroded at a faster rate than the hard rock layer.

> **Processes involved:**
> hydraulic action, abrasion, traction, eddying, solution, rejuvenation.

- The softer rock undergoes severe erosion due to **hydraulic action** and **abrasion**.
- This causes a vertical drop on the river's bed where the hard rock ends and the softer rock begins.
- As the falling water strikes the soft rock on the riverbed, its erosive power gouges out a deep pool called a **plunge pool**.
- This pool deepens gradually, caused by the **eddying** or swirling of the water and its **load**, which creates **abrasion** within the pool.
- **Large chunks** of the hard rock **break away** from the capstone and fall to the base of the waterfall. This occurs due to undermining or the opening up of the rock's joints by hydraulic action.
- In some regions where extremely cold conditions are experienced and the river freezes over, some **frost wedging** may loosen these rock chunks.
- In this way the waterfall **retreats upstream** leaving a deep, steep-sided narrow channel downstream from the waterfall. This landform is called a **gorge**.
- Some waterfalls are formed when sea level falls or land level rises and new profiles and waterfalls form at knickpoints.

Landform: Flood plain

Landform of erosion and deposition, middle and lower course

Example: River Shannon in the midlands, Blackwater Valley near Fermoy.

key point

Processes involved: undercutting, divagation, deposition.

Formation

- When a river reaches lowland it **slows down** and starts to swing from side to side. This lateral wandering of the river to and fro is called **divagation**.
- This creates **lateral erosion** and begins the process of removing its interlocking spurs. The processes of **hydraulic action, cavitation** and **abrasion** are very active at this stage.
- As the river flows around a bend it **erodes** most strongly on its **outside**, forming a **river cliff**.
- **Undercutting** of the bank occurs and parts of it **slump** into the river.
- Little erosion occurs on the inside of the bend, but there is often deposition, forming a gravel beach or **point bar**.
- Over time a wide and flat valley floor is created.
- During times of flood, such rivers **overflow** their channels and spread across this flat valley floor.
- Each successive flood over thousands of years builds up a thick blanket of the sediment called alluvium to form a level plain.
- High banks develop close to the channel. These are called **levees**.
- In delta regions these levees may retain a channel that is at a higher level than the surrounding floodplain.

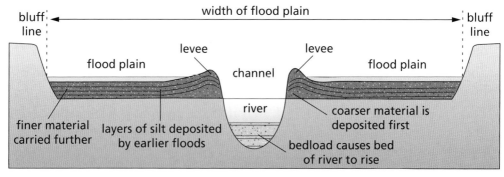

width of flood plain

bluff line — flood plain — levee — channel — levee — flood plain — bluff line

river

finer material carried further — layers of silt deposited by earlier floods — coarser material is deposited first — bedload causes bed of river to rise

Levee formation

Landform: Ox-bow lake

Examples: River Moy near Foxford, Co. Mayo; Shannon at Leitrim town.

A neck of land separates two concave banks where erosion is active

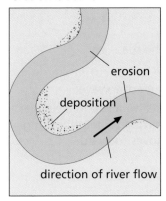

Neck is ultimately cut through: this may be accelerated by river flooding

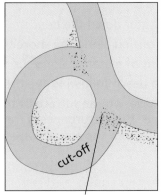

Deposition seals the cut-off, which becomes an ox-bow lake

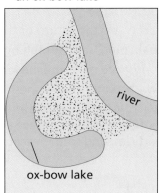

deposition begins to seal up the ends of the cut-off

Ox-bow lakes form in the lower stage of a river's course

Formation

- **Meanders** develop on mature and old river valleys where slopes are gentle or flat.
- As meanders move downstream they erode most strongly on the outside of bends by abrasion.
- This creates a loop in the river's course, enclosing a **peninsula** of land.
- Over time this peninsula develops a narrow neck as the meanders approach each other.
- Finally, during a period of flood the river cuts through this neck and continues on a straight and easier route, leaving the river loop to one side.
- Deposition occurs at both ends of this loop to form an ox-bow lake.
- After a long time these ox-bow lakes become filled with silt from floodwater, and finally they dry up.

> **key point**
>
> Processes involved: hydraulic action, corrasion/abrasion, cavitation, deposition.

OR

Coastal processes, patterns and landforms

Coastal Processes: see page 43.

> **DEFINITIONS**
> *Backwash:* the return of the water down the beach.
> *Load:* mud, sand and shingle carried along the shore by the sea.
> *Longshore drift:* the movement of material along the shore.
> *Swash:* water that rushes up a beach following the breaking of a wave.
> *Wave:* Wind causes water particles on the surface of the sea to move in a circular motion and form a wave shape. This disturbance is transmitted to neighbouring particles, and so the wave shape (not the actual water) moves forward.

- Always write at least 15 SRPs @ 2 marks each.
- Draw a simple diagram with a few SRPs as labels.
- Give an Irish example.

Landforms of coastal action

Landform: Cliff

Landform of erosion
Example: Cliffs of Moher, Co. Clare.

Formation

- Wave action cuts a **notch** on any new land surface that is exposed to the force of the sea.
- Air is forced into joints and bedding planes in rock surfaces that are exposed to wave action.
- The air is **trapped and compressed** by the force of incoming waves. This is called **hydraulic action**. As each wave retreats, the air instantly expands.
- Its 'explosive' expansion enlarges the cracks, and eventually shatters the rock into small and large blocks and boulders.
- The rock particles are removed by the crashing waves and fall to the seabed.
- **Strong waves** pick up these shattered rock particles and strike them off the coast. Most of this action takes place at or below high tide level. This process is called **abrasion**.

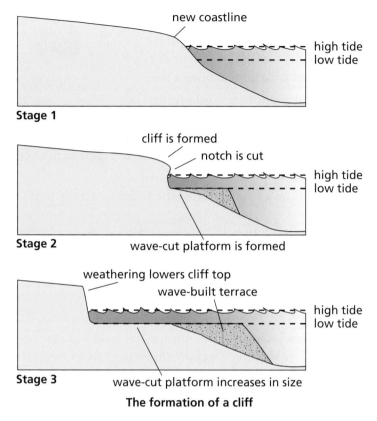

The formation of a cliff

- The combined processes of hydraulic action and abrasion eventually cut a notch in the coast that creates an **overhanging rock ledge**.
- Once this notch lengthens, the overhanging rock mass becomes too heavy to be supported and collapses into the sea.
- This leaves a vertical 'wall' of rock along the water's edge, which is called a cliff.
- As the cliff 'retreats', a level rock surface is formed at the base of the cliff. This surface is called a **wave-cut platform**. It may be exposed at low tide in some places.

Landform: Beach

Landform of deposition
Example: Tramore Beach, Co. Waterford.

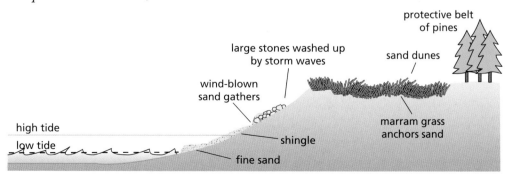

Composition of a beach

Formation

- A beach is formed by the process of **longshore drift**. This refers to the **zigzag movement** of beach material, such as sand and shingle, along a shore.

key point

Processes involved: deposition, longshore drift.

- As a constructive wave approaches a shore, part of the wave 'touches ground' and slows down. The remainder of the wave in deeper water continues at its original faster speed. So a wave tends to **bend** as it approaches a beach and breaks at an **oblique angle**.

- The water that rushes up a beach is called the **swash** and it deposits sand along the shore.

- Constructive waves commonly occur on beaches with a **low angle**. They have a wide area to cross, so their swash loses its energy quickly. This leaves a weak backwash, so sand and shingle is slowly, but constantly, moved up the beach. Less material is pulled down the beach by the **backwash**.

- The force of the backwash is called the **undertow**.

- During storms, sea level is higher than normal, due to low atmospheric pressure. Waves are also stronger and they regularly throw large rocks, broken shells and driftwood on to the shore above normal high tide levels. This forms the **backshore** or **storm beach**.

- The **foreshore** is composed of **fine sand** and small shell particles. It has a gentle gradient and is regularly covered by the tide each day.

- Some beaches may form in crescent-shaped pocket bays or coves.

- Others are long and narrow and may run parallel to the shore along spits or bars.

exam Q

Question 1B, SEC Sample Exam Paper 2006.

7

People's Interaction with Surface Processes

aims

You need to know how people interact with **one** of the following:

- mass movement processes: pages 41–43
- river processes: page 43
- coastal processes: page 43.

exam focus

- The easiest topic to learn and to write about is how people interact with river processes.
- You should make sure you are able to write about two examples, with 12 SRPs each.

Mass movement

The effect of overgrazing on mass movement processes

Desertification leads to soil erosion on a large scale

- The overstocking of land can lead directly to soil erosion. Overgrazing reduces heather and grass cover and the soil is no longer protected from the direct impact of raindrops. Rain strikes the soil and loosens it, causing it to be washed downhill.
- Since the 1990s Irish mountainsides such as the Galtee and Mweelrea mountains have been subjected to increased mass movement, as overstocking of sheep has led to soil erosion.

The effect of overcropping on mass movement

- Overcropping occurs when soils in areas that are not suited to tillage are exposed to wind and rain.
- The **Sahel** in North Africa, south of the Sahara, became vulnerable to erosion when overgrazing by cattle herders, overcropping by tillage farmers and drought conditions left the soil exposed to dry winds from the Sahara. This led to a cycle of drought, famine, disease and loss of life. This continues today.

OR

River processes (Fluvial processes)

The impact of hydroelectric dams

Hydroelectric dams are built across river valleys to dam water in order to generate electricity. This interferes with the natural processes of river action.

- How people interfere with river processes is the easiest option in this topic.
- Marking schemes will look for 12 SRPs. Try to name two examples and refer to river processes.

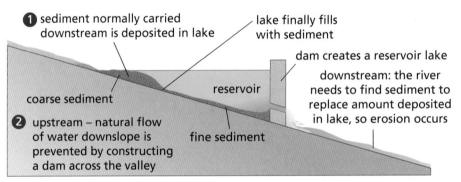

1 sediment normally carried downstream is deposited in lake

lake finally fills with sediment

dam creates a reservoir lake

reservoir

downstream: the river needs to find sediment to replace amount deposited in lake, so erosion occurs

coarse sediment

2 upstream – natural flow of water downslope is prevented by constructing a dam across the valley

fine sediment

Dams interrupt a river's natural processes

Case study: Ardnacrusha Dam on the River Shannon

- Ardnacrusha Dam was built in the 1930s.
- The dam was built below Killaloe to divert water to a **headrace** (man-made channel) to Ardnacrusha, where a hydro-power station was constructed. When it was first built it produced all our electricity, but today produces less than 1per cent.
- It created many environmental problems for the local region. For example, it diverted water from Castleconnell, once a world-famous salmon fishery, which then lost its tourism business.
- Large salmon of a species that once made the river famous were killed so that they would not interfere with the turbines.
- Much farmland behind the dam was flooded.

Common problems with hydro-dams

- Rivers slow down and are forced to deposit sediment in the reservoir lake behind the dam.
- This sediment should have been washed to the middle and lower stages, providing gravel, sand and alluvium supplies to flood plains and deltas.
- If a delta did exist at the river estuary before dam construction, it will now be prone to erosion, e.g. The Nile Delta, due to loss of alluvial soils in the reservoir lake upstream.
- Natural vegetation in regions behind dams is lost as the reservoir waters rise.
- Villages with all their historical character may be flooded and lost under the reservoir water. This has occurred at the Three Gorges dam project in China.

The impact of canalisation

Negative impact

Case study: The Aral Sea (see pages 198–199)

Fresh water was diverted by canal from Amu and Syr rivers for the purpose of irrigation. These rivers flow into and create the Aral Sea (which is really a freshwater lake).

Increased salt content

The Aral region is very hot in summer, which causes intense evaporation. Diverted water to canals reduced the inflow of the rivers. So evaporation increased the amount of dissolved minerals in the water, changing its nature from fresh to salty.

- This poisoned the sea's waters.
- It changed the sea's ecosystem, causing fish species and vegetation to die.
- The Amu and Syr lost so much of their water supply to canals and seepage that they now trickle to the sea.
- The Aral Sea shrank in size: its original coast is now 80 km from the sea.
- Fishing communities were wiped out and people migrated from the region.
- Seabed deposits were exposed to dust storms that caused sickness among remaining communities.

Positive impact: Improved agricultural output

- Dams were built on the Sacramento River in northern California and large reservoirs were created behind the dams.
- Canals and aqueducts were constructed to transfer water to the south of the Central Valley.
- This water is used for irrigation on a vast scale, producing crops such as oranges, lemons, cotton, vegetables and grapes.
- With the increased water supplies through irrigation from reservoirs, local areas that would otherwise be desert have become major farming regions.

Flood control measures

Levee construction

- Man-made levees are high banks of clay and stone, built parallel to a river's channel to contain floodwaters.
- Floodwaters no longer spread across a river's flood plain during times of heavy rain. This process naturally provided a flood plain with minerals needed by grasses to grow naturally and healthily. Levees deny a flood plain's natural mineral supply, which must now be provided by farmers themselves.
- Wildlife that once lived in marsh or wetland sections of the flood plains must find other nesting places.
- The bursting of levees can lead to severe loss of life.

OR

Coastal processes

The impact of recreation

What evidence in this photograph suggests that tourism may be hindered by this type of coastal development?

Groynes

- Long piles of large rocks are built at right angles to the coast in places to trap sand.
- These are called groynes. *Example:* Rosslare Strand, Co. Wexford.
- Longshore drift is interrupted by these barriers and coastal currents deposit sand, leading to the creation of new beaches.

Water quality

Naturally clean water may become polluted as recreation centres increase along a seashore. Water bodies can accept a certain level of pollutants and remain clean, since natural processes are able to break down pollutants such as human waste. However, when pollutants increase, seas become polluted, leading to poor water quality and contaminated beaches.

Coastal construction

The construction of hotels and holiday homes along sand dunes and sandspit environments leads to a change in natural ecosystems and damage to the coastal environment. Increased human traffic damages coastal grasses, leading to the erosion of sand dunes.

Coastal defences

An increase in coastal storms and surges as a consequence of global warming has led to great damage in some coastal areas. *Example:* Rosslare Strand, Co. Wexford. Groynes and breakwaters are used to reduce such storm damage by breaking the force and size of waves as they approach a shore.

Sand dune management

Wave energy is released by waves as they crash and run up a beach. It is a natural process that keeps coastal regions in balance – so beaches should be preserved in their natural form in order to maintain this balance.

Removal of sand by people, traffic, or any measure that interferes with this balance must be eliminated or reduced to protect coastal environments.

Natural wildlife protection

Mudflats, sandflats, coastal marshes and other environments that support wildlife should be protected as part of nature's heritage. They add to the attraction of coastal regions for bird watchers and tourists.

Questions 2C, 2006; 3C, 2007; 1C, 2008; 3C, 2009.

8 The Process of Isostasy, Adjustment to Base Level and Landforms

aims You need to understand that all landforms represent a balance between forces within and on the earth's surface; and that this balance may change over time.

The earth's crust is made up of rocks of different densities (weights).

- The continents are composed of light rocks, called **sial**.
- The ocean floors are made up of dense rocks, called **sima**. A continent 'floats' on a layer of sima that runs under the continents and along the floors of the oceans.
- When erosion of continents occurs, the eroded sediment is deposited on lowlands. This increases weight in this area, so lowlands are pressed down.
- This action also reduces weight in mountain regions, so the mountain regions float higher on the sima layer.
- Together these actions cause a levelling of the landscape. This process is called **isostasy**.

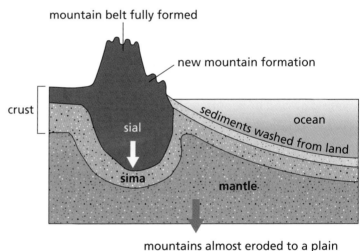

Erosion causes a levelling of the land surface over time

Landforms caused by changes in sea level

The process of **isostasy** causes raising and lowering of land relative to the level of the sea. This can lead to some landforms being drowned, or partially drowned, by the sea. Other landforms may be raised above sea level.

Emerged coastal features

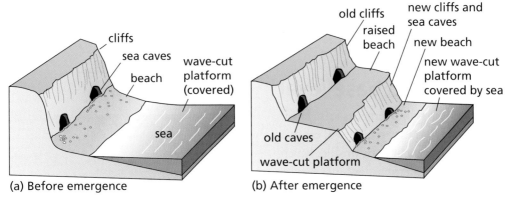

(a) Before emergence   (b) After emergence

Raised beach and wave-cut platform exposed due to isostatic uplift

Raised beaches and wave-cut platforms

- The sea level, relative to the land, changes over time.
- If the level of the sea falls or the land rises, coastal features such as beaches or wave-cut platforms may now be well above sea level.
- Step-like terraces may also form when sea levels change.

Submerged coastal features

Rias

Rias are submerged river valleys. They occur in south-west Ireland. *Examples:* Dingle Bay, Bantry Bay.

As the American plate moved away from the Eurasian plate, the west coast of Ireland lost its support, tilted seawards and was drowned by the sea. This process created the rias of the south-west.

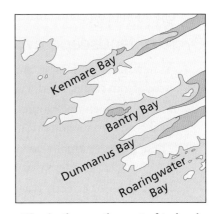

Rias in the south-west of Ireland

Fjords

During the last Ice Age, glaciers carved deep, U-shaped valleys in coastal mountain ranges. When the Ice Age ended, the water stored in the ice flowed back into the sea, causing the sea level to rise and flood some of these valleys, forming fjords. Killary Harbour is Ireland's best example of a fjord. There are many fjords in Norway.

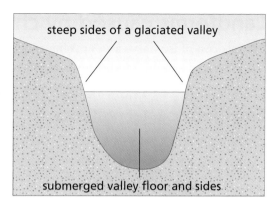

Features of a fjord

Adjusting to base level

- When earth movements raise land, the rivers in that region will erode to create a new curve or profile. Rivers begin cutting their new curve or profile from their estuaries upstream.
- This process is called **rejuvenation**.
- Waterfalls or rapids on a river near to its estuary indicate that **uplift** has taken place recently. In Co. Donegal in Ireland, the rejuvenation was caused by loss of weight on the landscape when the Ice Age ended.

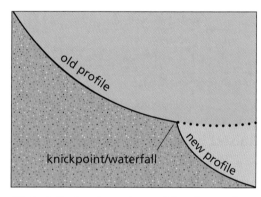

Waterfalls develop where old and new river profiles meet

- Waterfalls occur where the old profiles and new profiles meet. This is called the **knickpoint**.
- When rivers in their old stage are rejuvenated, they start to erode or cut into their old flood plain. This creates **incised meanders**.

Cycle of landscape evolution

- As new, level landscapes are exposed to weathering and erosion, they come under attack from rivers, wind, rain, frost and mass movement.
- The rivers open up channels, and the other processes combine to divide the original level land into separate ridges and valleys.
- These ridges gradually become worn down until they are just barely visible as raised land separating valleys that are in their lower stages of development.
- These almost perfectly flat landscapes are called **peneplains**. *Example:* South Cork.

Question 3B, 2009.

9 Ordnance Survey Maps, Photographs, Graphs and Charts

Scale

Scale is the relationship between a distance on the map and its corresponding measurement on the ground.

- Maps with a scale of 1:20,000,000 or 1:1,000,000 are **small-scale maps** showing large regions in little detail, e.g. major roads and cities (a road map).
- Maps with a scale of 1:2,500 or 1:1,000 are **large-scale maps** showing small areas in great detail, e.g. named streets and individual buildings.

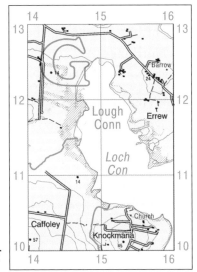

Area

To find the area of an OS map:

1. Count the number of grid squares across the top of the region.
2. Count the number of grid squares along the side of the region.
3. Then multiply the number along the side by the number across the top.

The area of this map is 3 × 2 = 6 sq km.

To find the area of an irregular-shaped region on an OS map (e.g. a water region):

1. Count the number of squares that have 50 per cent or more covered by water. Omit all others.
2. This number will represent the approximate area of the water region.

On this map, there are two squares at least half-filled with water. So the area of water is approximately 2 sq km.

Scale on a map

Scale on a map

- **Statement of scale.** The scale is stated. (In this case it is 2 cm to 1 km.)
- **Representative fraction** (RF) is given as a ratio. The RF 1:50,000 tells us that any one unit of measurement on the map corresponds to 50,000 similar units on the ground.
- **Linear scale** is a line divided into kilometres and parts of a kilometre (or miles and parts of a mile).

How to locate places on an OS map

Grid references

A grid reference is made up of:

1. **Letter (L).** It is coloured blue on every map and should be named first.
2. **Eastings (AT).** These are the vertical grid lines. They are numbered at the top and bottom. They should be named second.
3. **Northings (AS).** These are the horizontal grid lines. They are numbered along the sides. They should be named last.

How to locate a specific place on a map

Always look across the top first. Then look along the side. Remember **LATAS**:

L = letter
AT = across the top
AS = along the side.

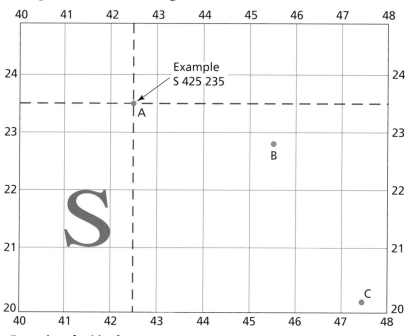

Examples of grid references: A = **S425 235**; B = **S455 227**; C = **S474 202**

Locating regions on maps

Four-figure grid references are used to locate a single square on a map.

The grid reference used to do this is:

- the sub-zone letter
- the easting on the west side of the square
- the northing on the south side of the square.

For example, the Mass Rock is located in region L 70 39.

Locating regions within Ireland

The **national grid** is used to locate places or regions on Ordnance Survey (OS) maps. This national grid is **displayed on the legend** attached to your OS map in an examination. By identifying the **sub-zone** letter on your map you can identify the location of that region in Ireland.

For example, the sub-zone letter on this map extract is **S. S** on the national grid is located in the **south of Ireland**.

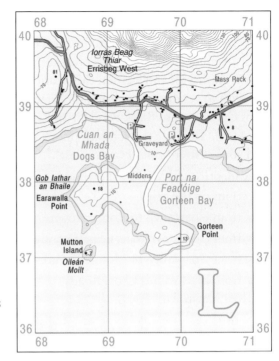

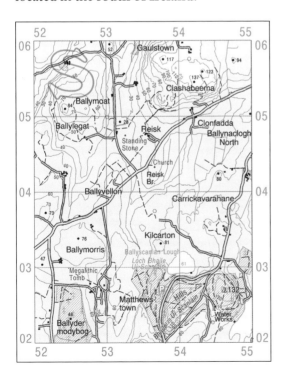

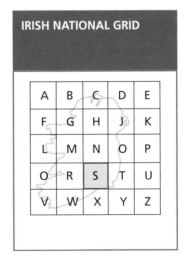

IRISH NATIONAL GRID

A	B	C	D	E
F	G	H	J	K
L	M	N	O	P
O	R	S	T	U
V	W	X	Y	Z

Directions on maps

Directions are usually given in the form of compass points. Place a cross representing north, south, east and west on the location you wish to get directions from, for example from Goatstown to Blackwood Cross Roads (see map). Then use the compass points to find your answer (*answer: north west*).

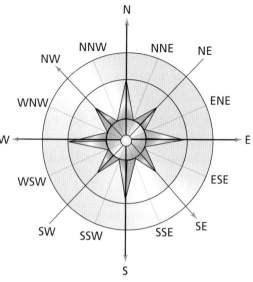

Now identify each of the following directions on the map:

- from Goatstown to Robertstown
- from Goatstown to its nearest graveyard
- from Goatstown to Mondello Park
- from Blackwoods Cross Roads to Goatstown.

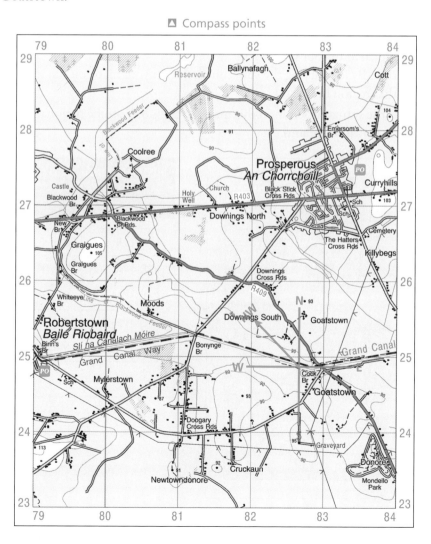

🔺 Compass points

How to locate places on photographs

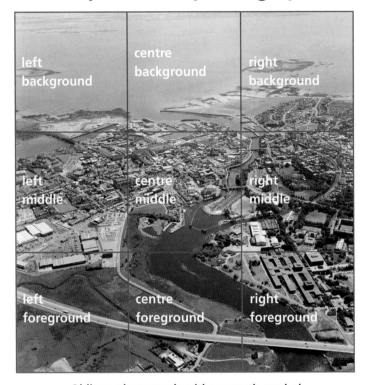

Oblique photograph with no north symbol

Oblique or vertical with north symbol

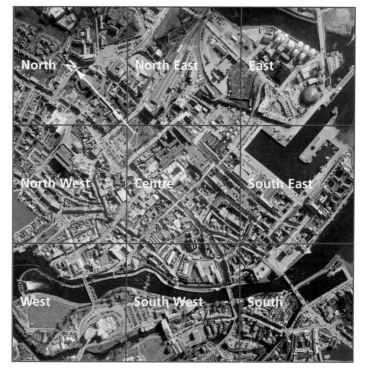

Oblique or vertical with north symbol

Drawing sketch maps

1. **Draw a frame** for your sketch map. This frame should be the **same shape** as the photograph or map.
2. Then draw in guidelines lightly on both the sketch map and the OS map or photo.
3. Alternatively, you can draw in the grid lines from your map. **Draw these lines lightly**.

Draw all sketch maps on the graph paper supplied in the exam.

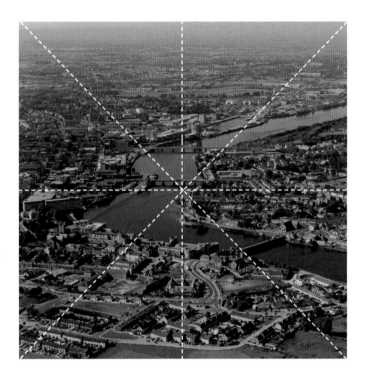

Drawing sketch maps from ordnance survey maps

1. Always draw – **on graph paper** – a frame similar in shape to that of the map.
2. **Never** trace a map. A sketch map must be drawn freehand.
3. **'Mark'** and **'name'** (or **'label'**) are different directions, and marks will be awarded for each separately.
4. Never draw a very large sketch map, as it is more difficult to draw and it takes up too much time.
5. Practise different types of sketch map, and time yourself.
6. Use a soft lead pencil.
7. Use colour **only** if you have enough time.
8. To identify individual physical regions on a map it is often helpful if you squint your eyes; the separate regions may then become clearer.

Drawing sketch maps of maps to half scale

1. Count the number of squares across the top and down the side. Suppose there are ten squares across the top and 12 squares down the side.
2. To draw to half scale all you need do is draw a box the same shape as the map, 5 squares across the top by 6 squares down the side.

A sketch drawn to half scale will be one-quarter the size of the original map.

Case study 1: Sligo coastal region

Sample question:

Study the map of the Sligo Coastal Region on page 75. Then draw a sketch map to **half scale** and on it mark and name:

(a) the physical regions

(b) Sligo urban region

(c) a coastal resort region.

Marking scheme:

Proportion – 2 marks

Graph paper – 2 marks

4 features @ 4 marks each (shown: 2 marks graded; named: 2 marks)

Required size is 12cm × 9 cm: allow a difference of up to 0.5 cm.

Key: physical regions

1. Coastal lowlands
2. Grange North upland
3. Drumcliff Bay
4. Sligo Harbour
5. Sligo Town urban region
6. Rosses Point resort region

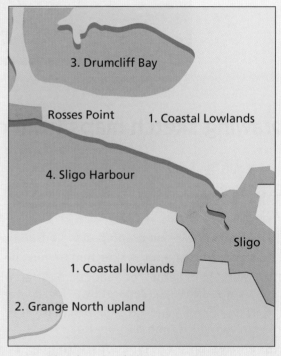

3. Drumcliff Bay

Rosses Point   1. Coastal Lowlands

4. Sligo Harbour

Sligo

1. Coastal lowlands

2. Grange North upland

Sketch map of Sligo coastal region

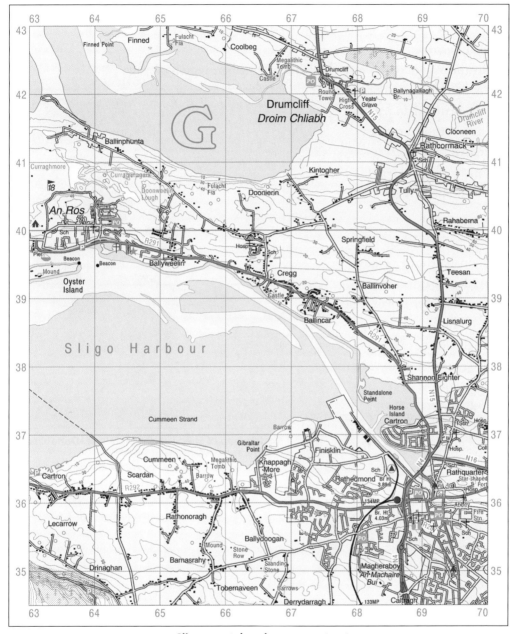

Sligo coastal region map extract

Case study 2: The Swords–Malahide–Donabate region

Sample question:

Study the map of the Swords–Malahide–Donabate region on page 77.

On a sketch map mark and name:

(a) the main urban regions
(b) a recreational region
(c) two nature reserves
(d) an agricultural region
(e) a woodland region.

Key: regions

1. Swords urban region
2. Donabate urban region
3. Malahide urban region
4. Portmarnock urban region
5. Golf links
6. Malahide Bay Nature Reserve
7. Rogerstown Estuary Nature Reserve
8. Agricultural region
9. Newbridge Demesne Woodland

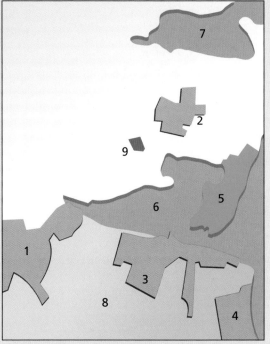

Sketch map of the Swords–Malahide–Donabate region

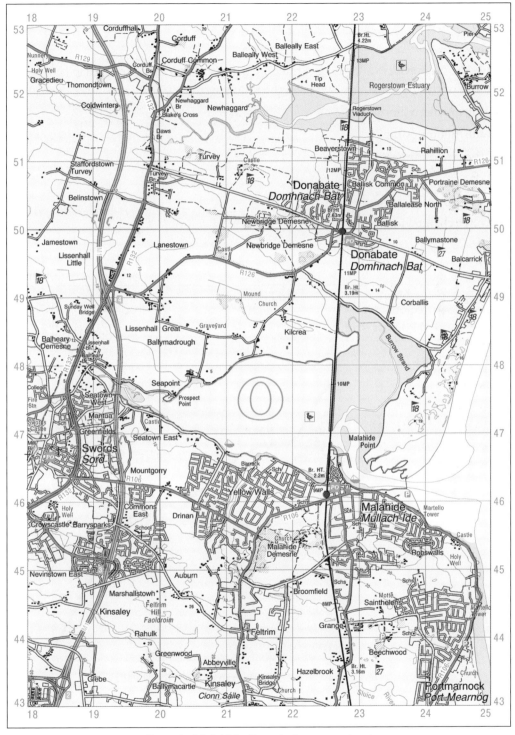

Swords–Malahide–Donabate map extract

Case study 3: The Nore River valley

Sample question:

Study the Nore River valley map extract on page 79. Then on a sketch map (not a tracing) of this region, mark and label the following:

(a) the upland regions

(b) the highest point

(c) the river Nore

(d) one regional road

(e) three third-class roads

(f) one urban region.

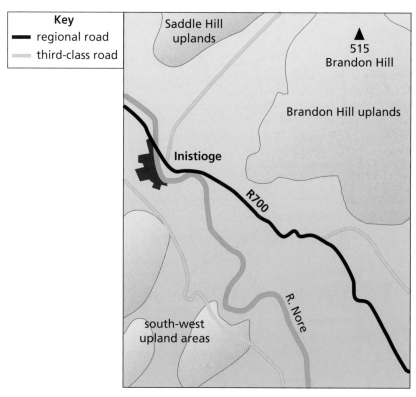

Sketch map of Nore River valley

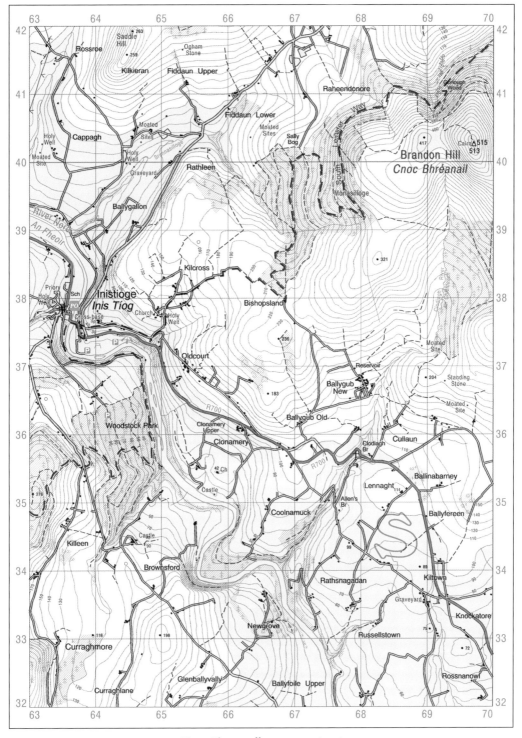

Nore River valley map extract

Case study 4: Drogheda urban region

Sample question: Using map evidence to support your answer, explain three reasons why Drogheda has developed as a growing economic centre.

Typical marking scheme:

Three reasons @ 10 marks each:

- reason identified – 2 marks
- map reference – 2 marks
- examination – 3 SRPs @ 2 marks each

Answer: **Evidence 1 – 10 marks**

There is an industrial estate (reason identified = 2 marks) located at grid reference O 07 74 (map reference = 2 marks).

- Industrial estates are industrial zones created and designed, for industry only, at the edges of cities and towns. This industrial estate is located at the south-western edge of Drogheda. (SRP 1 = 2 marks)
- Industrial estates were first introduced to Ireland during the 1960s under the Seán Lemass government. They were established to bring foreign direct investment into local economies such as that of Drogheda. (SRP 2 = 2 marks)
- Large industries and other manufacturers, locate in such estates and employ large numbers of personnel/workers, who come from the local housing estates or hinterland (give a good grid reference). (SRP 3 = 2 marks)

Then choose two other reasons and give evidence for them. For example in the case of Drogheda you could use Quay Grid Ref O 109 757 suggesting shipping/harbour facilities as a second reason and Regional Services centre, such as Hospital, route focus/nodal centre/market town, construction/housing estates. Any relevant aspect regarding growth is generally accepted.

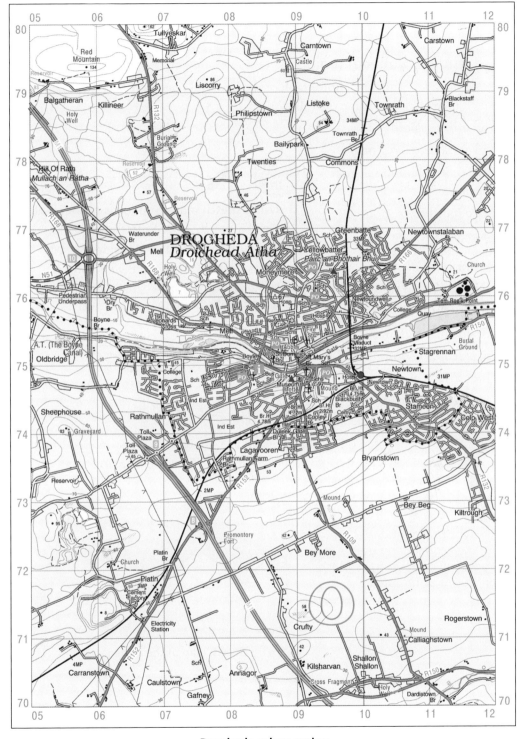

Drogheda urban region

Drawing sketch maps from aerial photographs

Case study 5: Donegal region

Sample question: Study the photograph of the Donegal region on page 83. Then on a sketch map mark and name the following:

(a) an urban region

(b) two residential regions

(c) the central business district region

(d) two industrial regions

(e) a green belt region.

Key: regions

1. Donegal urban region
2. Central business district
3. Residential region
4. Residential region
5. Industrial region
6. Industrial region
7. Green belt region

Drawing sketch maps of photos to half scale

To draw a sketch of a photo to half scale:

1. Measure the length and divide by two.
2. Measure the width and divide by two.
3. Draw a box (the same shape as the photo) with these measurements.

Always draw boundaries/an outline around land uses, e.g. woodland or housing estates, landforms or regions.

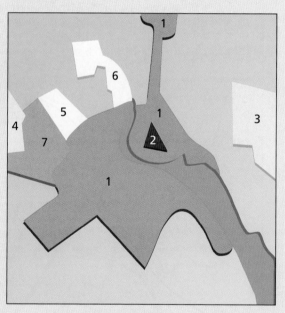

Sketch map of the Donegal region

Aerial photograph of the Donegal region

Case study 6: Donegal town

Sample question:

Study the photograph of Donegal town on page 85. Draw a sketch map (*do not trace*) of the area shown, and on it mark and label:

(a) the street pattern of the town

(b) five areas of different land uses/functions in the town

(c) the river.

1. Always draw a frame similar in shape to that of the map.
2. Never trace a map. A sketch map must be drawn freehand.
3. Draw the sketch to half scale (half the length and half the width).
4. Show and name only the features that you are specifically asked for.
5. Always outline your sketch with a soft pencil. This allows you to correct any errors you make.
6. Outline land-use zones with a heavy boundary line to limit the area.
7. Always mark and label each land-use area.
8. Use colour only if you have enough time.

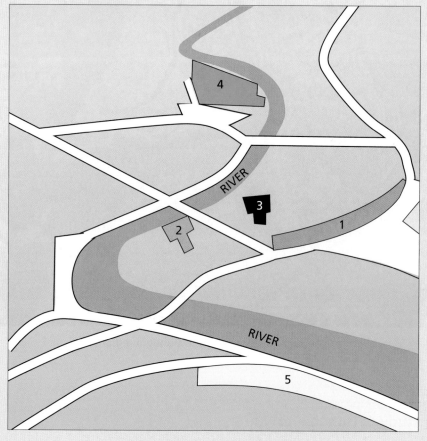

Sketch map of Donegal town

Key (land use/functions)

1. Shops/Commercial
2. Castle/Historical
3. Church/Religious
4. Factory/Industrial
5. Housing/Residential.

Aerial photograph of Donegal town

Case study 7: Ballybunion: A coastal town

Sample question:

Examine the aerial photograph of Ballybunion on page 87. Draw a sketch map based on the photograph (you may *not* use tracing paper), and on it mark and label:

(a) two areas where coastal erosion is evident

(b) two areas where coastal deposition is evident

(c) three regions of different land use that are related to the coastal location of this settlement.

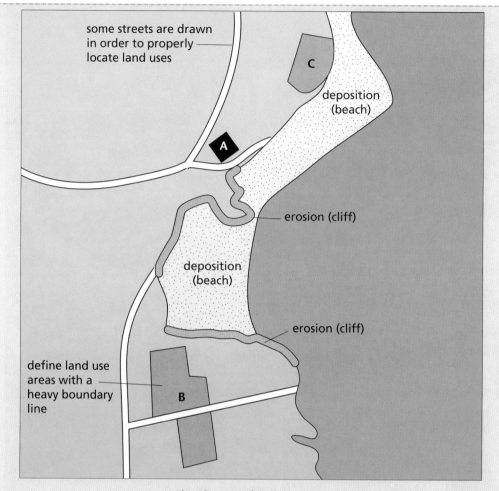

some streets are drawn in order to properly locate land uses

C

deposition (beach)

A

erosion (cliff)

deposition (beach)

erosion (cliff)

define land use areas with a heavy boundary line

B

Sketch map of Ballybunion

exam focus

Key (land use)

A. Hotel

B. Mobile home site

C. Pitch and putt course

These land uses are regularly found in seaside resorts.

For part (b), only include areas asked for; if in doubt include the name of the feature.

For part (c), land uses must be *directly* related to a seaside area.

1. Use a key or use labelled arrows to avoid overcrowding the sketch.
2. Limit the sketch size to half an A4 page to save time.
3. Always mark and label features to be identified.
4. Carefully examine the questions asked, and include only what is asked of you. If in doubt, add one extra example.

Aerial photograph of Ballybunion

Drawing graphs from tables

Questions that ask you to draw a graph from information supplied in a table appear regularly in the elective section of the exam, so you need to know how to draw simple charts and graphs.

SAMPLE EXAM QUESTION AND ANSWER

Question:

Energy in Ireland

Ireland's percentage share of energy requirements by Selected Sector for 1990 and 2006:

ENERGY USE IN IRELAND

Sector	1990	2006
Industry	27%	23%
Transport	22%	34%
Services	15%	16%
Agriculture	4%	2%

Answer:

Using graph paper, draw a suitable graph to illustrate this data.   (2009)

ENERGY USE IN IRELAND

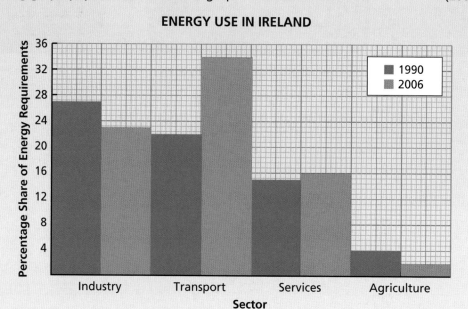

Types of graphs and charts

- **Bar charts.** The length of each bar represents the total or quantity of each factor. The bars can be simple, showing one single factor; or more complex, showing its component parts. Bar charts can also show gain or loss by showing bars above (gain) and below (loss) a central base line.
- **Pie charts** can show variations in size or composition of a feature/topic; for example the percentage share and total sales of cars in Ireland in a single year.
- **Line graphs** show change over time; increases or decreases; trends.
- **Scatter graphs** show relationships between two sets of data.
- **Flow charts** indicate at a glance occurring trends, e.g. numbers of migrants and their destinations.
- **Isoline charts/maps** show temperature (isotherms), rainfall (isohyets) or altitude (contours).
- **Choropleths** represent varying densities or population change.
- **Triangular graphs** are used to show information that can be divided into three variables, e.g. soil analysis; primary, secondary and tertiary industries.
- **Clock graphs** show activities/quantities of a recurring nature or pattern.

10 Types and Definitions of Regions

 aims — You need to know about different types of region.

What is a region?

A region is an area of the earth's surface that has human and/or physical characteristics that give it an identity and make it different from all the areas that surround it.

What is a climate region?

A climate region is an area whose unique weather system, temperature, precipitation, seasons, soil and vegetation make it completely different from all the surrounding regions. *Example:* cool temperate oceanic climate region.

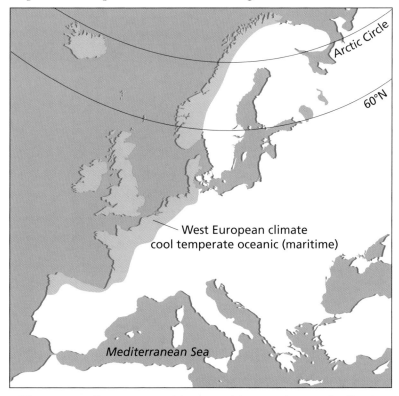

The western European coast has a cool temperate oceanic climate

What is a physical/geomorphological region?

Physical regions have unique surface characteristics, such as height, rock types, drainage patterns or internal rock structures, or a combination of these, that make them different from all surrounding areas. *Examples:* the Burren, Co. Clare; the Paris Basin.

The Burren, Co. Clare

What is an administrative region?

Governments divide their national territory into a hierarchy of local and regional areas that allows them to administer development more effectively. *Examples:* County Limerick, Waterford City, BMW region.

Ireland's regional authority regions

Definitions such as these may be required for the short-answer questions.

What is an urban region?

This is an area that includes a **town or city and its hinterland**. The hinterland that surrounds a human settlement is linked to it by interactions such as shopping, journeys to work, supplying farm produce. *Example*: the Paris Region.

What is a cultural region?

A cultural region is an area that has its own **unique identity** based on **human** rather than physical factors that are different from all surrounding areas. *Examples*: the Islamic World; Gaeltacht regions; the Walloon region, Belgium; Northern Ireland (a region of religious conflict).

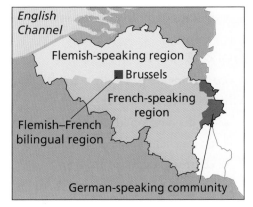

Belgium is divided into two cultural regions

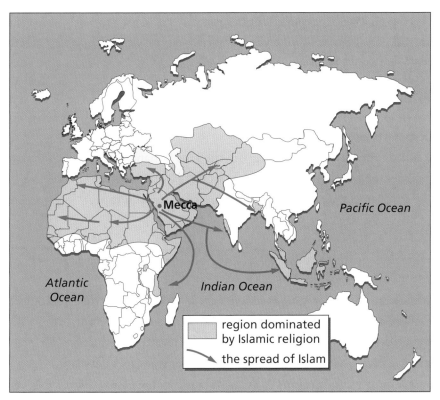

The Islamic faith spread from Saudi Arabia to other regions across Europe, Asia and Africa

What is a socio-economic region?

A socio-economic region is based on its **level of economic development**, defined by a combination of factors such as local supply of raw materials or local resources, strategic location for trade, or economic decline. There are three types of socio-economic region:

- less developed and peripheral regions, e.g. the BMW, the Mezzogiorno
- core regions, e.g. Dublin, Paris
- regions of industrial decline, e.g. Sambre-Meuse region, Cork region.

Core regions

Core regions are generally **centrally located** and **wealthy urban-industrial areas**. Characteristics of core regions:

- highly developed, centrally located and prosperous urban-industrial areas
- an excellent range of services and job opportunities
- centres of decision-making
- a highly urbanised society, with 80 per cent or more of the population living in cities
- a wide range of resources, e.g. excellent agricultural land; and deep, sheltered port facilities.

Most national cores are centred on capital cities and have a historic as well as a present-day role as core regions. *Examples:* Dublin, Paris.

Some national cores have evolved away from their capital cities. *Examples:* Northern Italy (Milan, Turin and Genoa).

International core regions

- Western Europe has an international core region where a number of national core regions have combined.
- It is called 'The European Dogleg' or 'The Hot Banana'.
- It includes the following core centres: Stuttgart, Milan, Lyons, Barcelona.
- These core centres are also called the 'Four Motors of Europe'.

Peripheral regions

Peripheral regions are the opposite to core regions. They are on the edges of the EU, far from wealthy core regions.

- Many are mountain regions. *Examples:* the West of Ireland, the Mezzogiorno.
- They have a higher dependency on agriculture than core regions.
- They suffer from out-migration and have low inward investment.
- They have high unemployment rates and a poor transport network.
- They are mostly rural regions with an average income of less than 75 per cent of the EU average wage.

Objective 1 regions

The Objective 1 regions of the EU, which receive special funding

Regions of industrial decline

Coal-mining regions

- These were once wealthy industrial regions based on coal mining and heavy industries, such as iron and steel manufacture. *Example:* the Sambre-Meuse region, Belgium.
- From 1750 onwards these regions experienced huge growth rates. Coalfields became the locations for manufacturing industry.
- Today they suffer from outdated technology, lack of high-quality coal, and high unemployment.

Coal-mining regions were once the major employment sectors in some countries, such as Belgium

Modern region of industrial decline in Ireland

- The Cork region suffered from industrial decline in the 1980s.
- Dunlop, Ford and Irish Steel closed their factories.
- New industries were attracted to create new sources of employment.

Short-answer questions: 8, 2006; 2, SEC Sample Exam Paper 2006.
Part 2 questions: 5A, 2007 Ordinary level (20 marks).

11 The Dynamics of Regions: Contrasting Regions in Ireland and Europe

aims You need to be able to:

- show how economic, human, and physical processes interact in a particular region
- explain how two factors influence primary, secondary or tertiary activities.

exam focus

You should study:

- Two contrasting Irish regions, e.g. the Border, Midland and Western (BMW) region *or* the West, **and** the South and East *or* Dublin region.
- Two contrasting European regions, e.g. the Paris Basin **and** the Mezzogiorno.
- One continental/subcontinental region, e.g. India *or* the American Southwest (see Chapter 12).

You need to be able to:

- draw sketch maps of two Irish, European and continental/subcontinental regions
- explain how two factors influence primary, secondary and tertiary activities in these regions.

The border, midland and western (BMW) region

Factors that created the environment

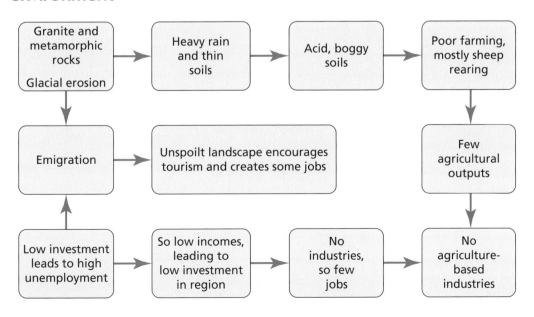

SAMPLE EXAM QUESTION AND ANSWER

Question: Draw an outline map of Ireland. On it, show and name the following:

- any two Irish regions
- any two urban centres
- any two rivers
- one lake
- two major routeways
- any two mountains.

Answer:

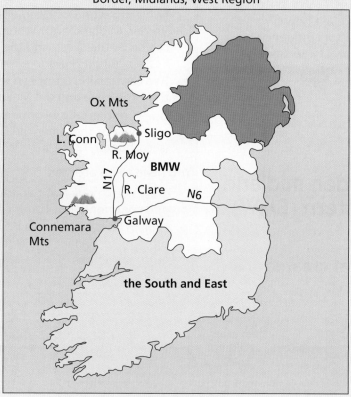

Border, Midlands, West Region

Ox Mts

L. Conn

Sligo

R. Moy

BMW

N17

R. Clare

N6

Connemara Mts

Galway

the South and East

The Border, Midland and Western region is a disadvantaged region in Ireland

Question: Draw a map of one Irish region. On it show and name the following:

- any two urban centres
- any two rivers
- one lake
- two major routeways
- any two mountains.

Answer:

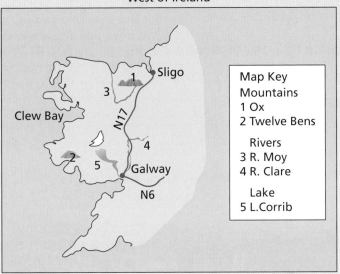

West of Ireland

Map Key
Mountains
1 Ox
2 Twelve Bens

Rivers
3 R. Moy
4 R. Clare

Lake
5 L.Corrib

The West of Ireland is a disadvantaged region in Ireland

Draw both of these maps and practise marking in some of the features, as shown. Drawing sketch maps is an important skill that's examined regularly in 20-mark questions.

The interaction of physical landscape, climate and human processes has made the BMW/West of Ireland an economically disadvantaged region.

Primary activities

SAMPLE EXAM QUESTION AND ANSWER

Question: Examine the factors that influence primary activities in one Irish region that you have studied.

Possible Marking Scheme:

- Named economic activity – 2 marks
- Two factors identified – 2 marks + 2 marks
- Region named – 2 marks
- Examination of 11 SRPs – 11 × 2 marks
- Give credit for examples (maximum 2 × SRP)

Answer:

Physical Factors: Relief and Soils

For this type of question, choose any two headings and always write at least 15 SRPs (30 marks). Make sure you emphasise how the headings interact with the economic activities.

The West of Ireland has a rugged landscape with poor soils, a wet climate and numerous sea inlets

- Much of the region has bleak, **rugged upland areas**, especially along the western coast. Example: The Twelve Bens in Connemara.
- Much of the **bedrock** of Western Galway, Mayo and Donegal is either granite or metamorphic rock. Many of these rocks cause waterlogging of the soil.
- The soil is composed of coarse **glacial moraine** or esker ridges. These soils lack sufficient nutrients for farming.
- Most of the upland areas and much of the lowland have a **blanket bog** covering, which is about 1–3 metres thick. These are waterlogged acid soils that have no nutritional value.

- Large areas are covered with **drumlins** of **fine heavy clays** that are not suited to tillage.
- Much of the midlands region of the BMW is low-lying in river **flood plains**. These lands are **prone to flooding**, especially in the flood plains of the Shannon river system.
- Farmers are encouraged to combine forestry with farming. They have been given grants to set aside lands for tree planting.

Climate

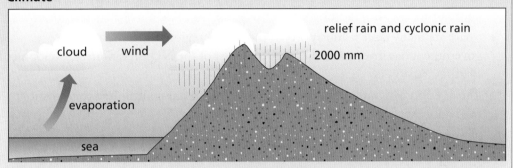

Relief rain in the West of Ireland creates over 2000 mm of precipitation in some places

- The West of Ireland has a cool temperate oceanic climate with most rain falling during the winter months. **Rainfall totals over 2000 mm** annually.
- **Frontal depressions** are forced to rise over the western mountains causing heavy relief rainfall. Many places have over 250 wet days per year.
- Heavy rainfall causes leaching of the soils.
- The prevailing winds of the region are the **south-west anti-trades**.
- Winter temperatures average 5°C; summer temperatures rarely average above 15°C. The low summer temperatures and heavy rainfall restricts the variety of crops that can be grown.
- The North Atlantic Drift keeps the **coastal waters ice-free** throughout the year. This influences Ireland's climate, keeping it mild with no extremes of temperatures.
- Tillage is not suited to most of the region due to high rainfall, low sunshine levels and poor drainage.
- Traditional farming in the BMW provides only **low incomes to most farmers**. Average farm income is only 50 per cent of that of the eastern region.

Factors influencing fishing and forestry

These points about fishing off the west coast could help you expand your answers on primary activities.

Coastal resources

- The **continental shelf** stretches for **480 km** off the west coast. This is a shallow sea region where sunlight reaches the ocean floor and encourages the growth of plankton, which provides food for fish.
- The warm waters of the **North Atlantic Drift** encourage the mixing of warm and cold waters along the coast. This provides a nutrient-rich feeding ground for a large variety of fish species.
- The **indented coastline** provides sheltered harbours, such as Killary Harbour, for aquaculture (e.g. fish farming).
- There are many large fishing ports in the BMW region, e.g. **Killybegs**. The government has invested in these ports as part of the NDP (National Development Plan).
- The development and promotion of inland fishing has contributed to tourism in the region, such as along the River Moy in Co. Mayo.

Manufacturing industry (Secondary activities)

Exam questions usually ask for primary, secondary or tertiary activities in 'one Irish region that you have studied', so you can choose the region for your answer.
Always choose two headings/factors when writing about primary, secondary or tertiary industries. The marking scheme normally specifies:
- two secondary activities identified – 2 marks
- two factors named – 2 marks + 2 marks
- examination – 10 × SRPs @ 2 marks each.

Government influence

- The **peripheral location** of the BMW West region **on the edge of Europe** in a country that lacks mineral resources such as iron or coal meant that industry on a large scale was very slow to develop.
- Most Irish industry is light and footloose industry, so it was suited to urban locations in the West such as Galway, Castlebar and Sligo.
- Membership of the EU in 1973 led to investment in an **improved transport and communications** system in the West.
- A growing and **well-educated labour force** and government policy, including low corporation tax, attracted foreign companies (multinationals) to locate in Ireland.
- In the 1960s and 1970s, multinational branch plants were attracted to rural areas by the IDA in the West, where the **costs of urban land and labour were lower** than in urban areas of the South and East.

Most government support in the West was invested in its urban regions, such as Galway

- Government policy encouraged a movement of industry from the Dublin region to the underdeveloped BMW region. This helped create 10,000 jobs in foreign-owned manufacturing companies by 1973.
- This region the past was able to benefit from Structural Funds from the EU. To qualify for this it had to have a GDP per person of less that 75 per cent of the EU average.
- The **National Development Plan** is focused on attracting future growth in the region through a network of gateways and hubs of Tuam and Ballina/Castlebar.
- The growth of **third-level colleges** in the towns of the West has attracted advanced technology companies, such as biomedical device manufacturers, to Galway and Castlebar.
- The government set up **Údarás na Gaeltachta** to develop industries in Gaeltacht areas. Industries receive special incentives such as grants to locate here.

Human/urban factors

- The population of the BMW/West is much lower than the East/Dublin region: 25–30 people per square kilometre.
- Even though the urban areas in the West continued to attract industry, the fact that most urban areas and larger urban areas were located in the South and East was the reason these regions continued to attract most industries.
- **Galway City**, however, became a centre for high-tech multinational companies such as Digital Galway, because of its **university** status.
- During the economic recession of the 1980s the manufacturing workforce in the BMW continued to grow to about 40,000 people, but this growth rate was slower than in the 1970s.

- Manufacturing employment peaked in the BMW region in 2001 at 60,000 workers. Since then this figure has fallen dramatically due to recession.
- **Dependence on foreign companies** is high, with 51 per cent of the workforce employed in foreign-owned factories in 2008.

Tertiary activities

Services/Tourism

In a developed economy, the majority of people are employed in the tertiary sector. These services are available in urban regions.

- The BMW West region is **mainly rural**, so the number of people employed in the service sector is lower than the national average.
- Apart from Galway, most towns in the BMW West region do not provide a good range of high-quality services. Many people from the region commute to urban areas, such as Galway, Dublin and Limerick, for work.
- The **decentralisation** of government departments to regional centres, such as the Department of Education to Athlone, helps to reduce the imbalance of service employment.
- The BMW West region has many advantages for **tourism**, such as scenic areas like Connemara and the Shannon waterway.
- The BMW West region has 52 per cent of the country's bed capacity, but generates less than 40 per cent of the country's tourist revenue.
- Tourism is **seasonal**, with July and August the most important months; many people in the catering and hotel trade become unemployed in the off-season.

Human processes

- The population of the BMW West region has been in decline since Famine times. This trend in migration will continue for some years to come due to the economic recession following the collapse of the Celtic Tiger.
- More than 18 per thousand of the population in Connacht are aged over 60 years. Death rates are 10.8 per thousand.
- Although the BMW covers 60 per cent of the country, it has only one-third of the population.
- Over **66 per cent of the people live in rural areas** and most of the Gaeltacht areas are located in this region.
- The **boundaries** of the **Gaeltacht regions** have reduced, as have their populations. Although the region is the heart of Irish culture, the number of native Gaelic speakers is in decline and the boundaries of Gaeltacht areas are shrinking.

The Southern and Eastern region

South and East region

exam focus

Practise drawing one of these maps of an Irish region until you can complete it in two minutes. Use pencil only: colour is not essential.

The South and East of Ireland is a prosperous/core Irish region

Migration to Dublin

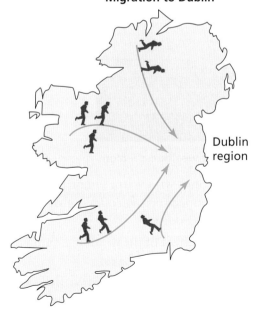

Dublin region

key point

The Dublin region is the core economic region in Ireland. It has more towns, more industries and more resources than the West/BMW. The South and East is richer, drier and has more developed infrastructure than the West.

The Dublin region is a prosperous/core Irish region

Primary activities

Physical factors: Relief, soils, climate

- Most of the land in this region is **undulating lowland**.
- **Brown soils**, formed from the original deciduous woodland cover and limestone glacial drift, cover much of the region. *Example*: Co. Kilkenny.

Many of these points are common to both the Dublin region and the South and East region. Choose **one** of these regions and make sure you can write at least 15 SRPs on it.

- Rivers, such as the Barrow, Nore and Suir are wide and deep, and drainage of the area is much better than in the BMW region.
- River valleys provide **natural routeways**, e.g. the valleys of Munster.
- Rivers such as the Liffey, Lee and Suir flow into the Celtic and Irish seas. They provide natural, sheltered inlets at their estuaries.

The East and South of Ireland is our wealthiest region

- The climate of this region is cool temperate oceanic, with warm summers (average 17°C) and mild winters (average 5°C). These temperatures encourage growth for eight months of the year. Little stall feeding is necessary.
- The lower level of the land and the **rain-shadow effect** of the western mountains results in much lower rainfall levels: less than 1000 mm in places.
- **Rainfall** is better **distributed throughout the year** than in the BMW. The south-westerly winds are milder and less severe because of the presence of trees and hedgerows, which are largely absent along the west coast.

- Winter temperatures are lower because of the effect of increased distance from the warm North Atlantic Drift; but **summer temperatures are higher** than in the BMW region.

Commercial factors

- To be competitive, **farms are more mechanised** in the South and East; they are larger and have a higher percentage of younger, more innovative farmers.
- Highly productive arable (tillage) and pastoral farming (cattle grazing) produce high-quality outputs. Grain growing has increased due to high prices for wheat and barley.
- **Farming is intensive** and specialised, giving better income levels and prospects for rural communities. Average farm income is 40 per cent above the national average.
- Because most lowland is used for farming, **only upland slopes are forested.** The most forested counties are Wicklow and Waterford.
- The largest fishing ports are **Dunmore East, Kilmore Quay** and **Howth.**
- The more polluted waters along the south and east coast limit the development of aquaculture.

Manufacturing industry in the South and East (Secondary activities)

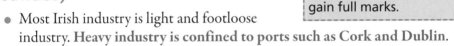

Try to write 15 SRPs for regional 30-mark questions/answers to gain full marks.

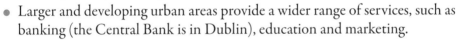

- Most Irish industry is light and footloose industry. **Heavy industry is confined to ports such as Cork and Dublin.**
- Larger and developing urban areas provide a wider range of services, such as banking (the Central Bank is in Dublin), education and marketing.
- A growing and well-educated labour force and a government policy, which included low corporation tax, attracted foreign companies (multinationals) to locate in Ireland.

Natural resources in the Cork region

- Cork harbour is a natural deep-water port capable of accommodating ocean-going shipping, including oil tankers.
- During the 1980s many of Cork's established industries closed due to their high production costs.
- During the 1980s over 5,500 people were made unemployed in the Cork region and it became a region of industrial decline.
- Cork's industries were **revitalised in the 1990s.** Chemical and pharmaceutical industries have located around Cork harbour.
- A deep port facility was developed at **Ringaskiddy** to benefit **Pfizer** and other heavy industries.
- Cork's success occurred because its infrastructure, such as education (Cork Institute of Technology), port facilities, airport and roads were all modernised.

Many industries have located in industrial regions around Cork harbour

The national capital: A core region

- Membership of the EU in 1973 led to investment in an improved transport and communications system. This led to the construction of **dual carriageways**, such as the Naas dual carriageway, and improved surfacing of national routeways.
- All the national primary routes pass through the South and East because they all lead to Dublin. Most industrial estates are located close to or on these routes.
- Dublin remains Ireland's largest industrial centre. The Celtic Tiger encouraged many high-tech industries around Dublin.
- In the 1990s, **60 per cent of Ireland's net growth** in manufacturing was in the Dublin region.
- The **National Spatial Strategy**, as part of the National Development Plan, has focused on attracting new growth industries through a network of **gateways** and **hubs**.
- Many new industrial estates and business parks, such as Park West in Dublin, were established to cater for the growth in manufacturing and service industries.
- **Most industrial jobs** are located in the South and East because most of Ireland's urban areas are in the region.
- Dublin's region has a **high population density**: 43 per cent of the population are aged under 25, which provides an educated labour force and market.
- People are wealthier in the GDA (Greater Dublin Area), making the region attractive to producers of high-value luxury goods.
- There are, however, many problems for industry, including traffic congestion on the M50, which disrupts the delivery of raw materials and manufactured goods.
- Poor planning laws and corruption have led to urban sprawl with few or no definite boundaries.

- Spiralling house prices have driven young people out of the city to dormitory towns, increasing Dublin's urban hinterland.
- Because over 50 per cent of Ireland's manufacturing employment is controlled by foreign companies, Ireland's industrial base is prone to downturns.
- In recent years some Irish companies, such as Dell Ireland, have relocated much of their manufacturing to Poland and other cheaper locations.

Tertiary activities

Services

- In 1981 Ireland became defined as a service economy when, for the first time, more than half the working population was employed in the tertiary sector.
- By 2002 approximately 70 per cent of all employment was in services, and three-quarters of these jobs were in the eastern and southern region.
- In the 1990s, four out of every five jobs created were in the services sector.
- The three most important of the internationally traded service (ITS) industries are:
  o computer software
  o data processing (including telesales)
  o international financial services.
- By 2002, some 56,000 jobs were available in ITS, and Greater Dublin benefited most.
- Its well-developed communications systems have been vital in attracting data-processing operations, while the many third-level colleges and universities have attracted computer software companies.
- The most notable new development in Dublin has been the **International Financial Services Centre (IFSC)**.
- Dublin is the country's capital city and the decision-making centre for many public and private enterprises.
- It is the dominant shopping centre, with a range of major educational, health and recreational facilities, and it is the hub of the country's transport system.
- Over 60 per cent of the country's €4.9 billion of tourist revenue is spent in the South and East region. This is directly related to air access: 93 per cent of all scheduled flights to Ireland land in Dublin.
- The South and East region has more developed transport systems than the BMW region, including:
  o most of the country's ports
  o two of the three international airports
  o the national rail and road networks, which meet in Dublin.

Human processes

- The south and east has increased its share of the national population, owing to people migrating from the BMW region in search of work. Its population is now three times greater than that of the BMW.
- Its **towns are more numerous**, larger and more evenly distributed, and three-quarters of its population lives in these urban centres.
- An estimated 86 per cent of Ireland's third-level places are in the region, and 90 per cent of the region's graduates find jobs here.
- The population is younger, with only 14 per cent aged over 60 years.
- Birth rates are higher and death rates are lower than in Connacht.
- The region provides an **above-average prosperity** level, higher than the EU average.

A European region (Not Ireland)

When a question asks you to write about 'a European region (not Ireland)', it refers to a region of a country on the **continental landmass of Europe**, e.g. the Paris Basin, the Mezzogiorno.

The Mezzogiorno in Italy

Mezzogiorno

key point

The Mezzogiorno is a peripheral/ disadvantaged region in Europe.

The Mezzogiorno has suffered from out-migration for over a century

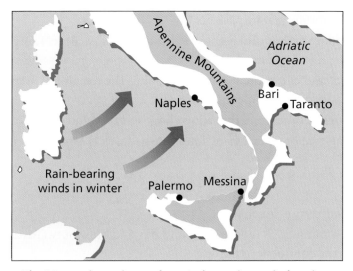

The Mezzogiorno in southern Italy receives rain-bearing
winds in winter

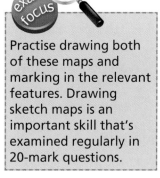

Practise drawing both
of these maps and
marking in the relevant
features. Drawing
sketch maps is an
important skill that's
examined regularly in
20-mark questions.

Always choose two headings/factors
when writing about primary,
secondary or tertiary industries. The
marking scheme normally specifies:

- two secondary activities
  identified – 2 marks
- two factors named – 2 marks
  + 2 marks
- examination – 10 × SRPs
  @ 2 marks each.

Physical factors: Relief and soils

- Southern Italy is dominated by the steep slopes of the **Apennine mountains**, which stretch 1,500 km along the spine of the peninsula.
- The **Mezzogiorno** stretches from Rome to Sicily.
- The **rich, fertile, alluvial (river) and volcanic soils** from weathered lava are mostly located in **valley flood plains** or **narrow coastal plains**.

The Mezzogiorno has many villages perched
on high ground to avoid the wastage
of precious farmland

- Calabria, in the toe of Italy, is mostly granite plateaux with poor, thin soils.
- The Apennines were formed from the **collision and subduction of small tectonic plates.**
- The Tiber is the largest river and enters the sea south of Rome. The remaining rivers are small, fast-flowing streams from the Apennines.
- Much of the **bedrock is porous limestone** that allows little surface drainage.
- The high Apennines are **karst** landscapes, where limestone bedrock is exposed over large regions.

Climate

- The Mezzogiorno has a **Mediterranean** climate.
- High pressure dominates in summer. **Winds are hot and dry** and blow outwards as north-easterly winds from the continent of Europe.
- Summer rains fall as **intense downpours** accompanied by thunderstorms. These create rapid runoff and erosion, often leading to landslides and mudslides.
- Temperatures are high, with an average of 29°C.
- Winters are mild, about 17°C, and moist. South-west winds bring cyclonic rain. Rainfall amounts range from 500 mm to 900 mm annually.
- The lowest rainfall occurs along the Adriatic coast, because it is in the rain shadow of the Apennines.

Primary activities

Human factors

- Until the 1950s, the majority of the working population was employed in farming and fishing. The people were poor and incomes were low.
- The system of land ownership was called **latifundia**: most of the best land was owned by absentee landlords. A lot of land was farmed but yields were low. It was an **inefficient** system and farmers were poor.
- Peasant farmers lived in hilltop villages and travelled daily to work on the latifundia.
- Only one-quarter of the farmers owned their own land.
- By 1950, 70 per cent of these farmers' land holdings were smaller than three hectares. To support their families they overworked the land, leading to overgrazing, overcultivation and eventually soil erosion. This system was called **minifundia**.
- Most of the original pine woodland cover was cut down for agriculture, leaving the steep Apennine slopes without vegetation, the roots of which had bound soil particles together.

Government influence

- From 1950 onwards, most of the estates were bought by the State and the land was redistributed to the landless labourers.
- Holdings of **5–50 hectares** were created.
- Farmers were trained to work their newly family-owned land efficiently, growing a mix of crops such as cereals, citrus fruit and traditional crops of olives and vines.
- Three related factors were put in place to support this new farming system:
  - an irrigation network to promote growth in summer
  - improved transport systems, such as **autostradas**, to get high-value, perishable crops to market quickly
  - new villages and towns were built with all the important services such as schools, healthcare centres and leisure facilities.
- Today only one in ten of the region's workforce is involved in farming. The move to more intensive farming by fewer farmers has also increased rural prosperity. The Mezzogiorno is now a leading supplier of **citrus fruits**, vegetables and **olives** to European markets.
- The most successful farming areas are on coastal lowlands and river valleys where irrigation water is available.
- The **Metapontino** is a coastal strip in the Gulf of Taranto. It was once a malarial swamp, but was drained as part of the land reform programme.
- Using the waters of the five rivers that cross the plain, irrigation produces cash crops such as citrus fruits, peaches, table grapes, strawberries, flowers and salad crops.

Secondary activities

Government influence

- Because it is a peripheral region, the Mezzogiorno is an Objective I status region.
- By the 1950s, only 17 per cent of Italy's workforce was located in the Mezzogiorno. Just as with agriculture, industrial development here has had its successes and failures.
- **Government help** was needed to encourage industrial development. This help included:
  - generous grants and tax relief
  - state-controlled companies had to make 80 per cent of new investment in the South
  - a number of key industrial development areas were created to act as a basis for regional growth.

Some results of the reforms

- Between 1960 and 2000 the region's industrial workforce almost tripled, to 1.4 million, and over 300,000 new jobs were created. This has reduced dependence on agriculture and increased the prosperity of the people.
- Almost 75 per cent of all new jobs have been in heavy industries such as steel, chemicals and engineering. Because the heavy industries are located on the coast, the inland rural areas have remained depressed.
- The most successful region is the **Bari–Brindisi–Taranto** triangle, where oil refining, chemicals and steel form the basis of this major industrial zone.
- The construction of a new deep-water port at Taranto was vital in the selection of this site for the country's largest iron and steel mill.
- **Latina–Fronsione** is the fastest growing industrial area in the South. Over 250 new factories, including a car plant, employ over 16,000 workers.
- **Catania–Augusta–Siracusa** is one of the largest oil-refining, chemical and petrochemical complexes in Western Europe. Local deposits of potash, oil, natural gas and sulphur favour this type of industry.

Transport infrastructure

- Major improvements in roads, autostradas, and **modernisation of ports** such as Naples and Taranto.
- Major investments were made to **improve transport systems**. The backbone of the system is the **Autostrada del Sole**, which runs from the Swiss border in the north of Italy to the 'toe' of Italy in Calabria. Another motorway runs along the east coast.
- Bridges were built over deep gorges and valleys; tunnels were drilled through steep mountain spurs to shorten journey time to this peripheral region.
- The supply of fresh food in winter and early spring, such as early vegetables, fruit and fish, to the much colder northern region (e.g. the Plain of Lombardy) was made possible and viable by this investment in 1,000 km of road way.
- Port developments have improved access to the South, and these regions have become core industrial centres.

Tertiary activities

Tourism

- The long, hot, dry summers, dramatic coastal scenery, extensive beaches, and historic cities have much to offer the tourist. The South also tends to be cheaper and less crowded than other Italian regions.
- Hotels have been improved to cater for the 12 million tourists who visit the south annually.

- More than 9 million of these tourists come from other parts of Italy.
- Sorrento, near Naples, is a major tourist centre. Located near **Mount Vesuvius**, **Herculaneum** and **Pompeii**, it is a busy coastal resort on cliffs that overlook the old town's fishing village and the Isle of Capri, another major tourist resort even in Roman times.

Human processes

- Migration within Italy is a major factor, influencing population patterns in the country. Between 1951 and 1971 over 4 million migrants left the South because of unemployment and poverty. Most of those who left were attracted to the cities of Milan, Turin and Genoa, or to the USA.
- Over 1 million people left the Mezzogiorno in the 1980s, and this **outmigration** trend continued into the 1990s.
- Since the 1990s, increasing numbers of migrants from other countries, such as Albania and the former Yugoslavia, have been attracted to Italy.

The Paris Basin

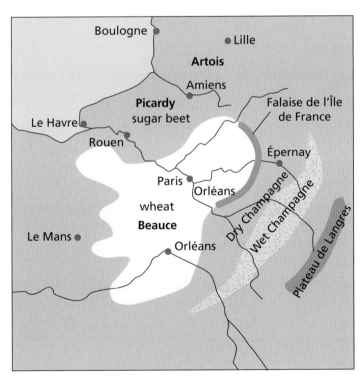

The Paris Basin

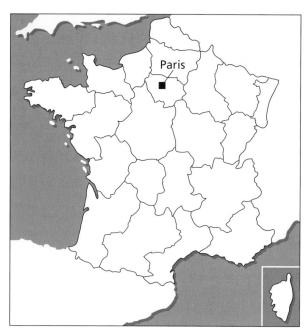

- Always draw a box around your sketch map and give it a title.
- Always mark and name each feature you are asked for.

The location of the Paris Basin

Primary activities

Primary activities are influenced by the following factors.

Physical factors: Relief, drainage and soil

- The Paris Basin occupies 25 per cent of France and is larger than Ireland.
- Structurally it is a broad, shallow **downfold** (depression) consisting of layers of sedimentary rock, one inside the other, and it might be described as a series of stacked saucers.
- In the centre are **sandstones and limestones**, which are surrounded by belts of chalk and clay.
- In the east and south-east the edges of the chalk and limestone stand out prominently.
- Erosion has exposed the sedimentary rocks and has produced a landscape of alternate **scarps** (Côte de Meuse) and vales (Dry and Wet Champagne).
- The Paris Basin has a covering of **limon**, a wind-blown soil. Limon soils are fine-grained, rich in minerals, and level.
- Champagne Pouilleuse (Dry Champagne) is named after the permeable nature of the chalk.
- East of Champagne Pouilleuse is an outcrop of clay, once an area of marsh, shallow lakes and damp soils, called Champagne Humide (Wet Champagne).
- The Paris Basin is drained by the River **Seine** and its many tributaries (e.g. the Rivers Oise, Marne, Aube and Yonne).

Climate

The Paris Basin experiences two types of climate:

- Along the English Channel (coastal strip) there is a **maritime climate**.
  - South-west anti-trade winds blowing over the English Channel and the North Atlantic Ocean bring rain throughout the year.
  - These warm, moist winds keep the climate mild in winter and warm in summer.
  - Because the Paris Basin forms part of Continental Europe, its summer temperatures are higher than average for its 49° latitude.
- Inland, towards Paris and the scarplands, a **transitional** type of climate is experienced. This means that it forms a middle zone between the maritime climate on the coast and the continental type in central Europe.
  - Paris has average temperatures of 2.5°C in January and 18.6°C in July, and annual rainfall of 570 mm.
  - It has cool, dry winters and hot summers, with maximum rainfall in spring and summer.

Agriculture

- The rolling expanses of **loamy limon soils** grow wheat and sugar beet on the Île de France. In Beauce, large farms and level, open landscape allow intensive mechanised cultivation of cereals: wheat, barley and sugar beet.
- Many farms **exceed 80 hectares** (200 acres) and have large fields where a high degree of mechanisation is achieved. The area is called the **granary of France**.
- The scarp slopes of Falaise de l'Île de France are sheltered and sunny, so this is a region of vineyards famous for **champagne**. Reims and Epernay are market centres for the wine industry.
- Mixed farming is carried on in Dry Champagne, with animal farming and cereals such as wheat. In Wet Champagne, dairy farming is practised on the valley floor.
- Surrounding Paris, intensive market gardening supplies the conurbation with a large variety of vegetables.
- The population of the Paris Basin is approximately 22 million people. This population provides a large market for farm produce grown in the region.

Secondary activities

Transport centre

- Paris is a focus of routes – air, water, road and rail – on a **bridging point** on the River Seine.
- It is the centre of an important inland waterway system, and is connected by canal to the Rhine, the Loire and the Saône, and to the sea at Le Havre. All these waterways are used by barges to transport goods.
- Although it is 160 km from the sea, Paris is an extremely busy **inland port**.

- Products from the Paris Basin, as well as imports, are stored on the quays upriver from Le Havre and Rouen.
- Paris has 20 per cent of the national workforce and a highly diversified economy: craft industries, such as perfumes and fashion clothing, vehicle assembly, oil refining and chemicals.
- Industry in Paris has been successful because:
  - (a) it is in the centre of a rich agricultural hinterland, with processing such as milling and canning
  - (b) it is the centre of French rail, including the high-speed TGV system and road networks, so it is the ideal location for assembly-type manufacturing as components can be brought from all parts of France and other European markets
  - (c) it is built on a wide and deep river, the Seine, and has excellent dock facilities for the export of products and the import of raw materials.
- **Le Havre** is an important port at the estuary of the Seine. It has many industries, such as **oil refining and chemicals**. Ship repairs and maintenance are also important in Le Havre.
- **Rouen** on the River Seine is an inland port with large oil-refining and chemical industries.

Tertiary activities

Transport

- Paris is the centre of the French transport system.
- All routes meet in Paris and the **autoroutes** and rail networks connect Paris to other regions.
- Paris is the hub of the **TGV** rail system, a high-speed train network on which trains can reach speeds of 300 km per hour.
- Paris is also connected by the TGV system to London, via the Channel Tunnel, and to Brussels.
- There are about 350 TGV trains in operation, making it a very efficient system.

- Transport systems within Paris create thousands of jobs. Part of this service is the **Métro**, which is the underground rail system in the city.
- The Métro is connected to the national network, the SNCF, and the Réseau Express Régional, an underground rail system that extends into the suburbs.
- The périphérique is a ring road in Paris that helps reduce traffic congestion.

Urban planning

- Poor, old housing in Paris was demolished and replaced with modern high-rise apartments in **urban renewal projects**, e.g. near Montparnasse.
- Five new towns (e.g. Melun Senart), each catering for over 100,000 people, have been built north and south of the Seine near Paris.

Tourism

- About 30 million tourists visit Paris annually.
- Its **wide boulevards**, which meet at the Arc de Triomphe, ornate buildings, art galleries such as the Louvre, monuments such as the Eiffel Tower and street attractions such as Montmartre on Sundays all add character to the city.
- **Disneyland Paris** is located 30 km to the east of the city.
- To the west of the city is the **Palace of Versailles**, the former royal palace of Queen Marie Antoinette and King Louis XVI.
- The Paris Basin has many other attractions, such as the cathedrals of **Notre Dame**, Chartres and Rheims. Paris has been described as the most beautiful city in the world.

Human factors

- One of the most successful developments in Paris has been at **La Défense**, to the west of the city centre. Large office complexes have been built, creating thousands of office jobs in the tertiary sector.
- The total population of the Paris Basin is 22 million people. This is more than one-third of the population of France.
- The Île de France, the centre of the Paris Basin, has 11 million people. This creates high densities in the centre, in stark contrast to the edges of the basin, where densities are much lower.
- The birth rate for the Île is 15 per 1,000: a large proportion of the population is young. The death rate here is only 7 per 1,000, so **natural increase is 0.8 per cent**.
- The edges of the Paris Basin are suffering from out-migration and these migrants are moving towards Paris because of its attracting forces.

Racial composition

- A shortage of labour in cities along the River Seine after World War II attracted migrant workers. **Portuguese and Algerian migrants** came to France in large numbers, along with migrants from other North African countries.

- About 1.2 million foreign workers live in the Paris area.
- Famous people of French colonial origin include the soccer player Zinedine Zidane (from Algeria) and the rugby player Serge Betsen.
- Some North African countries were colonies of France and so their people were entitled to enter France.
- Large numbers of migrants live in **inner-city ghettos** or **poor suburban neighbourhoods**.
- Unemployment in France has led to racial tensions in the past.
- The rise of Islamic fundamentalism has led some Islamic women to adopt more traditional codes of dress, and this has resulted in some tension in schools and with school authorities.

12 The Dynamics of Regions: A Subcontinental Region (India or the American Southwest)

You need to be able to:

- Study **one** continental/subcontinental region only: **either** India (pages 121–132) **or** the American Southwest (pages 132–138).
- If you have not studied either of these regions, use this chapter as a guide to how to lay out your notes.
- Make sure you know everything about your chosen region under the headings in the chapter. *Note:* culture appears regularly in exam questions.

The Indian subcontinent

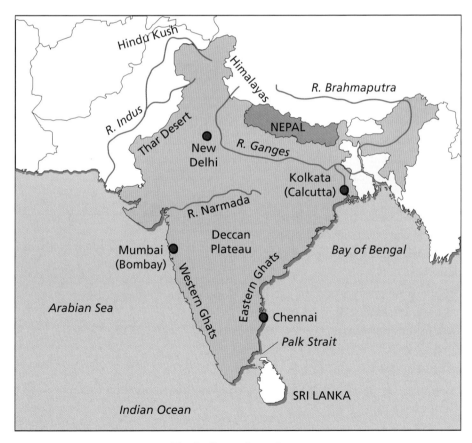

The Indian subcontinent

India is a subcontinental region. It is one of the most heavily populated and also one of the poorest regions in the world. The physical environment and human activities have a profound effect on each other.

Primary activities

Physical factors: Relief, drainage and soils

There are three main physical regions in India:

- Northern Mountains
- Indus–Ganges Plain
- Southern Plateaux.

Northern mountains

- Extremely high mountains in the north of the country separate India from its neighbours.
- They extend from the **Hindu Kush** in the north-west, through the **Himalayan range** to the extreme north-east of the country.
- Mount Everest, the highest mountain on earth, and the next 23 highest peaks are all in this range.
- They were formed by the **collision** of two of the earth's **crustal plates**, the Eurasian plate and the Indian plate.
- This collision compressed the earth's crust and buckled it upwards to form these fold mountains.

Indus–Ganges Plain

- The Indus–Ganges Plain is a **huge depression** or syncline that formed south of the mountain chain.

Draw a sketch map of India. On it show and name:
- the outline of the region
- two seas
- two rivers
- two cities
- two upland regions.

Then practise and practise this until you can do it in two minutes.

Always choose two headings/factors when writing about primary, secondary or tertiary industries. The marking scheme normally specifies:
- two secondary activities identified – 2 marks
- two factors named – 2 marks + 2 marks
- examination – 10 × SRPs @ 2 marks each.

Focus on how the physical landscape and climate affects agriculture. This shows an examiner that you understand the interaction between these forces.

- It is covered with thousands of metres of **alluvial (river) soils** that have been washed into the depression by India's three most important rivers – the Indus, the Ganges and the Brahmaputra – and their tributaries.
- About half of India's people live in this region.
- The rivers are swollen in summer by melt-waters from glaciers and monsoon rains from the surrounding mountains.
- Extensive areas of lowland are flooded by these waters, which deposit highly fertile soils on their flood plains.

Southern plateaux

- Southern India is made up of a number of plateaux. The **Deccan plateau**, the largest, is tilted from west to east. Its basaltic black soils retain moisture and are suited to growing cereals.
- Two mountain ranges, the **Western Ghats** and **Eastern Ghats**, border narrow coastal lowlands. Both of these increase rainfall amounts for peninsular India.

exam focus

Always give at least 15 SRPs in a 30-mark answer and explain the relationship or interaction between the statements you make.

Climate

- **Temperature and rainfall levels vary** according to altitude and distance from the sea.
- The climate of India is **tropical continental monsoon**. Most of India is in the tropics.
- Only the mountains of the north and north-west have frost. Temperatures are high year-round.
- India's climate can be divided into two main seasons: the dry monsoon and the wet monsoon.

The dry monsoon season

- This occurs from **October to June**, when cold winds blow outwards from a high-pressure area in the centre of Asia. They are land winds, so they are dry. They bring freezing temperatures and snow to the mountains in the north.
- From March to June these winds become warmer, and by June temperatures can be as high as 49°C in the Ganges valley.

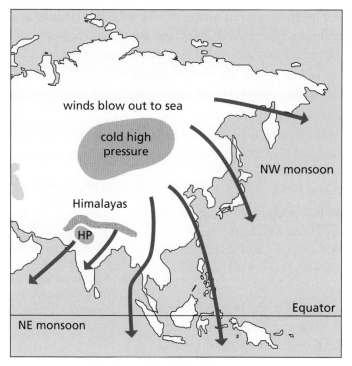

October to June is the dry season

The wet monsoon season

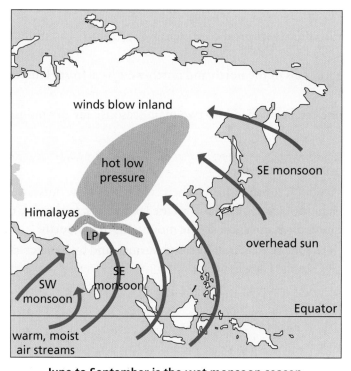

June to September is the wet monsoon season

- From **mid-June to September**, warm ocean winds are sucked into a **low-pressure** area in the continent. One wind blows as a south-west monsoon from the Arabian Sea. Some of this air is forced to rise over the Western Ghats and intense rain falls. The second wind blows from the Bay of Bengal and veers north to blow along the Ganges and Brahmaputra valleys. In some areas, up to **10,000 mm of rain** can fall in a six-week period.

- As the winds move west along the Ganges valley, rainfall reduces. When they reach the extreme north-west, the winds have become dry, leading to desert conditions.

exam focus

Exam questions often ask you to explain how climate and soils have influenced farming in a continental or subcontinental region.

- The monsoons bring essential water supplies to India's population. If they don't arrive it can mean widespread famine in the country.

- The rains provide the ideal environment for the production of rice, which needs flooded fields in its early stages of growth.

Farming

India's farming output has increased substantially, but most of its farms are tiny and output is low

- India's cultivated land is equal in area to the total cultivated land of the EU countries. Arable farming, especially cereals, is the main type of farming.
- Two-thirds of India's one billion people depend directly on the land for their living. Almost half of rural families have farms of less than 0.5 hectares, or no land at all.
- A quarter of India's agricultural land is owned by less than 5 per cent of farm families. Most family farms are broken up into tiny, scattered plots.
- Farming is mainly intensive subsistence. This means people depend on their own food supplies to feed themselves.
- Rice is the chief crop. Cereals such as wheat and millet are grown in drier areas.

- Almost all planting, weeding and harvesting is **done by hand**.
- Double cropping is practised: rice is grown in the wet season, and other crops, such as cereals, are grown in the drier season.
- The country's rapidly growing population places a huge demand on annual output.
- **Genetically modified**, high-yield varieties of rice and wheat have been introduced and are now grown. These varieties are resistant to many diseases and pests.
- India has the largest livestock population in the world. Many are in poor physical condition.
- The slaughter of cattle is illegal in many states because of the Hindu belief that the cow is a sacred animal.
- Most of the beef that is eaten comes from cattle that have died of old age.
- Many cattle are malnourished and old livestock are allowed to roam as strays or may be sent to special compounds until they die.

key point

India's 'green revolution' is the government's aim to make India a net exporter of food to ensure political stability and security. The green revolution has led to India becoming a net food exporter.

Mining

- India has **large reserves of iron ore and copper**. Other mineral ores are bauxite, from which aluminium is made, and zinc, gold and silver.
- Most of India's oil comes from Mumbai (Bombay) High Field in the Arabian Sea.
- The most important coal-producing regions are Bihar and West Bengal.

Secondary activities

Government influence

After independence in 1947, only 2 per cent of the labour force was employed in industry. Industry was concentrated in the major cities of Mumbai (Bombay), Kolkata (Calcutta) and Chennai (Madras).

Indian industry has three factors in its favour:

- a large home market
- a wide range of natural resources, such as coal and iron ore
- a cheap labour force.

The government has focused on new industries such as:

1. Agri-industries: the manufacture of fertilisers and machinery and food processing to benefit rural communities.
2. Consumer goods industries and small-scale, labour-intensive craft industries which can be competitive in export markets.
3. Community-based developments and self-help schemes in rural regions: this was intended to create jobs in rural regions where over 70 per cent of the people lived.

4. High-tech industries: the growing educated workforce is attracting computer software companies to India. India produces more university graduates than the USA and Canada combined. Most of these new industries are located in urban regions such as Kolkata, Mumbai and Chennai and their hinterlands.

Planning programme in urban centres

- Following independence, national planning recognised the importance of urban centres for economic development.
- A new capital, New Delhi, was set up.
- Major urban growth centres were also established, based on existing cities.
  - **Mumbai.** Over the centuries Mumbai became a region of in-migration because it practised a policy of religious tolerance. Mumbai has attracted growth industries such as electronics and pharmaceuticals. It also has traditional industries, e.g. food processing and textiles.
  - **Chennai.** Chennai forms the core of the southern industrial zone. Textiles and light engineering are important industries. Many multinational computer software companies have set up here. The region is called India's 'Silicon Valley'.
  - **Kolkata.** Heavy industries such as iron and steel are long established, owing to local sources of coal and iron ore. The Indian-owned Tata Iron and Steel Company is one of the largest in the world.
- India is ranked thirteenth worldwide in manufacturing output and the manufacturing industry employs 18 per cent of India's total workforce.
- India's iron and steel industries are based on large reserves of iron and copper ores in the north of the country.
- Government investment in education has driven India's increasing industrial production and services.

Tertiary activities

Services

India's service sector is underdeveloped. So many of India's population are poor and do not have the money for education, healthcare, or much else, even if these services were available. As with similar economies, there are two levels of services:

- One type caters for what are regarded as the rich; for them there is the full range of services.
- The other type caters for the poor, or underclass. It is similar to what you would find in any large city, and is the informal sector. There are the unlicensed street sellers such as shoeshine people and street vendors, alongside illegal activities such as prostitution and drug dealing.

Transport

In 2009, half of India's villages did not have access to tarred roads suitable for vehicles. These communities use dirt-track roads and carts drawn by cattle.

Tourism

India's varied landscape, its history and its natural wonders offer vast potential for the tourist industry. Attractions include:

- the Himalayan mountains
- the many palaces and religious temples of the Hindu, Buddhist, Sikh and Muslim religions
- the physical landforms of the major rivers
- a wide variety of wildlife.

Tourism is on the increase. However, much remains to be done, especially when there is such pressure of population numbers. The obvious poverty of many of the people can be upsetting for the visitor.

Human processes and culture

Population dynamics

- India's population is greater than **one billion people**. With a **natural increase of 1.6 per cent annually**, its population increases by 16 million people every year, and could reach 2 billion by 2040.
- The country has only recently **entered the third stage of the population cycle**.
- Even though healthcare has improved and the death rate has reduced, death rates are still high.
- Because rural families are large, it is **difficult to control population**. Large families are seen as a positive aspect of life, rather than as a burden to feed and clothe.
- Because India has a very young population, it will continue to have a large natural increase for the near future.
- India's population is very unevenly distributed. There are high population densities in the Ganges valley, along coastal lowlands and in cities and their hinterlands. The interior regions have low population densities.
- India has many different cultural groups. A number of outside factors have complicated matters. These include:
  - the migration of Europeans
  - the spread of Islam
  - British occupation.

Languages

- The people of India speak many different languages: there are over **1,600 different languages and dialects**. Schools teach in 58 different languages.

A 30-mark question on culture regularly appears in the exam. The marking scheme in 2009 asked for the following.
- Aspect of culture identified – 2 marks
- Region named – 2 marks
- Examination – 13 × SRPs @ 2 marks each
- Other aspects of culture may be credited from SRPs.

- The constitution of India recognises 18 languages.
- National newspapers are published in 87 languages and radio programmes broadcast in 71 different languages. This creates difficulties and disunity between cultural groups.
- The two main language families in India are **Indo-European** (the largest language group) and **Dravidian**.

- **Hindi** is the official state language, but its position of importance is resented by other language groups. It is spoken by over 250 million people.
- Dravidian languages are spoken by 200 million people, mainly in the south of the country.
- English, which is spoken by about 2 per cent of the population, is a legacy of British colonialism.
- Language differences in India emphasise cultural divisions rather than unity within the state.

> **exam focus**
>
> A question asking you to explain cultural differences appears regularly in exam papers. Use any two headings, (e.g. religion, language, customs, etc.) to structure your answer.

Clothing

Indian clothing is distinctive and colourful

- Many Indian people, especially in cities, wear Western-style clothes, but most Indians wear traditional clothes:
  - men wear a **dhoti**, a simple white garment wrapped between the legs, like loose trousers

- o women wear a **sari**, a straight piece of cloth draped loosely over the shoulders and head and around the body like a long dress. Wealthy women may wear saris of silk, with borders of gold thread.
- Indian men of the **Sikh** tradition wear a turban and a beard.
- Many women wear a **kumkum**, a round dot usually made with a red or black powder, in the middle of the forehead. The kumkum is considered a mark of beauty.

Religions

- Asoka, an ancient Indian ruler, converted to Buddhism and helped to spread it throughout India, in the 4th century BC.
- Three other outside influences that affected India are: European migrations (Europeans moved to India, bringing their languages with them); the spread of Islam; and British colonisation.

Hinduism

Every year, millions of Hindus gather at the steps in Varanasi to wash in the sacred River Ganges

- Hinduism is the dominant religion in India.
- In Hinduism there is a multi-layered society in which people are divided according to class or **caste**. At the top of society are the priests or Brahmins, and other high-ranking people such as officials or professionals. At the bottom are the lowest castes (e.g. the **Dalits**), who do the menial or dirty work.

- Belonging to a caste is decided by birth and one cannot move up the system in a single lifetime. Caste members often only socialise or marry within their own group; but education has helped to change this perspective and today many educated Hindus of various castes mix freely, especially in urban regions.
- The castes help preserve and pass on various skills in the arts and crafts from generation to generation.
- Hindus are forbidden to kill cows or to eat their flesh, because cows are considered sacred. Many cattle are undernourished and roam freely, even in cities.
- **Hindus** believe that all living creatures will have many lives on earth after they die. This philosophy is called **reincarnation**.

While Hinduism is the main religion, other religions are also important.

Islam

- There are about 200 million Muslims in India. Islam was introduced through trade to India and it is most common in the Indus and Ganges basin. It is rare in peninsular India.
- Islam accepts all converts as equal and rejects the caste system, which is why it was attractive to many Indians.

Sikhism

Sikhism was founded in the 15th century. It does not have a caste system. The Sikhs are a powerful cultural group and are centred in the Punjab, an important farming region.

Buddhism and Christianity

Buddhism and Christianity are minority religions in India.

The political–religious divide in India (see p. 153)

- India was a **colony of Britain**. After **independence in 1947** it was **divided into two states**: India, a Hindu state, and Pakistan, an Islamic state. This division was based on religious grounds and caused many minority religious groups to remain within the Indian state.
- Large-scale migration resulted, due to fears of persecution. Over 15 million people moved home. Many Muslims left India for Pakistan, and many Hindus left Pakistan for India.
- Pakistan was initially divided into two parts: West Pakistan, in the Indus valley; and East Pakistan, in the Ganges valley. They were separated by a long distance, with northern India in between.
- In 1956 East Pakistan broke away from West Pakistan and became **Bangladesh**.

- Some territory is still in dispute between Pakistan and India; this disputed region is called **Kashmir**.

OR

The American Southwest

The American Southwest

The American Southwest is a region that borders Mexico, stretching from California in the west to Texas in the south. Its states include **California**, **Nevada**, **Arizona**, **New Mexico** and **Texas**.

American Southwest states

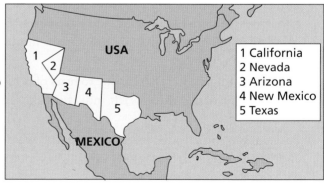

1 California
2 Nevada
3 Arizona
4 New Mexico
5 Texas

States in the American Southwest

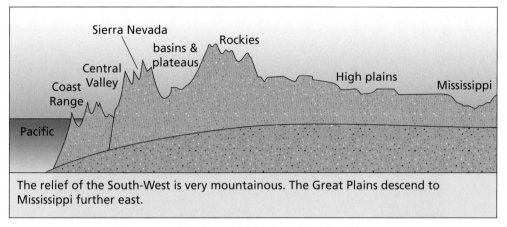

Sierra Nevada

Rockies

basins & plateaus

Central Valley

Coast Range

High plains

Mississippi

Pacific

The relief of the South-West is very mountainous. The Great Plains descend to Mississippi further east.

A cross-section through the American Southwest

Primary activities

Physical factors: Relief, drainage and soils

The physical landscape of the American Southwest varies enormously.

- To the west in California is the Central Valley, which separates the **Coastal Range** from the **Sierra Nevada Mountains**.
- Further east are the highlands and **mountain plateaux and basins** of the mountain states of Nevada, Utah and Arizona, the largest of which is the Great Basin of Nevada.
- Further east still are the **Rocky Mountains**, which fall on to the High Plains of Texas.
- The **Great Basin** is the largest basin of internal drainage in the USA.

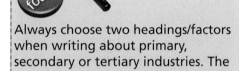

Always choose two headings/factors when writing about primary, secondary or tertiary industries. The marking scheme normally specifies:

- two secondary activities identified – 2 marks
- two factors named – 2 marks + 2 marks
- examination – 10 × SRPs @ 2 marks each.

- **The Great Salt Lake,** near Salt Lake City, was formed from salts that resulted from the evaporation of river waters flowing towards this depression.
- The **Colorado** and the **Rio Grande** are the two largest rivers in the region.
- The Colorado flows through the Grand Canyon gorge, which formed as the river eroded vertically through this barren landscape in northern Arizona.
- The Rio Grande separates Texas from Mexico. The soils in the lower stage of the Rio Grande are rich in alluvial deposits.

Climate

Large regions of the American southwest have desert characteristics, with drought-resistant plants

- Much of the Southwest is **arid** or **semi-arid**, with average annual precipitation below 250 mm. Southern California, Arizona and New Mexico are either desert or semi-desert.
- **Death Valley** in southern California, which is below sea level, has recorded the hottest temperatures in the western hemisphere.
- Central Valley in California has a Mediterranean climate of hot summers and warm winters with temperatures somewhat like our summer days.
- Farmers must practise irrigation in many places to overcome drought for crop production.
- Climates range from sub-tropical along the Gulf Coast to mountain climate in the Sierra Nevada and Rockies, and cover a vast region that stretches 3,000 km from coastal Texas to California.
- The region forms part of the **Sun Belt** of the USA. Many regions that border Mexico have over 2,500 hours of sunshine annually.

Agriculture

- The availability of water supplies and altitude influence agriculture in the region. Many family farms exist here.
- The industry is dominated by large farm units, in many cases owned by **agri-companies**.
- Agriculture is very market-focused and highly industrialised, with heavy investment in machinery.

- The greater proportion of the region is dominated by **cattle ranching** in the dry lands of Nevada, Utah, New Mexico and Arizona.
- Rainfall is uncertain and the low stocking rates means that cattle numbers per hectare are few.

This is an extensive form of farming and is very different from the intensive form of agriculture practised in the **Central Valley in California**:

- Irrigation is widely used for intensive farming in response to the rapid rise in population in this region over the past 40 years.
- About one-third of the fruit crops and one-third of the truck crops of the entire United States are produced in California.
- One of the largest networks of irrigation systems in the world supplies water to the farms in California.
- The farms specialise in **fruit and vegetables**.
- **Citrus fruits** are widely grown: California is the second largest producer in the United States, after Florida. The other fruits that are grown include dates, peaches, grapes, cherries, tomatoes and plums.
- Many regions specialise in a single crop, such as the Napa and Sonoma valleys, which specialise in vines and the wine industry.
- Much of the agricultural labour is carried out by migrant Mexican labourers.

Natural resources

- In the past many people were attracted to the Southwest because of its minerals, such as gold and silver.
- The discovery of gold in 1848 led to the **Californian Gold Rush**.
- Today, **oil and natural gas deposits** are the main employment providers. Texas, in particular, has enormous deposits.
- The wealth of the region fluctuates and depends on the value of oil. During periods of high oil prices profits soar and employment improves, while when oil prices are low the level of employment falls.
- **Mining** is still important. Uranium, sulphur, gold and copper, lead and zinc are all mined.
- The mineral deposits owe much of their origin to igneous activity associated with subduction of the Pacific plate under the North American plate. This region is **part of the leading edge of the American Plate**.

Secondary activities

Manufacturing

In recent years manufacturing has moved away from the north-east USA to southern California and Texas. This is because of the large numbers of **Mexican migrants** who have settled in towns along the Mexico–USA border region.

The advantages of the region for manufacturing are:

- There is plenty of cheap land for factories.
- On the Pacific Rim it is close to Asian markets, and it is close to the Atlantic Ocean for access to European markets.
- There are many industrial raw materials in the area, such as oil and gas for the petrochemical industry.
- Cities do not suffer from urban decay and the quality of life is good.
- The **US Air Force bases** in the region have given rise to many factories making military equipment. San Diego is a military naval base and the largest in the country.
- The south and west is well connected by road to markets in the USA.

Manufacturing in Texas

- Texas is eight times the size of Ireland. It is the most important state in the USA for the production of the oil and gas that form the basis of many industries.
- The coastal cities on the Gulf are known as 'the chemical crescent'.
- There are 30 oil refineries on the coast, as well as numerous petrochemical works and fertiliser plants. Offshore oil and gas platforms are located off the coast.
- The **aerospace industry** is centred on **Houston** – so aircraft, space-related technology and satellite equipment are manufactured in the region.
- Much industry is located in the industrial triangle of Houston, Dallas–Fort Worth and Austin–San Antonio.
- Austin, the home of Michael Dell, is the corporate headquarters of the Dell Corporation, which manufactures PCs.

Silicon Valley in California

- Silicon Valley is the best-known centre for **information technology** in the Western world. Famous companies, including Hewlett-Packard, Intel, Sun Microsystems, Apple and IBM, are all located here. Silicon Valley is located south of San Francisco.
- Stanford University and the University of California are central to the growth of Silicon Valley.
- Approximately 50 per cent of all high-tech equipment in the USA is manufactured here.

Manufacturing on the Mexican border

- Multinational companies locate twin manufacturing plants on each side of the Mexico–USA border.
- The Mexican companies supply products that are made with low labour costs to their American companies, which then export the finished product.
- These manufacturing centres on the Mexican side are called **maquiladoras**. Many of them have experienced rapid growth in recent years.
- In 2000, 23 per cent of all Mexican manufacturing production came from maquiladoras.

Tertiary activities

Tourism

- Tourism is a major industry in the Southwest. The Grand Canyon, Zion National Park, Yosemite, and Carlsbad Caverns, one of the largest limestone caverns in the world, are all located here.
- Many cities, such as San Francisco and Las Vegas, and Hollywood in Los Angeles, are also major tourist attractions.
- Las Vegas is the gambling capital of the world. It is a city built especially for entertainment, in a desert landscape.
- San Francisco is a major tourist town. The prison of Alcatraz on an island in San Francisco Harbour, the trams on Powell Street and Chinatown attract many visitors.
- Public transport is a problem for Los Angeles. The lack of an underground system, as well as few bus routes, have led to an extreme form of car culture where everybody has a car.

Human processes – Culture

The total population of the American Southwest is about 60 million people. Many cities are affected by **urban sprawl**, and large numbers of people have difficulty travelling to work because of traffic problems.

The Southwest is a **multi-cultural society**.

Native Americans

- Most Native Americans live on reservations. Some have become farmers, stockmen and truckers.
- Native Americans were dispossessed from their traditional hunting grounds in the nineteenth century by Eurasian migrants in search of farmland.
- The spread of the railway system and the destruction of the buffalo herds that the Native Americans depended on for their food supply helped reduce their population numbers.
- European diseases, alcohol and wars dramatically reduced the native population.

The Hispanic community

- The term 'Hispanic' refers to people of the Spanish-speaking world who come from Mexico and other countries in Central and South America, south of the USA. There is a large Hispanic community in the Southwest.
- Even though there are Hispanics who have become wealthy in the USA, the majority stay in poverty for many years after arriving.
- Numerous television channels are broadcast in Spanish.
- Many Hispanics live **illegally** in the USA but aspire to the American way of life and so learn English and American customs very quickly.

- Immigration laws have favoured Latin American and Asian migrants rather than Europeans in recent decades.
- Hispanic culture thrives in the Southwest and the border region is known as Mexamerica.

Chinatown in San Francisco displays many distinctive Oriental-style buildings and signs

The Asian community

- A large number of people from **Asian ethnic groups** live in the Southwest. They include Chinese, Japanese and Vietnamese.
- The majority of these people live in California, the American region nearest to where they originally came from.
- Many Chinese live in ghetto areas for social security; originally they lived in ghettos as a refuge against abuse. Over 30,000 live in **Chinatown in San Francisco**.
- Many Asians have been very successful in third-level education and business.

The African American community

- Large ghettos of African Americans live in cities such as Los Angeles.
- The riots in Watts in south-central Los Angeles occurred as a result of discrimination in housing and jobs.

Use the Web to find out about Rodney King and the 1992 riots in Los Angeles.

Questions 4B and 6C, 2009.

Primary/secondary/tertiary activities in an Irish region: 4B, 2008; 4B, 2007.

13 The Complexity of Regions 1

aims You need to know about:

- the interaction between cultural groups within countries in Europe and within Ireland
- the European Union, its future expansion and its effects on Ireland.

Case study 1: Northern Ireland

Historical background

- Scottish settlers were brought to the region during the Ulster Plantation.
- These settlers had a **different culture**, religion and traditions from the local Catholic population.
- In the nineteenth century, Ulster experienced the development of heavy industry based on coal supplies from Scotland.
- So when partition occurred in 1921 the Republic had an underdeveloped economy, while the north-west was a thriving industrial society.
- The majority of Irish people saw that political independence was essential for the economic and cultural development of the other three provinces, Connaught, Leinster and Munster.

> **key point**
>
> Economic, cultural and political processes interact within regions.

See also Religious Conflict in Northern Ireland, page 298–299.

Changing relationships on the island of Ireland

Economic trends

- Migration was dominant throughout the decades up to 1960.
- Since then the Republic has attracted foreign multinationals to Ireland.
- Ireland has a developed, modern, industrial economy with high-tech industries. Some industries, however, have reduced their workforce to remain competitive in the recent recession.
- Northern Ireland, on the other hand, has a depressed economy. Its old textile and shipbuilding industries have gone, although modern green energy generators for wave power are manufactured here.
- Civil unrest and religious bitterness have discouraged foreign investors.

Political interaction

- Tensions between the Republic of Ireland and Northern Ireland faded somewhat between 1921 and the 1960s.
- The refusal of the British government to grant full civil rights to Catholics in the North led to a state of near civil war that persisted virtually continuously until the 1990s.
- The signing of the **Belfast Agreement** led to new political interactions based on the 'Strands'. These new political bodies are a new Northern Ireland Assembly, a North–South Ministerial Council and a British–Irish Inter-Government Conference.
- These bodies are designed to create inter-relationships and encourage co-operation rather than division.

The interaction of cultural groups within political regions (Countries)

Some minority culture groups with a strong self-identity feel their interests are not represented by the larger host country in which they live; so the links that tie these regions together become weakened.

What emerges are nationalist groups that look for more powers of self-government.

This is called **autonomy** or **devolution**. A more extreme agenda would involve a new and separate state from the majority population.

The syllabus requires you to study the interaction of cultural groups in Ireland and in Europe.

Case study 2: The Basques

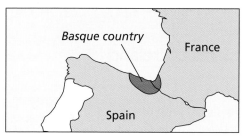

Most of the Basque region is in Spain; the remainder is in France

Always write your answers in paragraphs. The bullet points here are purely to help your revision.

The Basques may be used as an example to answer a range of related questions on changes of political boundaries, cultural conflict and political conflict.

The scenic landscape of the Basque region contributes to its attraction for tourists

A cultural group without nationality

- The Basque country is a region at the western end of the Pyrenees, the mountains that divide France from Spain.
- It is made up of seven districts, four of which are in Spain and form the largest section, while the other three are in France.
- Three of these historic Basque territories – Araba, Bizkaia and Gipuzkoa in the north of Spain – are grouped together to form a political unit, known as **Euskadi**, or the Autonomous Community of the Basque Country.
- Euskadi has a population of 2.1 million people. They have their own president and parliament but are represented internationally by Spain.
- Spain's other Basque district, Navarra, is its own region, separate from Euskadi and less troubled politically.

Who are the Basques and why are they different?

- The Basques were living in the Pyrenees over 4,000 years ago, long before the Celtic tribes of central Europe moved west to Britain and Ireland.

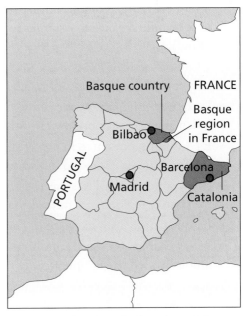

Spain, showing the location of the Basque country

- Basque cuisine is based on seafood, especially cod and hake.
- Basque dishes are very popular throughout Spain and most major cities have Basque restaurants.
- The annual bull run has made **Pamplona**, a city in Navarra, famous.
- Every year, six bulls are allowed to run freely through Pamplona's streets before being killed later that day by matadors in a bullring.
- Many people run ahead of the bulls and some get hurt or killed.

Language

- The Basque language forms a crucial part of their unique identity. It is called **Euskara**, and it is spoken by about 520,000 people.
- It is one of the **oldest living languages** and is not known to be related to any other language.
- It was spoken in the Basque region in Neolithic or Stone Age times.
- The first written texts in Euskara date from the tenth century.
- The language was forbidden after the Spanish Civil War in the 1930s, when the dictator General Franco was in power.
- Basque schools, called **iskastolas** started in the 1930s in defiance of this policy.
- Because there were many dialects of Euskara, steps were taken in 1964 to create a unified Basque language.

Basque conflict with the Spanish government

- A small number of violent extremists are represented by **ETA** (in Euskara it stands for 'Basque Homeland and Freedom'), an **armed nationalist group**.
- They believe that complete independence from Spain and France can be achieved only by military means – similar to what the IRA believed about the reunification of Ireland.
- ETA was founded in 1958 because the Basque people were oppressed during the reign of the fascist dictator Franco in Spain.
- In the beginning they were a non-violent group, but their every move for independence was put down by force. This made them opt for armed resistance.
- ETA is not represented in power sharing in government. So ETA has returned to violence, the very method it discarded as hopeless in 1998.
- A key concept of ETA is the 're-nationalisation of the Basque country' – to restore the Basque region to its full cultural identity.
- Basque nationalism has risen in France, an area that was formerly stable.
- Policy changes on social conditions and welfare and the loss of influence by trade unions has led to discontent.

The future of the European Union

New developments in the EU will influence trade, politics and sovereignty issues.

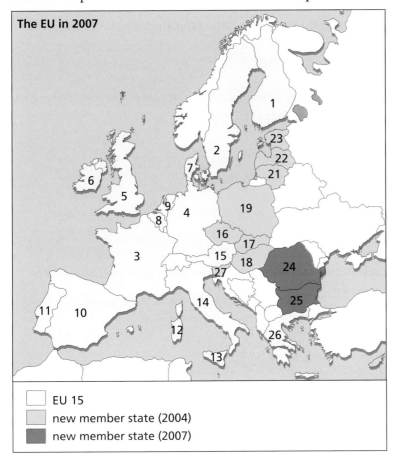

The EU in 2007

EU 15
new member state (2004)
new member state (2007)

Name each country of the EU numbered 1–25

exam focus

Make sure you can name all 27 EU countries.

Recent treaties/agreements

- **Maastricht Treaty** (1992) – established the three 'pillars' of the EU (economic, political, social).
- **Single European Market** (SEM) (1993) – allowed for the free movement of goods, services and people within the Economic and Monetary Union (EMU).
- **Amsterdam Treaty** (1997) – placed employment and citizen rights at the heart of the EU.
- The **euro** – introduced in 2002.
- **Nice Treaty** (2002) – allowed for change in the institutions and voting systems so that the EU could be further enlarged.
- **The Lisbon Treaty (2009) made changes to the way the EU is run and how it makes decisions:**
  - Each member state will continue to nominate a Commissioner.
  - Many decisions on legislation are to be made by the Council of Ministers in co-operation with the European Parliament.

- A new post of President of the European Council was created.
- The European Parliament and the Council of Ministers to have joint decision-making powers over the entire EU budget.
- The European Parliament and the Council of Ministers to make co-decisions on agriculture, asylum and immigration.

Sovereignty

Each member had to give up some degree of independence or sovereignty, so four main political institutions were created to regulate the Union:

- European Commission in Brussels
- European Parliament in Strasbourg, Brussels and Luxembourg
- Council of the European Union (Council of Ministers)
- European Council.

Development and expansion of the EU

In 1957 the **Treaty of Rome** created the European Economic Community (EEC). Its purpose was to increase trade between six countries in the core of Europe. Since then there have been six enlargements:

- **1973**: Denmark, UK, Republic of Ireland
- **1986**: Spain and Portugal
- **1990**: East Germany became part of Germany
- **1995**: Austria, Sweden and Finland
- **2004**: a number of Eastern Bloc countries (Czech Republic, Estonia, Hungary, Latvia, Lithuania, Poland, Slovak Republic, Slovenia), plus Cyprus and Malta
- **2007**: Bulgaria and Romania.

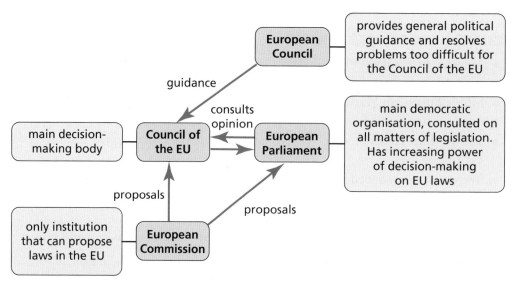

How decisions are made in the EU

SAMPLE EXAM QUESTION AND ANSWER

Question: Examine the impact of European Union expansion on Ireland's economy and/or culture OR examine the impact of EU expansion on any one EU country.

Note: Use what you have learned in your Junior Cert CSPE course to develop these statements about the EU.

Answer:

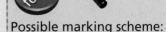

- Ireland joined the European union in 1973 and became one of nine members. Before 1973 the EU had only six members. This allowed greater access for Ireland to foreign markets.
- Ireland achieved Objective 1 status, which allowed access to Structural Funds for economic and social development.
- The Irish government invested large sums into the road network of the West as well as funding a new airport in Knock to allow easier access to core regions for the western counties.

Possible marking scheme:
- two impacts identified – 2 marks
- examination, 13 x SRPs @ 2 marks each
- discussion without reference to Ireland or EU country – 0 marks
- discussion without reference to enlargement – maximum 6 marks.

- Agriculture was the first Irish industry to benefit from EU expansion. Farms were modernised, improved breeds of cattle were introduced, and grants were given to farmers to improve their farms, e.g. milking parlours were built (the Guidance Fund).
- Rationalisation for the EU single market encouraged agricultural co-operatives to join and become some of the largest agri-based companies in the world.
- The Common Agricultural Policy created a Guaranteed Fund to maintain high prices for farm produce.
- Ireland became a major player for **foreign direct investment** (FDI) as industries that located in Ireland had direct access to the EU market.
- Ireland's new **branch plants** involved the processing or assembly of imported raw materials and component parts, e.g. Krupps in Limerick in the 1960s and more recently Dell Ireland in Limerick.
- The dependence on Britain as our main market for goods changed and mainland EU is now our major market area.
- Originally agricultural goods dominated Ireland's trade and this has been replaced by a range of manufactured goods, such as computers and computer parts.
- As almost all production by multinational companies (MNCs) is for export, membership of the EU has been and is crucial for the long-term success of Irish industries.
- Ireland has a **more diverse culture** as a consequence of migration from eastern European countries such as Poland as well as African-Europeans from former colonial powers such as Britain and France.

Disadvantages

- Membership of the EU allowed **foreign trawlers** access to Irish territorial waters: these caused over-fishing in areas such as the Celtic Sea.
- While **farm income has increased**, the number of family farms and farmers has declined.
- Increased agricultural production has led to river, ground-water and lake **pollution**.
- Since 2007 the EU has had 27 members. This has had a major effect on Ireland. Some Irish regions have **lost their grant status**, e.g. the BMW region has lost its Objective 1 status. This means less income from the EU.

The future of EU Expansion

Advantages

- As the EU becomes a larger region its increased population will provide a growing market for Irish products.
- The increasing area of the EU will provide a greater supply of raw materials that can be accessed by Ireland without extra import taxes being paid.
- The enlarged EU will provide new opportunities for highly skilled Irish graduates establishing new companies in these new states.

Disadvantages

- Newer member states have lower production costs and this encourages existing Irish companies to locate **replacement plants** in Central and Eastern Europe.
- New EU member states create **increased competition** for foreign direct investment (FDI).
- Higher levels of unemployment and lower living standards in **newer member states** encourages out-migration. This may have a negative effect if many people migrate to Ireland.
- The large new **eastern periphery** will take a large percentage of Structural Funds. This will lead to a reduced take for Ireland.
- Ireland has **lost its status** as a problem region, which has led to reduced support funds for roads and other developments.

Questions 5C and 6B, 2006; 6C, 2008; 5B, 2009.

14 The Complexity of Regions 2

aims You need to know:

- that the boundaries and size of regions may change over time
- how the size of some cultural regions has changed over time
- how one Irish urban region and one European urban region have expanded over time
- how cultural groups have been affected by changes to the political boundary of a country.

Changing boundaries in language regions

The size and shape of language regions can change over time.

The Irish language regions

The boundaries of Gaeltacht regions have reduced over the past century

- There were 1.5 million Irish speakers in 1851. Most of them lived in the western half of Ireland.
- From 1861 the number of Irish speakers declined to 544,000. This was due to:
  - large-scale emigration
  - the growing popularity of English.

From 1926 to the present

After independence the Irish government was committed to supporting Irish:

- Irish became the official language of the state
- Irish was compulsory at school
- official Gaeltacht regions were identified.

The present

- About 1.5 million people can speak some Irish. However, few are fluent.
- The largest number of Irish speakers are in Leinster.
- The Gaeltacht boundaries have diminished to tiny pockets that are located on peninsulas in the West of Ireland.

Urban growth and city regions

World urban growth

- In 2004, half of the world's population of 6 billion people lived in cities.
- By 2025 about 80 per cent of people will live in cities.
- The growth rate of this trend is fastest in the developing world.

Urban growth in the EU

- About 80 per cent of the population lives in cities.
- Urban sprawl is a problem in every EU country.
- Rush hours create traffic jams in most city regions.

exam focus

You are expected to study urban growth and expansion of one city region in Ireland and Europe. Dublin and the Randstad are the examples chosen in this chapter.

SAMPLE EXAM QUESTION AND ANSWER

Question: 'The boundaries of city regions have expanded over time.'

Discuss this statement, with reference to **one** example you have studied.

The Growth of Dublin – An Irish urban region

Answer:

- Founded by the Vikings, Dublin has become Ireland's largest city with a population of 1.3 million people in the Greater Dublin region, 35 per cent of Ireland's total population.
- The original settlement of Dublin occupies a low-lying site on both banks of the Liffey where it enters Dublin Bay. This is the lowest bridging point on the River Liffey and so was a natural focus of coastal and inland routes.
- Dublin became the focus of the country's roads, rail and canal networks over the centuries. Today all national primary routes and rail routes meet in Dublin.
- Before World War II Dublin was a compact city. The built-up area did not extend more than 5 km from its centre.

1960s expansion

- Dublin underwent a period of rapid expansion during the 1960s. Most of this expansion occurred within 8 km of the centre of Dublin.
- Many inner city communities were removed from decayed slum regions such as The Liberties and relocated in new housing estates and apartment complexes in places such as Tallaght and Ballymun.
- Dublin's expansion continued throughout the 1970s due to the development of three new towns: Blanchardstown, Clondalkin and Tallaght. About 40 per cent of Dublin's population now lives in this zone.

Dublin region

The urban area of Dublin has expanded dramatically over the past 20 years

Recent expansion

- As competition for land and the cost of living continues to rise in Dublin, more and more people are encouraged to look farther from the city's edge. Many small towns and villages more than 16km from the city centre have therefore increased in size.
- For people who live close to or on transport routes to the city, long-distance travel to work has become an accepted part of their daily lives. Dublin's hinterland has expanded, so many people commute from as far away as Arklow or Athlone.

Solving Dublin's urban problems

- Dublin is a primate city and it contains ten times the population of our next largest city, Cork.
- The National Spatial Strategy formed part of the National Development Plan (2007–2013) with a fund of €184 billion to invest in new developments.
- The National Spatial Strategy proposed large-scale developments in a series of gateways, and hubs to encourage the dispersal of population and employment out of the Dublin region.

○ Gateways, such as Limerick, Galway, Athlone and Mullingar offer the best prospects for countering the dominance of Dublin. These developments include:

1. Hubs, such as Kilkenny, Castlebar and Monaghan. These are smaller urban centres that will help disperse development from gateways into their regions.
2. Strategic road corridors that provide efficient links between gateways, hubs and Dublin.

○ Dun Laoghaire Corporation and Dublin County Council were abolished and three new counties – Fingal, South Dublin and Dun Laoghaire-Rathdown – were created to administer to the needs of Dublin's population.

SAMPLE EXAM QUESTION

Describe and explain the growth of one major urban area in a European region (not Ireland) that you have studied.

Marking scheme:
- region named – 2 marks
- urban area named – 2 marks
- examination – 13 × SRPs @ 2 marks each.

Case study: The Randstad

Growth of the Randstad

- The western part of the Netherlands is one of the **most urbanised** regions in Europe. It has a radius of approximately 50 km.
- Most of the country's major cities are in the Randstad: they include Amsterdam, Utrecht, Rotterdam and The Hague.
- The Randstad contains **40 per cent** (6 million) of the Dutch population living on only 17 per cent of the country's land area.
- The growth and expansion of the towns and cities of the Randstad have created a sprawling urban region which can be classed as a **megalopolis**. This means that many conurbations have grown towards each other.
- The Randstad is shaped like a horseshoe and is a **polycentric** city region. This means that it is made up of a number of major cities, with no single city being dominant.
- At its centre is an important agricultural and recreational area that contains small towns and villages. This is called the **Greenheart** of the Randstad.

The Randstad – urban region

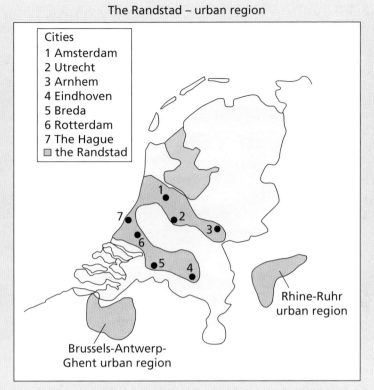

Cities
1 Amsterdam
2 Utrecht
3 Arnhem
4 Eindhoven
5 Breda
6 Rotterdam
7 The Hague
□ the Randstad

Rhine-Ruhr
urban region

Brussels-Antwerp-
Ghent urban region

**The Randstad is a horseshoe-shaped urban region in the
Netherlands**

- Since the end of World War II, the Randstad has grown rapidly. This has been
  due to the region's strategic location at the core of the EU, its excellent transport
  systems and Rotterdam, the EU's largest port.
- As this urban region developed, competition for land increased and caused
  urban sprawl to occur around the Randstad's cities. This in turn put huge
  pressure on the Greenheart.

Planning for the Randstad

- At the national level, **five regional centres** have been designated for major
  investment in infrastructure, such as transport and housing. Planners hope these
  will attract any new residential and economic developments.
- The greatest difficulty for the Randstad's planners is the **control of urban
  sprawl** and the prevention of urban growth in the Greenheart.
- Urban sprawl will be strongly controlled by **buffer zones** or **green belts** to
  prevent continuous urban sprawl and create areas of rural atmosphere in urban
  regions.
- New urban developments will also be encouraged along its eastern edge to close
  off its open end between Nijmegen and Eindhoven.

New villages have been planned in circles around centrally placed towns on land recently reclaimed from the sea

- New **overspill towns**, such as Almere on the south Flevoland polder, have been developed to cater for the overflow of people from Amsterdam and to control Amsterdam's outward expansion.

EU Concerns for the Randstad

- If uncontrolled urban growth is allowed eastwards along the river Rhine, the Randstad could eventually join up with the expanding cities of the Rhine–Ruhr industrial region in Germany.
- To the south, unplanned expansion could link up with the **Brussels–Antwerp–Ghent growth zone** of Belgium.

Changing political boundaries and cultural groups

Changes in political boundaries can have an important effect on cultural groups. Some people, as a result of changes in a country's boundaries, find themselves living under a different government or political system.

Case study: The problem of Kashmir – a religious conflict

- Remember your study of how India, Pakistan and Bangladesh became independent countries as a consequence of partition in India after independence. Different religious beliefs was the main reason for this partition.

- Once independence was achieved, the ruler of each state had to decide whether to join India (if there was a Hindu majority) or Pakistan (if there was a Muslim majority).

- Violence broke out in the Kashmir valley between the minority Hindu population, who looked to India for support, and the majority Muslim population, who looked to Pakistan for support.

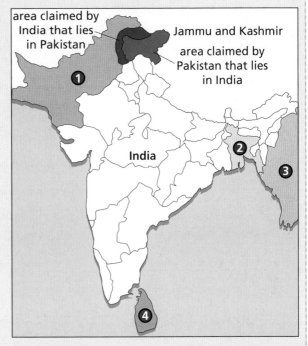

Name the countries 1–4 that surround India

- War broke out when the ruler opted to join India.

- Pakistan claimed Kashmir because there was a majority Muslim population. India claimed it because the ruler had decided to join India.

- Today the region is divided into two parts:
  - The part nearest India is under Indian control and has a Muslim majority who wish to be part of Pakistan.
  - The part nearest Pakistan is under Pakistani control and has a Hindu majority who wish to be part of India.

- The two areas are separated by a political boundary called the **line of control**. This boundary was agreed by both sides after the United Nations negotiated with the two nations.
- Regular clashes occur, as armies on both sides build up their arms in the face of a political threat. Relations between the two nations are sensitive because:
  - India controls 80 per cent of the Kashmiri population, where there is a majority of Muslims who want to be part of Pakistan.
  - The headstreams and many tributaries of the Indus river rise in the Indian-controlled part of Kashmir. The Indus is Pakistan's most important river and it depends on it for its water supply and for irrigation. It wants to gain control of this water source, which is vital for its future needs.
  - An increase in Muslim fundamentalism is creating unrest and fighting in the region.
  - Both India and Pakistan have **nuclear weapons** that could create massive damage and loss of life in a subcontinental region where one-sixth of the world's population lives.

Questions 4C, 2006; 6B, 2007; 5C, 2008; 6B, 2009.

SECTION 2
Electives

All students must study **either**

Patterns and Processes in Economic
Activities (pages 156–190)

or

Patterns and Processes in the Human
Environment (pages 191–226)

Elective 1: Patterns and Processes in Economic Activities

15 Patterns in Economic Development

aims You need to be able to:

- explain the uneven patterns in the distribution of economic activities
- assess the accuracy/usefulness of varied indicators as measures of economic activity.

key point

Economic activities and wealth are unevenly distributed over the world.

What does economic development mean?

Economic development refers to the total quality of life of a population. It includes the standard of its education, medical care and diet. The greater a country's economic development, the better the living standard of its people should be.

Measurement of economic development

Gross National Product (GNP)

- The GNP of a country is the total value of all output produced by that country's economic activities, including any income from abroad.
- It is measured in US dollars, so that relative comparisons can be made.
- For example, in Ethiopia US$1 will buy far more than in the USA.
- This is called **Purchasing Power Parity** (PPP).
- Purchasing Power Parity converts a national income to its equivalent in the USA.

Human Development Index (HDI)

The Human Development Index has a range of values from 0.0 to 1.0. The closer a country's HDI is to 1.0, the higher the value of the HDI and the better the quality of life in that country.

Three factors are used as a way of measuring development:

- life expectancy
- GNP per person
- adult literacy rates.

Uneven economic development

- About one-fifth of the world's population lives on less than US$1 per day and the world's richest 1 per cent of people receive as much income as the poorest 57 per cent.
- In general, people who live in the northern hemisphere have a high living standard, because of the development of industry and the gradual urbanisation of the population.
- The majority of people who are in poverty live in the southern hemisphere.

Regions differ in their levels of economic development.

Uneven patterns of agricultural and industrial activities

A country's wealth depends on its levels of:

- agricultural development
- industrial development.

The role of agriculture

Agriculture is more important in a developing economy than in an industrial economy because:

- there are few alternative employers
- it supports many people with the basic necessities, even though living standards are at subsistence level.

But agriculture does not improve living standards, as do industry and other occupations, because:

- only low levels of education are needed to improve output
- difficult conditions such as drought or flooding add to the problems of production
- there is often poor access to markets
- the price of cash crops is unstable and generally low.

In India, almost all planting, weeding and harvesting is done by hand, and all family members are involved.

The role of industry

In contrast to agriculture, the growth of industry improves living standards throughout a population because:

- once industry is established it encourages a wide range of services that provide well-paid jobs
- transport networks are improved
- a large home market for products is created by the high wages in industry
- industry educates its workforce by introducing new skills.

Uneven development in the EU

- Uneven economic development exists between the different EU member states. It also exists within member states.
- There is a core region in the EU where living standards are high. This region includes the Manchester–Milan axis.
- There are peripheral regions where living standards are lower. *Examples:* the West of Ireland, the Massif Central in France.
- There are rich and poor regions within individual countries. In Ireland, Dublin is a rich core region and the West of Ireland or BMW is a poor peripheral region.

1. Explain the global distribution of uneven economic development.
2. Examine the various methods of measuring economic development. Use examples where appropriate.

16 Changing Patterns in Economic Development

You need to understand that:
- the economies of regions grow and change over time
- colonisation has had an impact on the level of economic development of a country.

Stages in economic development

Five changes are necessary for a country to improve economically.

1. *Change in structure*. Primary industries become less important. Industry and services improve.
2. *New technologies* are introduced.
3. Companies join together to create *larger companies*, to compete better at home and abroad.
4. Overall *quality of life* is improved. Better living standards prevail.
5. *Volume and value of trade increases*.

Fourteen of the 20 poorest countries in the world are located in sub-Saharan Africa. Their poverty is due to:

- political instability. Many are former colonies of European powers
- warfare and civil disturbances
- droughts, famines and diseases
- failure to attract industry
- a health crisis linked to Aids.

Some countries have shown a measure of improvement. These are called **newly industrialising** countries: they include Hong Kong, South Korea, Singapore and Taiwan.

Case study: Changing patterns of economic development in Belgium

The core region of Belgium has changed from Wallonia in the south to Flanders in the North. The formerly important industrial centres of Liège and Namur are located in the Sambre–Meuse Valley.

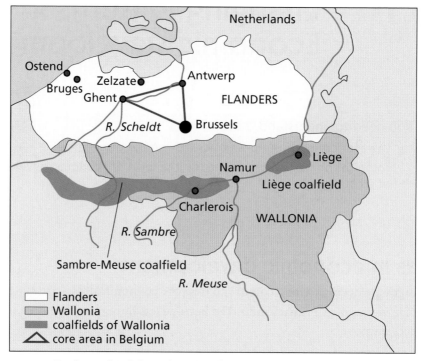

Regions of Belgium showing the Sambre–Meuse coalfield

This change was due to:

- The decline in coal mining and iron and steel production. In the 1950s new oil-burning engines replaced steam engines, so there was less demand for coal.
- New heavy industries preferred coastal locations, where iron ore could be easily imported.
- The quality coal seams of the Sambre–Meuse valley were exhausted.
- Rising costs of mining made coal uncompetitive as a fuel.
- The growth of service industries created new wealth in the Flanders region.

Now Wallonia, in the south of Belgium, is a **depressed region**. However, financial support was given by the EU to aid redevelopment. This included:

- modernising its declining steel industries
- retraining workers in new industries
- improving transport routes and the environment
- attracting new industries and services.

Why did flanders become the new core region in Belgium?

The principal reasons were:

1. its central location in Belgium and the EU

2. its location on one of the world's busiest shipping routes, the English Channel and North Sea

3. Antwerp, Belgium's third largest port, is in Flanders

4. its attractive landscape, with the historic towns of Bruges, Ghent, Antwerp and Brussels

5. a new steelworks at Zelzate near the coast.

Colonialism and development

Brussels is a bilingual city in the prosperous Flanders region

Colonialism led to the exploitation of a large number of countries in the interests of a few colonial powers.

Learn the effects of colonisation on one country that you have studied.

SAMPLE EXAM QUESTION AND ANSWER

Question: Examine the impact of colonialism on a developing economy you have studied and its adjustment to globalisation. (2008)

Marking scheme:

- impact identified – 2 marks
- named developing economy – 2 marks
- examination – 13 × SRPs.

Answer:

India during British rule:

- India was a British colony from the late 1700s until its independence in 1947. It was known as 'the jewel in the British Crown'.
- In pre-colonial times it specialised in the production of raw materials.

- Its industries were all run down to allow British goods to gain access to a large, new market.
- From then on, India specialised in **exporting primary unprocessed commodities**, such as cotton, to Britain.
- Manufacturing industries were not encouraged to develop, and this helped keep India's economy underdeveloped.
- Most of India's trade was with Britain.
- High taxes that were returned to Britain helped increase Britain's wealth.
- India's railroad system was one of the positive results of colonialism and today it is one of the largest systems in Asia.

After independence:

- In 1951, India introduced the first of many **five-year plans** to expand industry and raise living standards.
- Manufacturing industries that were established included iron and steel, sugar refining, cotton mills, mining of iron ore and coal.

Today's India

- Since 1990, India has adopted **free trade** to cash in on expanding world markets.
- It **borrowed wisely** to modernise its economy, upgrade infrastructure and expand its education programme.
- India has **attracted FDI** to modernise industry and create wealth-generating jobs in high-tech goods and services, e.g. IBM.
- The value of industrial exports has increased dramatically and India is now classed as a **newly industrialised country** (NIC).
- Its major industrial centres include **Kolkata** and **Mumbai**.
- As exports of higher-value industrial goods and services have increased, India's dependence on exporting primary goods has decreased.

Global issues of justice and development

The developing countries have been unfairly treated in three main areas:

- fair trade
- health services
- gender discrimination.

Fair trade

1. Commodity prices

- The prices of primary goods such as coffee and copper have fallen, so poor countries must export more to retain present income.
- Long working hours, child workers and unfair wages are involved.

key point

- There are justice issues involved in global development.
- Many countries have not shared equally in the development of global trading.
- Large numbers of people have failed to benefit equally from growing world development.

2. Terms of trade
The price of manufactured goods from developed countries has risen. This is a double injustice.

3. Percentage profit
- Producers of the raw materials receive only a tiny proportion of the final price of the product sold to the public.
- Most profit goes to the multinationals.

Health services
Poor quality of life and low life expectancy are the norm in underdeveloped countries. Aids has become a **disease of the poor**.

Gender discrimination
- In some countries, such as certain Arab societies, the law discriminates against women.
- Women do not have equal rights in marriage.
- Many women are not allowed to work outside the home.
- Males have a better chance of going to school than females.
- Arranged marriages often force young girls into unwanted relationships.
- Women are seen as a cheap source of labour, especially in the developing world.

Questions 7C, 2008; 8C, 2006.

17 Globalisation

 You need to understand that:
- multinational companies play a central role in the development of a single global economy
- individual economies are linked in a global framework
- decisions and actions in one part of the world can have significant consequences in distant places.

Causes of globalisation

- Improvements in transport.
- Improved telecommunications.
- More multinational companies.
- Global banking.
- Free trade.

 The world is now a workplace where decisions made in one part of the world can have major effects on people living in another part.

Economic globalisation

The two key factors in understanding economic globalisation are: **multinational companies** (MNCs) and their **foreign investments**.

Multinational companies invest huge sums of money to set up factories or mines in many countries. This is called **foreign direct investment** (FDI).

Increased international trade

More and more goods and services are being traded worldwide than ever before.

The growth of multinationals

Some of the largest MNCs have sales that exceed the GNP even of some wealthy countries. Exxon-Mobil, an American MNC, has a business turnover equal to the GDP of a rich country such as Belgium. Other MNCs include Dell, Microsoft, Toyota.

Footloose locations

Multinational companies may move part or all of their production from one country to a new location in another country where they can manufacture their products more cheaply.

The product cycle and global assembly line

1. Initial research and development occurs in the major cities of a developed country.
2. Skilled graduates and a large market are needed for early product development and sales.

Dell, a large MNC, is located in Ireland

3. As the product becomes simpler, less skilled workers, lower-cost labour, become desirable.

4. As the product becomes more basic and easier to assemble, the branch plants are moved to less developed regions, such as India and South-East Asia, for cheaper production.

key point

Individual economies are linked in a global framework.

This pattern of location or production can be viewed as a global assembly line.

Location of MNCs

There are two main desired locations:

1. major industrialised regions
2. peripheral regions.

exam focus

Carefully look at the marking schemes that apply to questions in this elective.

Major industrialised regions – The Global Triad

About 70 per cent of all MNC investment is located in industrialised regions such as the USA, Japan and Western Europe. These are the **Global Triad**. They control 75 per cent of world trade today.

Peripheral regions

Some 25 per cent of world manufacturing production comes from branch plants located in developing countries. The most successful of these developing countries are called **newly industrialising countries** (NICs).

What are branch plants?

- Branch plants are factories of an MNC that are located in foreign countries, often developing countries.
- This is done to keep profits high and remain competitive.

Advantages and disadvantages of branch plants

Advantages

- They provide work for many people in each factory, e.g. Wyeth Nutritionals in Askeaton in Co. Limerick has a workforce of 600 people.
- People learn new skills and new technologies.
- They bring a lot of investment money from abroad.
- They increase exports.
- They create many types of factories and services that help an economy to modernise.

Disadvantages

- Wages can be low. *Example:* Nike was forced to change its wage rates after criticism of sweatshop tactics in Indonesia.
- MNCs may trade only with their branch plants abroad and may not create back-up services locally.
- Much profit is returned to the MNC's headquarters in its home country.
- If branch plants close, large numbers of people may become unemployed. *Example:* Dell in Limerick reduced its workforce by 2,000 people in August 2009.
- Decision-making is generally done elsewhere and the host country has no control over these decisions.

The international division of labour

What is meant by the division of labour?

- All jobs or tasks need workers. If workers specialise in certain tasks they become more efficient at those tasks so costs fall.
- More profits can be achieved if different areas specialise in certain products or services.
- Infrastructures and land use are designed to suit this type of production.

What is meant by the international division of labour?

When a country specialises in producing certain goods or services for which it has an advantage over other regions, its productivity increases, its exports increase and its profits increase. This creates money for the country to import goods or services.

What is meant by comparative advantage?

Comparative advantage means that a region has some particular advantage that enables it to produce specific goods more cheaply than other regions. The advantage may be the presence of **raw materials**, a **specialised labour force** or some other advantage.

What has led to the development of the global economy?

There are two key factors:

1. multinational companies and the development and location of their branch plants
2. increased global trade.

Phases in the development of the global economy

Division of labour

1. The traditional international division of labour

During the Industrial Revolution colonies supplied raw materials to colonising countries, such as Britain. In turn the colonial powers sold their manufactured goods back to the colonies. In this way the colonial powers became richer.

2. The newer international division of labour

From the 1990s onwards a range of back-office services have been relocated from core countries to peripheral and developing countries. The developed countries then specialise increasingly in high-tech industries and higher-order services.

3. The most recent international division of labour

MNCs are subcontracting an increasing number of key functions from highly paid locations in core countries to peripheral regions where workforces are becoming well educated.

This prevents workers having to migrate for work to core countries and causing a brain drain at home.

Why do MNCs locate their branch plants and back-office services in peripheral regions?

- Labour costs are low.
- There are large workforces due to high birth rates.
- There is little union input, so workers can be exploited.
- Many developing countries have increasingly tried to educate their people so as to attract higher-value jobs.

MNCs in the EU and Ireland

Many foreign multinational companies have invested in factories in Ireland and in the EU.

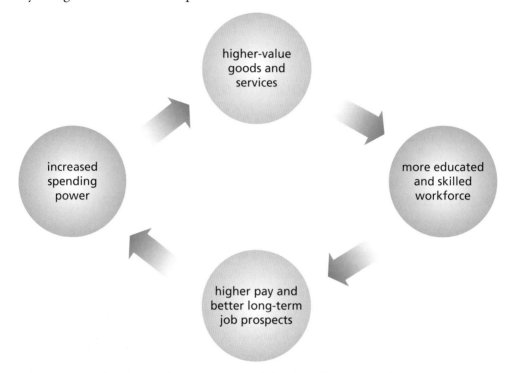

Advantages of the phases of the international division of labour for developing countries

European MNCs and their global investments

Multinational companies from the EU have been investing in branch plants in other regions for a long time.

Now the EU is the largest source region of MNC investment.

About 90 per cent of investment comes from the USA and Japanese companies, e.g. Toyota.

More and more MNC funds are used to set up branch plants and back-office services in newly industrialising countries (NICs) in South-East Asia and Latin America.

MNCs in Ireland

- MNCs laid the foundations of our industrial development in the 1960s in the Shannon Industrial Estate.
- Production is focused on high-value goods and services such as electronics, pharmaceuticals and internationally traded services.
- New plants were set up for key areas such as research and development.

Why do MNCs invest in Ireland today?

Because of:

- a large supply of well-educated, skilled young workers
- support from high-quality research facilities and universities

- low corporation tax rates for companies
- direct access to the large EU market.

Why do MNCs leave Ireland?

- Uncompetitive because wages are high.
- Less expensive graduates are available in NICs
- Recession causes some MNCs to contract and close branch plants to protect their market share.
- Other countries offer better incentives to relocate.
- Corporation tax rates may increase.

SAMPLE EXAM QUESTION

Question: In the case of one multinational company (MNC) that you have studied, examine the global nature of its activities. (30 marks)

Marking scheme:

- naming MNC – 2 marks
- naming two global locations – 2 marks + 2 marks
- examination – 12 × SRPs @ 2 marks each
- discussion with no obvious reference to global nature – maximum 6 × SRPs.

Write out a case study of one MNC that you have studied. Use the Wyeth case study below if you have not completed this exercise in school.

Case study: Pfizer – a multinational company

Always refer to the global nature of an MNC. Name some branch plant locations.

- Company name: Pfizer
- Headquarters: New York, USA
- Main products: Pharmaceuticals and Healthcare
- Global employment: 100,000
- Offices in 90 countries

Pfizer in Ireland

Pfizer (founded in 1849) is one of Ireland's leading employers and the largest pharmaceutical sector investor and employer. One of the first pharmaceutical companies to locate in Ireland (1969), Pfizer has a rich heritage of innovation and expansion over a forty year period. The business boasts almost 5,000 colleagues across 10 locations based in Cork, Dublin, Kildare and Limerick.

Pfizer's business interests in Ireland are diverse. There is a manufacturing presence in Active Pharmaceutical Ingredients, Solid Dose Pharmaceuticals, Sterile Injectibles,

Pfizer has given stable, consistent and well-paid employment to Irish workers since the 1970s

Nutritionals, Vaccines and Biopharmaceuticals; commercial Human Prescription, Animal Health and Consumer Health products businesses; Global Financial Services centre and a global Treasury operation.

Ireland is a leading manufacturing base for Pfizer globally, exporting to global markets. Total capital investment by the company in Ireland exceeds $7 billion.

Pfizer, Askeaton (Co. Limerick)

In 2009 Pfizer acquired the Wyeth Plants in Ireland as part of a Global acquisition.

- The Askeaton Nutritional Plant (formerly Wyeth) commenced commercial production in 1974.
- Today, the Askeaton plant is one of the largest infant nutritional production facilities in the world.
- 600 people are employed at the site in County Limerick.
- The plant produces both powdered baby food and liquid food.
- It has an annual capacity of 50 million kg, and uses milk from 160,000 cows to meet its annual milk demand.
- More than one-third of the company's output goes to Europe.

Reasons for locating in Limerick

- Located near the Golden Vale, Ireland's most important dairying region.
- A large supply of dairy science and general science graduates from Irish universities, especially UCC.

- Excellent transport systems, such as Shannon International Airport nearby, access to Dublin and Rosslare to export products.
- In the 1970s Ireland was trying to expand its industrial base and so offered lucrative government grants and a low tax rate to companies such as Pfizer.
- Well-developed telecommunication systems.
- English-speaking country.

Pfizer Ireland Pharmaceuticals (Newbridge, Co. Kildare)

- This plant opened in 1992, on a 40-hectare site at Newbridge, Co. Kildare and employed 50 people. Today it employs 1,000 people on a 120-hectare site. It manufactures a wide range of pharmaceutical products, such as antibiotics and hormone-replacement drugs.
- It imports its key inputs from companies in Europe such as in Germany.
- It outputs are exported to more than 100 countries across Europe, Latin America, Asia and Africa.
- Western European countries such as Britain are some of Pfizer's most important markets.
- Pfizer has plants in 90 countries including Canada, Mexico, Brazil, India, China and Australia.

SAMPLE EXAM QUESTION

This is a popular question, so learn in detail about one MNC of your choice.

Sample question:

With reference to one multi-national company (MNC) which you have studied, examine how its distribution is influenced by global factors/the global nature of its activities. (2007, 2008)

Patterns of world trade

World trade has increased hugely, especially between the EU, Japan and the USA (The Global Triad).

Two factors have been responsible for the increased volume and value of world trade:

1. the number and power of MNCs
2. improvements in transport and communications.

Merchandise trade (Trade in products)

Trade is best developed in the developed world. Regions such as South Asia and sub-Saharan Africa trade little with developed regions because:

- they were colonies until recent times.
- they produce mainly low-value raw materials
- the prices of most raw materials have declined.

The three developed regions of the EU, Japan and the USA (the Global Triad) control half the value of world merchandise trade. The EU is the most dominant of these three regions.

Patterns in the location of service industries

Globalisation has increased demand for a wide range of services, such as:

- legal and financial services
- marketing
- research and development
- back-office services.

1. Offshore financial centres

Many wealthy people use banks in island states, such as the Cayman Islands, to avoid taxation in their own countries.

2. Geographical centres of control

Major cities (London, New York, Tokyo) in the most developed regions attract the most service industries.

These cities and the global trading triad have used their power to increase their influence over poorer regions of world.

What has helped increase the trading power of the Global Triad?

- The USA has increased its influence throughout North and South America through **NAFTA** (the North American Free Trade Area).
- The EU is increasing its trading area through the eastern expansion of the EU and by creating closer ties with Russia.
- Japan is extending its influence throughout South-East Asia, Australia and New Zealand.

Questions 8C, 2007; 8B, 2008.

18 Ireland and the European Union

Trading patterns in the European Union

The EU accounts for 40 per cent of all trade in goods and services worldwide. Because a number of European countries were colonial powers, many of their former colonies are still major trading partners with the European Union. Forty per cent of the growing global trading patterns still focus on Western Europe. Patterns of EU trade can be divided into two types:

1. **Internal-EU trade** – trade between member states
2. **External-EU trade** – EU trade with the rest of the world.

Internal-EU trade

Since World War II, the growth of trade between member states has grown rapidly because of:

- the **Treaty of Rome**, which created free trade between member states
- enlargements of the EU
- well-developed rail, road, pipeline and air routes
- the large size and wealth of the EU
- the creation of the **Single European Market** in 1993
- eastern expansion of the EU.

External-EU trade

1. **Colonial links** have created a web of trade routes with the EU.
2. **Japan and the USA** are the EU's most important trading partners, creating a Global Trading Triad.
3. The **Lomé Convention** in 1963 created trade links between countries in Africa, the Caribbean and the Pacific (ACP countries). Most of them were former colonies of EU countries.
4. There is increased trade between the EU and **MNC branch plants** in Asia and Latin America.

Ireland's trading patterns in the EU

- Before the 1960s, Ireland imposed a tariff or tax on imported goods to protect home industry from competition.
- Today it is part of a tax-free open market in which all EU countries export to each other without any additional tax.

key point

Ireland is a member of the EU and so is part of a major trading bloc within the global economy.

1. Ireland's Changing Pattern of Trade
   - Until the 1980s, Ireland was dependent on Britain for over 50 per cent of the value of its exports. Today it's 36 per cent.
   - MNCs have created a global trading pattern with Ireland through their branch plants.
2. Changes in the Make-up of Ireland's Export Trade
   - Until the 1970s, food and live animals formed the largest part of our exports.
   - EU membership and MNC operations, such as electronics and chemicals, increased industrial goods and services.
   - Agricultural products now make up only 6 per cent of exports.
   - Almost all MNC products are for export, and the EU market is hugely important to them.

EU policies and the Irish economy

The Common Agricultural Policy (CAP) and its impact on Ireland

It was introduced in 1962:

1. to increase production and productivity
2. to provide a fair living standard for all its farmers.

At that time farming made up 24 per cent of Irish jobs and 43 per cent by value of Irish exports.

What policies were needed to achieve these aims?

It was necessary to:

- introduce a **common tariff** (tax) on all imports from outside the EU, to protect farmers from cheaper imports
- establish a **Guarantee Fund** and a **Guidance Fund** to finance the CAP.

What did the guarantee fund do?

- It bought any surplus farm produce within the EU to maintain high prices that were fixed each year.
- It subsidised exports throughout the world and so reduced stored surpluses. These stored surpluses were called 'intervention'.

What did the guidance fund do?

It provided money to modernise farm buildings and machinery and to organise farms into single, larger farm units rather than scattered smaller ones.

Later changes to the CAP

1. A reduction in prices guaranteed to farmers.
2. Diversification of farm activities, so as to create more income for farmers, e.g. tourism, cheese-making.
3. Making farmers more competitive.
4. Creating more direct income support for small farmers.
5. Protection of the environment.

The Irish farming sector was given a guaranteed sale price by the EU for its products

Impact of the CAP in Ireland

Positive effects

- Farms were modernised and productivity was increased.
- Subsidies encouraged some farmers to change from dairying to sheep rearing, especially in upland regions and the West.
- Farm incomes increased as their output increased.
- The number of small farms was reduced.
- Farm sizes increased and farms became more specialised.

Negative effects
- Greater inequality between small and large farmers.
- The number of farmers was reduced.
- Increased migration from rural areas.

The effects of CAP on the environment

Negative effects
- Increased use of fertilisers led to soil and water pollution.
- Hedgerows and stone walls were removed to increase field size.
- Habitat for wildlife such as plants and animals was reduced.
- Overstocking of the land led to overgrazing and soil erosion in hilly areas.

Positive effects

The Rural Environmental Protection Scheme programme (REPS) was introduced in 1994 to protect the environment.

The scheme's objectives:
- Establish farming practices and production methods to preserve the traditional landscape.
- Protect wildlife habitats and endangered species of flora and fauna.
- Produce quality food in an extensive and environmentally friendly manner.
- Produce a 5-year plan that protects the environment.

Find out more about REPS at: www.agriculture.gov.ie/ruralenvironment/

The Common Fisheries Policy and its impact on Ireland

How has the Common Fisheries Policy (CFP) affected the Irish fishing industry?

- The Common Fisheries Policy was introduced in 1983 and Ireland was allocated only 5.8 per cent of the total allowable catch (TAC).
- Irish fishermen have exclusive access to waters within 19 km of the Irish coast only, they must surrender exclusive fishing rights to remaining territorial waters.
- This exclusive zone was kept to a minimum as a consequence of pressure from Spain, which has one of the largest fishing fleets in the EU.
- The Irish Conservation Box (ICB) has replaced the former Irish Box. The ICB is smaller than the previous box area but extends much farther south than before.

Negative effects

Ireland undervalued its rich fishing resources in return for getting a better deal from the CAP. This has restricted the development of the fishing industry in the following ways.

- It has exposed Irish waters to major fishing fleets of countries such as Spain.
- With 11 per cent of EU waters, Ireland has less than 6 per cent of the total allowable catch (TAC).
- Over-fishing has almost wiped out many fish species, such as cod and herring.
- The number of days that Irish fishermen can operate at sea is currently 55 per year under the Common Fisheries Policy rules.
- Larger vessels have led to further over-fishing.
- Fishing is concentrated out of a small number of major ports.

Positive effects

- The total value of fish landings has increased significantly.
- Killybegs port in Co. Donegal is now the largest seafood port in Europe.
- Some sea areas are closed off to protect spawning adult fish and help small juvenile fish reach adult size.
- Escape panels form part of trawl nets to reduce the catch of small fish.
- Reduction of fishing time at sea helps protect stocks.

The Common Regional Policy (CRP) of the EU and Ireland

When Ireland joined the EU it was the poorest of the member states. Since then, large transfers of **Structural Funds** have been responsible for Ireland's development.

Structural funds of the common region

- **ERDF:** European Regional and Development Fund – to aid industrial development and upgrade roads.
- **ESF:** European Social Fund – to train/retrain workers who become unemployed in problem regions.
- **FIFG:** Financial Instrument of Fisheries Guidance – helps the fishing industry and fishing regions.
- **Guidance Section of the Agricultural Fund:** to improve farm structures.

The reformed CRP of 1989–99

This helped Ireland in the following ways:

- In 1989, Ireland was designated an **Objective 1** region for guaranteed Structural Funds. Objective 1 regions are least-developed regions and must have a GDP per person of less than 75 per cent of the EU average.
- Ireland had to submit National Development Plans to receive funds for:
  1. modernising high-tech industry
  2. improving transport and communications
  3. increasing labour skills for future challenges of change.
- Recently, structural funds were reduced because of Ireland's increased wealth.

The European Social Fund (ESF)

Through its National Development Plans, the ESF hopes to:

- reduce employment through training schemes
- provide affordable housing
- integrate minorities
- create gender equality in the workplace
- provide community support schemes for people in disadvantaged urban areas.

Questions 7B, 2006; 9C, 2007; 9B, 2008; 9C, 2009.

19 The Environmental Impact of Economic Development

You need to understand that economic development, which sometimes involves the exploitation of natural resources, may have negative impacts on the environment.

Renewable and non-renewable resources:
- **Renewable resources** are those such as water that, when used wisely, can be used over and over again.
- **Non-renewable resources** are those such as oil and natural gas, which cannot be renewed.

Trends in energy resources in the EU
- Oil and natural gas have replaced coal as the main source of energy.
- Nuclear power use has increased rapidly for those countries that lack other energy resources.
- Owing to increasing affluence, almost half of EU energy demands must be met by imports.
- Most EU countries must import energy supplies to meet their needs.

Ireland's energy resources
- Bord na Móna – provides low-grade fossil peat fuel for domestic use and for three peat-fired power stations.
- Six hydroelectric power stations.
- One coal-fired power station.
- Three oil-burning power stations.
- Three natural-gas power stations.
- Three gas fields: Mayo, Seven Heads and Kinsale.
- New wind turbine locations.
- Only 15 per cent of energy needs met by home resources.

The environmental impact of burning fossil fuels

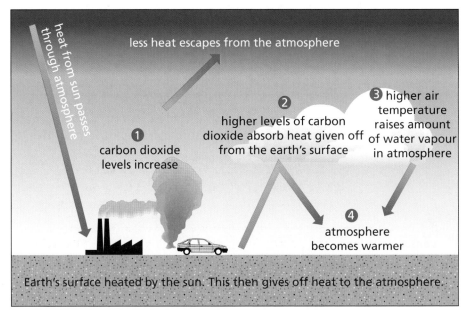

heat from sun passes through atmosphere

less heat escapes from the atmosphere

① carbon dioxide levels increase

② higher levels of carbon dioxide absorb heat given off from the earth's surface

③ higher air temperature raises amount of water vapour in atmosphere

④ atmosphere becomes warmer

Earth's surface heated by the sun. This then gives off heat to the atmosphere.

The effects of increased carbon dioxide in the atmosphere

Smog in urban areas

- Burning of fossil fuels, such as **coal and oil**, releases nitrous and sulphurous gases into the air.
- Smog is a yellowish-brown haze that forms when sunlight 'cooks' air pollutants to chemically react with each other.
- The main air pollutants that react together are **nitrogen oxides** and **sulphur dioxide**, produced by traffic and power stations.
- **Volatile organic compounds** (VOCs) from paint and solvent plants also add to the cocktail.
- The reaction of sunlight with these air pollutants causes lung/breathing difficulties (e.g. asthma) and reduces plant growth.
- Los Angeles and Athens are still affected by this problem.
- The biggest threat to air pollution in Ireland is now exhaust fumes from vehicles.
- These gases are also the cause of global warming.

exam focus

The marking scheme for any question on the impact on the environment of burning fossil fules is likely to be:

Environmental impact named – 2 marks

Examples of two fossil fuels named – 2 marks + 2 marks

Discussion – 12 × SRPs @ 2 marks each

Discussion must refer to the environmental impact

Credit a max of 3 × SRPs for economic references.

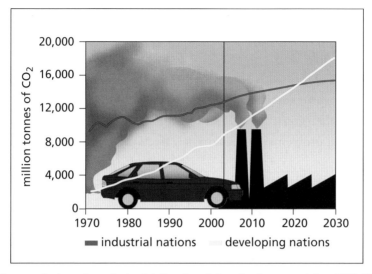

Carbon emissions from industrialised and developing countries 1970–2030

Some consequences of global warming

Note: global warming is also covered in Section 3, Option 1: Global Interdependence (see pages 234–236).

- Further information is available at www.microsoft.eu/environment
- Play the DVD of *An Inconvenient Truth* and see the devastating potential of global warming.

Acid rain

The increased rain comes from two kinds of air pollutants: sulphur dioxide and nitrogen oxides. These gases are produced by fossil fuel power stations, cars, trucks and buses. They dissolve in rainwater to form sulphuric acid and nitric acid. These acids return to earth in rain and snow.

Effects of acid rain

- Forests are damaged:
  - tree growth is stunted
  - leaves are discoloured and fall early
  - bark splits and is affected by cold weather.
- Acid levels in rivers and lakes rise and kill aquatic life.
- Essential nutrients are leached from soils.
- Toxic minerals enter rivers and lakes.
- Buildings are damaged.
- Respiratory diseases such as asthma increase.

Renewable energy and the environment

Hydroelectric power

There are a number of difficulties in increasing the use of hydroelectric power supply:

- Most of the best sites are already developed.
- High costs of dam construction and reservoirs.
- Environmental problems such as adverse affects on wildlife habitats and fish migration.
- Local community disruption. People may have to be relocated and rehoused.
- Loss of land due to flooding behind the dam.
- Visual pollution from dam structures.

Wind energy in Ireland

- Wind energy is the most preferred clean energy alternative in Ireland at present.
- Only 2 per cent of Ireland's energy was generated by wind in 2005. By 2008, this figure had grown by 55 per cent.
- Ireland generated 15 per cent of its energy needs from renewable sources in 2010.
- Over 1,000 megawatts came from wind turbines in 2009, and the growth rate in wind turbines is increasing rapidly.
- Two hundred wind turbines are to be built offshore on the Arklow Bank, which will generate enough energy to meet

Wind turbines are new, attractive features on the Irish landscape. Do you agree?

10 per cent of our total needs or the needs of 500,000 people along the east coast.
- The most suitable sites for wind turbines are:

  1. large, uninhabited or regions with a low population density, e.g. hill tops

  2. exposed coastal or inland sites with constant strong winds

  3. offshore shallow water banks such as the Arklow sand bank.

Disadvantages of wind farm development

- Noise caused by rotating turbine blades.
- Visual impact of turbines.
- Mass movement of surface material (e.g. peat) when disturbed for development.
- Damage to homes and life due to mass movement.

Wave energy

The world's first tidal turbine was installed and anchored to the seabed in Strangford Lough in Northern Ireland. Its 300-tonne turbine will generate enough electricity to power 1,000 homes. Due to its success, others are expected to be built in many rapid tidal currents worldwide.

Environmental pollution

Pollution at local and national levels

Waste disposal

> **key point**
>
> Pollution can occur at local, national, international and global levels.

As Ireland's prosperity has increased, so have its levels of pollution. There is an urgent need to find new ways to dispose of waste because:

- most existing waste-disposal sites are already near capacity levels
- most communities are opposed to new landfill sites nearby.

Ways of disposing of waste

Incineration

Advantages:

- takes up little space
- capable of huge volume of waste disposal
- generates heat for additional energy supply
- burning at high temperatures creates only limited pollution.

Disadvantages:

- increases air pollution
- releases dioxins into the air that may cause cancer
- toxic ash must be disposed of.

Six major incinerators, one for each of six regions, are planned to deal with waste in Ireland.

One at Poolbeg in Dublin could treat 25 per cent of the city's waste, and generate energy for 35,000 homes.

Most people are afraid that incinerators would damage the local environment and people's health.

Recycling

- Ireland's volume of waste is unsustainable for the future.
- Irish people are the least committed in the EU to recycling. We need to become more committed to recycling.

Sustainable economic development and environmental issues

Environmental impact studies in Ireland

These form a vital and integral part of national and county development plans.

They are carried out by independent researchers, who:

- assess and report on the state of the environment
- look at the costs and benefits of any new project
- estimate its possible impact on the environment.

> **key point**
>
> Sustainable economic development is a long-term plan that is vital for reducing the impact of people's activity on a region's natural resources.

The role of the EPA (Environment Protection Agency)

1. To promote and implement the highest practical standards of environmental protection and management for sustainable and balanced development.
2. To license and control all large-scale activities that could impact on the environment.
3. To ensure that all waste-disposal sites apply for a pollution-control licence to operate.
4. To record and monitor all industrial emissions from individual factories.

Irish fish stocks and sustainable development

Why have Irish fish stocks decreased?

- Irish fish landings have increased four-fold over a 30-year period.
- There has been an increase in the size and efficiency of fishing vessels.
- Unrestricted access has been granted to Irish waters by large EU fishing fleets.
- New research and monitoring of fish has provided details of shoal movements at various times of the year.

How can fish stocks be sustained?

- Allow spawning stock to reproduce at an effective level.
- Allow young fish to reach maturity so they can breed and multiply.
- Increase mesh sizes on nets.
- Make the use of all monofilament nets illegal.
- Reduce net sizes.
- Reduce the existing total allowable catch and national quotas for each fish species in EU waters.
- Create exclusion zones where fish can spawn.
- Provide protection vessels to control and enforce conservation measures.

Mining and environmental impact

Tara Mines has attempted to reduce the environmental effects of its mining operation on the local environment. Can you identify some of these efforts from evidence in the photograph?

Past mining operations created unsustainable development because:

- High-waste tip-heaps that encircled settling ponds were owned by the mines. These created visual pollution.
- Water used for treating mineral ores was released into nearby rivers.
- Exposed mining pits filled with polluted water once the mines closed.
- A high dust content was created in the air close to the mines.
- Local mining villages with a high unemployment rate depended on the mine for unskilled work (e.g. Silvermines village, Co. Tipperary) but created a spoiled landscape that discouraged new industry from coming to the area.

Case study: Tara Mines, Co. Meath

Began operation in 1977 and is the largest zinc ore mine in the EU. Severe planning restrictions were applied to planning permission. The reasons for this were because the area is:

- a fertile farming region for fattening cattle
- close to the Blackwater, a major fishing river
- near large urban regions such as Navan town.

Planning restrictions included:

- new tree plantations to screen the development from public view and reduce dust distribution
- noise and air pollution to be closely monitored
- water used in the mine to be purified before being released into the Blackwater
- large quantities of mining waste to be returned underground or contained in environmentally friendly settling ponds
- water from the tailings pond to be recycled in the mine.

Conflicts of interest due to resource development

Fish farming in Ireland

Reasons for the growth of fish farming

- The introduction of quotas on fishing fleets led to a shortage of fish supplies.
- Higher living standards led to a need for a balanced diet that includes fish products.
- Ideal conditions exist in Ireland for fish farming, including:
  - pollution-free waters off the west and south coasts
  - numerous sheltered bays and estuaries
  - regular tides that help flush out toxic waste from fish populations.

What negative visual effects do these fish cages have on the locality?

Economic advantages of fish farming

1. It creates employment for many coastal communities in the West of Ireland. Over 1,800 people are directly employed in fish farming.

2. Spin-off industries such as fish-cage manufacture, preparation of fish feed and fish processing add to employment numbers.
3. Generous government incentives are available for setting up fish farms.
4. There is local expertise in the fishing tradition.
5. Large quantities of fish can be reared in numerous coastal bays.

Environmental objections to fish farming

1. Water quality declines owing to the addition of chemicals for flesh colour and prevention of fish diseases.
2. Toxic waste from excess chemicals, fish excrement and dead fish builds up directly under the fish cages.
3. Disease spreads to local natural fish populations: for example, the spread of fish lice to sea trout has almost wiped out this species in Irish waters.
4. Scenic locations can be visually polluted by fish cages.
5. Interbreeding of farmed salmon with wild salmon can interfere with the salmon's ability to survive as a species.

SAMPLE EXAM QUESTION AND ANSWER

Question: Conflict may develop between economic interests and environmental interests. Examine this conflict with reference to one example you have studied.

Marking scheme: Conflict identified – 2 marks.

Reference to one example – 2 marks.

Examination – 13 × SRPs @ 2 marks each.

Discussion on one side of the argument only – 6 SRPs maximum.

Example can refer to region/conflict.

Answer:

The Mayo gas terminal development: local/global interests

This development highlights the conflict between the development of a natural energy resource at sea by Royal Dutch Shell and the need to protect the safety of local people in north-west Mayo where the gas is brought ashore.

> exam focus
> Be aware of the marking scheme and time when preparing and answering the question. Remember, you have about 13 minutes for a 30-mark answer.

The gas project

- The Corrib gas field is located 70 km off the Belmullet coast in Co. Mayo.
- It will supply 60 per cent of Ireland's gas needs for 20 years, so it will also reduce our gas import bill.
- Royal Dutch Shell, Statoil and Marathon have invested in the development of an off-shore gas terminal and pipeline to link the gas field to the Irish gas grid.
- The high-pressure gas pipeline surfaces near Rossport and continues to a terminal at Ballinaboy, where the gas is processed.

The cause of the conflict

Some local people fear:

- the danger of the high-pressure pipeline so close to people's homes
- the danger of the possibility of bogbursts or landslides in the local bogland environment during the development of the terminal
- the dangers to Carrowmore lake and the local water supply posed by removing 500,000 tonnes of wet bog.

Some local people also wanted the gas processed in an off-shore terminal and then transported in a lower-pressure pipeline to the national grid.

Few benefits to local people or the state will accrue as a consequence of the development e.g. no royalties are being extracted; no equity share taken; no windfall tax levied; companies are not obliged to employ Irish workers.

Royal Dutch Shell

The exploration company states that:

- there is no threat to the local community as a consequence of a high-pressure gas pipeline
- they have taken community interests on board by adjusting the pipeline route to cater for local concerns.

Consequences

- Campaigning by local people has highlighted the method by which the government has granted exploration concessions over the past few decades.
- Five locals, the Rossport Five, were imprisoned for their refusal to co-operate with a court ruling.
- An Taisce also objected to parts of the development.
- The Corrib consortium agreed to re-route the pipeline.
- Local opposition continues, but on a reduced scale.
- The natural gas supply from this field has yet to come ashore to reduce our reliance on imported energy.

Development of Irish bogs

Conflict arises over the way Ireland's bogs should be used.

Economic advantages of bogland development

1. It creates employment in Ireland's Midland region, where few industrial jobs are available.
2. Peat is a major source of cheap fuel for many disadvantaged communities in the Midlands and West.
3. Energy is generated from peat-fired power stations, reducing the amount of imported fuels needed.
4. Many families depend on turf supplies for winter heating.

Environmental Advantages of Unspoilt Bogs

1. They support a wide range of rare plants and animals.
2. They act as bird sanctuaries at night for many migratory birds, such as wild duck.
3. Many of Ireland's archaeological sites are preserved under their peat cover.
4. They are natural landscapes that attract many specialist tourists to study their flora and fauna.

Global environmental concerns

Deforestation

Economic advantages of deforestation

- Powerful logging companies have much profit to gain by this activity.
- Developing countries such as Brazil finance other development by exporting forest products.
- Large ranches are developed on cleared forest soil to graze cattle for low-cost meat for markets in the developed world.
- New farms can be supplied to poor, landless peasants.
- Consumers in the developed world provide a major market for tropical hardwood products.

Economic and environmental disadvantages of large-scale deforestation

- Large-scale loss of soil is caused by exposure to torrential tropical daily downpours. Upper soil layers are washed away.
- The absence of large quantities of tree litter leads to a quick loss of natural humus that enriched the soil through decomposing leaves.
- The felling of trees for agriculture leads to slash-and-burn activities, fast loss of soil fertility and, finally, abandonment of farms.
- There is a loss of vast quantities of plant, animal and human environments that were in balance with nature.
- There is also a loss of pharmaceutical products from plant life that could lead to medical cures for cancer and other diseases.
- Contact with modern society threatens the survival of ancient forest tribes who live in the rainforests.
- Tropical forests supply a large amount of oxygen to the atmosphere. They also absorb massive amounts of carbon dioxide from the atmosphere, so reducing global warming.
- Forests add a large quantity of water vapour to the atmosphere through the process of transpiration. An imbalance due to loss of forest cover could dramatically affect our human and wildlife habitat and even threaten our existence.

Policies for sustainable development

1. Promote the resources of the rainforests as a source of employment, health and wealth by selectively harvesting plants for medicinal needs and food supply.
2. Establish national parks so the natural landscape is preserved and for the development of high-income tourism.
3. Give financial incentives to countries that preserve their natural forests by offsetting debt against preservation.

Desertification

(See under Global Interdependence, pages 236–237.)

Questions 7B, 7C, 8C, 8B, 2006; 7B, 7C, 8C, 9C, 2007; 7C, 8B, 9B, 9C, 2008.

Elective 2: Patterns and Processes in the Human Environment

20 Population

aims You need to know how population statistics change over time and over regions of the world.

World population distribution and density

key point

Population density and population distribution change over time due to physical, social, political and economic factors.

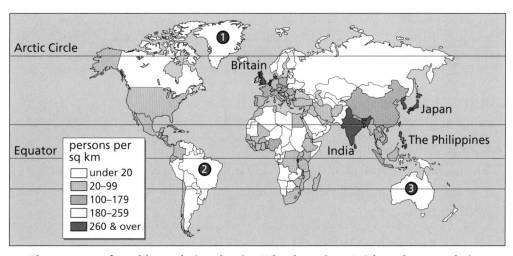

The patterns of world population density. Why do regions 1–3 have low population densities? In your answer refer to (a) climates and (b) vegetation.

SAMPLE EXAM QUESTION AND ANSWER

Question: Describe and explain, using examples which you have studied, the difference between the terms *population density* and *population distribution*.

(2008)

Marking scheme:

Identify terms – 2 marks + 2 marks

Two named examples – 2 marks + 2 marks

Explanation – 11 × SRPs @ 2 marks each

Answer:

Population density refers to the average number of people per square kilometre in a country or region.

- It is calculated **by dividing the population** of a country or region **by its land area.**
- Some regions have a low population density, e.g. Ireland (58 per square kilometre).
- Other regions have a high population density, such as the Island of Java in Indonesia, which has a density of 5,000 people per square kilometre. Some regions, such as hot desert areas, contain few or no people at all per square kilometre.
- Density per square kilometre may be misleading.

Population distribution describes where people are located in a country.

- It shows areas where lots of people live as well as areas where few people live.
- In Ireland, for example, most people live in the east while few live in the west and north-west of the country.
- Population distribution may show the relationship between where people live and the height of the land. Mountain regions may have few or no people, while lowland regions have many people.

The world's surface is very unevenly populated. About 80 per cent of the world's population occupies about 10 per cent of the world's living space.

Four most populated regions of the world

1. Western and Central Europe.
2. Eastern USA and South-Eastern Canada.
3. The Indian subcontinent, including Pakistan, India, Sri Lanka and Bangladesh.
4. East and South-East Asia, including China, Korea, Japan, Malaysia, the Philippines and Indonesia.

Least populated regions of the world

1. The cold tundra of Northern Canada, Greenland, Siberia and Antarctica.
2. Mountainous lands such as the Rocky Mountains in the USA and Canada, and the Himalayas.
3. The plateau lands of Tibet and Central Asia.
4. Hot desert regions of Australia, the Sahara and the Arabian peninsula, and the deserts of Iran and Pakistan.
5. The equatorial rainforests of the Congo basin in Africa and the Amazon in South America. The Amazon basin includes much of Brazil and parts of Peru, Ecuador, Colombia and Venezuela.

Physiologic density refers to the ratio of people in a country per unit of area of agriculturally productive land.

The effects of urbanisation on world population distribution

- In 1950, 29 per cent of the world's population lived in urban areas.
- In 2000, 50 per cent lived in towns and cities.
- By 2030, more than 60 per cent of the world's population will live in urban areas.
- In 1960 there were two cities with a population in excess of 10 million people.
- In 2015 there will be 26.
- All mega-cities lie within 500 kilometres of a coastline.

key point

The growth of cities has changed population density and distribution on a world scale.

Some effects of migration on population distribution and density

1. Millions of Europeans migrated to the United States and Canada in the eighteenth, nineteenth and twentieth centuries. This created a high density of population in eastern USA and south-eastern Canada.

key point

The large-scale movements of people changes the density and distribution of world populations.

2. Over 6 million people from southern Italy have migrated to northern Italy over the past 50 years. This has had two effects:
   - it has increased the population of northern Italy
   - it has reduced the population of southern Italy.
3. Millions of people have migrated from Ireland since famine times. This has reduced the overall population and density especially in the west, north-west and midlands regions.
4. Spanish and Portuguese colonisation of Latin America has led to:
   - a large density of people of European ancestry in this region
   - a low density of Native Americans in this region, due to the spread to the area of European diseases that wiped out native populations.

Patterns in the growth of population

key point

Why did world population grow rapidly from 1750 onwards?

The world's population was low until 1750. Then large cities developed during the Industrial Revolution and numbers grew rapidly.

- New farming methods, such as selective breeding and creation of individual farm units, prevented the spread of animal diseases.
- Improved technology, such as seed drill machines, created increased output from farm units.

- The invention of the steam engine led to increased employment, affordable and better housing in urban regions and a corresponding rise in population.
- Hygiene improved and medical knowledge was gained.
- There was increased land supply in the New World.

Why did world population grow rapidly in the twentieth century?

- There were great improvements in medical care, such as antibiotics and the control of many diseases, e.g. tuberculosis.
- New high-yielding seed varieties increased food supplies.
- Increased clean water supplies and better sewage-disposal systems were developed, leading to control of infectious diseases.
- Lower death rates and increased life expectancy led to rapid population growth rates.

Why do population growth rates vary between regions of the world?

- Growth rates for developing countries such as India are high because they are in the early, expanding phase of population growth.
- Birth rates are very high, e.g. 2.8 per cent growth rate for Pakistan, which causes a population to double in 25 years.
- Growth rates for developed regions such as the EU are stable. Growth rates for individual countries are declining, as in Germany. They are in the final or senile stage of the population cycle.

Changing population characteristics

Analyses of population pyramids

These are useful for the following reasons:

Birth rates indicate the potential:

- population of a country for many years ahead
- school-going population and the number of teachers required for the future
- paediatric care needed in hospitals and the number of doctors needed.

Death rates indicate:

- the standard of medical care, which reflects the wealth of a country
- the number of pensioners or elderly dependants
- the number of nurses, doctors and nursing homes needed for the future.

Population pyramids indicate:

- migration patterns reflecting movement into and out of the country
- dependent age groups and size of working population
- balance between males and females.

> **key point**
>
> Population pyramids display a population's structure in age groups and these statistics are used by governments to plan for future services and predict population trends.

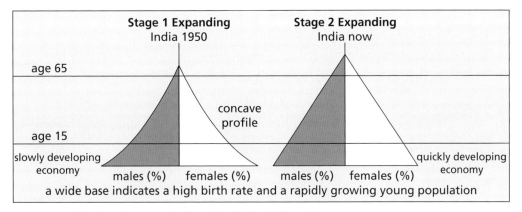

Age pyramids showing population of India in 1950 and now.

Stage 1

1. Few old people. Death rates high in all age groups.
2. No social welfare system.
3. High birth rates and high death rates indicate a poor, undeveloped country. Few industries.

Stage 2

4. Longer life expectancy. Larger number reach over 65 years.
5. Fall in death rates causes growth in middle age groups. Fast-growing population.
6. Still high birth rates.

Dependency ratio:

- This ratio is the number of children under 15 and people over 65, relative to the working age group.
- In developed countries the young dependency group rises as school- and college-going ages rise.
- The greater the number of the dependent age group relative to the workers, the larger the number of people being supported by a smaller number of workers.
- As populations grow older, so the cost of caring for the elderly in that country rises. This increases taxes on the workers in order to provide for them.

Patterns of population change in Ireland

Stages in Ireland's population growth pattern

1. Famine and emigration led to a rapid fall in Ireland's population in the 1800s.
2. Improved food supply and medicines slowed population fall. Many people continued to emigrate because of a lack of jobs.
3. A new economic policy and attraction of MNCs led to increased employment that halted emigration in the 1960s.
4. An economic depression in the 1980s forced many to emigrate, especially the young.
5. The Celtic Tiger economy attracted many foreign nationals and returning Irish from abroad. This led to a rapid rise in population.
6. The end of the Celtic Tiger has caused both Irish and foreign nationals to leave Ireland for work abroad.

key point

The Republic of Ireland's population declined from 6.5 million in 1841 to under 2.8 million in 1961. Since then Ireland's population has grown to approximately 4 million people.

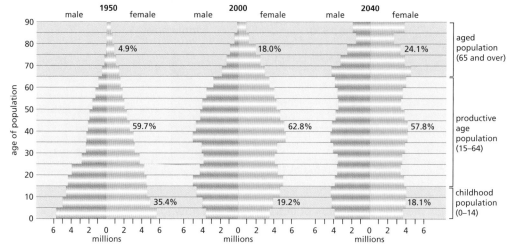

Population pyramids showing Ireland's population growth patterns, 1950–2040.

Age-structure changes

There are clear changes in the age structure of Ireland's population since 1961.

In 1961 there was a high dependency ratio

exam focus

These points provide background information on graphs and population pyramid-type questions.

- A large number of children in the 0–14 category had to be supported by workers with low income.
- Huge numbers of young people emigrated to the United States, Australia and Britain once they reached working age. This left a great shortage of educated people of working age. The country suffered from a 'brain drain'.
- Ireland had a very high birth rate at this time. Few people went to third-level colleges.

In 2010 there is a lower dependency ratio

- There are more people in the 65+ category. Medical care is improving, resulting in fewer deaths.
- There is a very large educated workforce, but high emigration is increasing the dependency ratio.
- Ireland has become a multi-ethnic society for the first time.
- Many mothers work outside the home.
- The birth rate is low and stable, but still 2 per cent greater than in Japan, indicating an industrialising economy in Ireland.

Life expectancy for both males and females in Ireland remains low compared with many other EU countries.

exam Q

Questions 10A, 12A, 2006; 12C, 2007; 10A, 10C, 2008.
Graph exercise: 12A, 2008.

21 Overpopulation

aims You need to:
- understand the meaning of overpopulation
- study examples of overpopulation.

key point

Optimum population is the number of people working with all the available resources of that area, who will produce the highest standard of living and quality of life available to them.

Overpopulation occurs when there are too many people in an area for the resources of that area to maintain an adequate standard of living.

exam focus

Learn this definition of overpopulation: you could be asked for it in the exam. *Example:* the Sahel in Africa is overpopulated.

SAMPLE EXAM QUESTION

Question: Examine one cause and one effect of overpopulation, with reference to an example(s) you have studied.   (2006, 30 marks)

Marking scheme:
   Cause stated – 2 marks
   Effect stated – 2 marks
   Example – 2 marks
   Discussion – 10 SRPs
   Overall cohesion – 4 marks
      graded
   A second example may be
      credited from the SRPs
   If cause only or effect only –
      0 marks

When the waters of the Syr and Amu were reduced due to irrigation, the size of the Aral Sea was also reduced

Overpopulation in the Aral Sea region

The Aral Sea region is located in central Asia. Two large rivers, the Amu and Syr, flowed through a desert region to feed the Aral Sea with fresh water. This water supply was in perfect balance with the amount lost from the sea through natural evaporation. For thousands of years this ecosystem was in perfect harmony with the demands by the local population on its resources.

The main cause of creating overpopulation was the **over-development of water supplies for irrigation**. Numerous canals were built to divert the water from two rivers, the Amu and Syr, to provide water for irrigation. Over seven million hectares of cotton, rice, and melon fields were irrigated to increase agricultural production for the markets of the former Soviet Union.

Consequences

Only tiny amounts of fresh water now reach the Aral Sea. This has had a 'domino' effect on every living creature in its environs. The ecosystem of a freshwater sea was destroyed because:

- Its fresh water gradually **changed to salt water**.
- As a result, fish life, delta farmland, forestry and swampland were destroyed.
- Coastal fishing communities were economically devastated as fish life disappeared from the sea.
- Much of the sea bed became dry land.
- Respiratory diseases and cancers increased.
- Migrants fled from towns that were once coastal settlements and are now 50 km from the sea.

Overpopulation has also occurred in the **Sahel** as a consequence of **desertification**, while in parts of India where population density is extremely high (e.g. Kolkata), other **social factors** as well as a **lack of infrastructure** play their part. See page 236 on desertification.

The influence of society and culture on overpopulation

(a) Religious influence causes overpopulation

The combination of the following factors cause overpopulation:

- India's Hindu religion and traditions restrict it from creating extra food supplies and resources to employ more of its people and create more employment.
- Hindus are mostly vegetarians and prohibit the eating of pork. For Hindus the cow is a sacred animal, so the slaughter of cattle is illegal
- Many of India's cattle are poorly bred and undernourished. Old livestock are allowed to roam as strays.

(b) Cultural influence causes overpopulation

- Much of India's poverty is influenced by high fertility rates and the status of women. Half of India's population live on less than $1 per day.
- They enter marriage in their teens with the prime task of producing children. 62 per cent of adult women are illiterate and have little influence in their family structure.
- Women are severely discriminated against and married women are often secluded from other males.

Low incomes cause overpopulation

- People who live in poor underdeveloped regions generally have large families. These high birth rates are generally driven by the need to ensure enough financial support for parents in their old age.
- Large families in India and south-east Asia are seen as an economic advantage. In India the northern states are the least educated and the poorest and they have the largest families. Its southern states, e.g. Kerala, are the richest and most educated and have the smallest families.
- Industries are poorly developed and a subsistence way of live is the norm.

The influence of technology on overpopulation

- The invention of the steam engine however, provided vast numbers of jobs for Britain's population that were migrating to coalfields and factories at that time.
- Over the past 100 years and especially the past 50 years Japan has invested vast resources in developing a highly sophisticated technology-based society.
- Japan is an exporter of flawless computers, cars, and electronic equipment and these industries allow it to purchase all its material needs to maintain the highest living standard in the world.
- Genetically modified foods offer the prospect of a limitless world food supply or at least an increased supply for the most highly populated countries such as India and China.

Your knowledge of India from your regional geography studies should help you develop these points on its society and culture.

For questions on overpopulation you should refer to population numbers, resources and culture.

Questions 12B, 2006; 10A, 2007; 11C, 2009.

22 Migration

aims You need to understand:
- changing migration patterns in Ireland
- migration policies in Ireland and EU
- ethnic, racial and religious issues that arise from migration
- contrasting impacts of rural/urban migration.

Migration and changing migration patterns in Ireland

Migration patterns in Ireland

> **key point**
>
> **Push factors** force people to leave a region. They may include financial, religious, social or environmental reasons.
>
> **Pull factors** attract people to a region. Again, they may be financial, religious, social or environmental.

exam focus

Ordinary level students should focus on two reasons why people migrate from their home in the West of Ireland and two problems caused by this migration on the Dublin region.

Higher level students should study two impacts, in detail, of rural to urban migration.

Marking scheme (2009): Two impacts named – 2 + 2 marks
One migration named – 2 marks
Examination – 12 × SRPs (6 × SRPs per impact) @ 2 marks each.

From west to east
- The Leinster region's population has increased each year since 1926.
- Connacht's population has fallen from 1.4 million people in 1841 to 433,000 today, a 70 per cent drop.

From rural to urban regions
- In 1926, 68 per cent lived in rural regions; 32 per cent lived in cities.
- In 1961, 54 per cent lived in rural regions; 46 per cent lived in cities.
- Today, 60 per cent of Irish people live in urban areas.

Reasons why people leave the west of Ireland for Dublin

1. Farms in the west of Ireland are small and unprofitable. People leave the land for jobs in the cities.
2. Industry is reluctant to set up in an area where the workforce is limited. So jobs are few and people leave to find employment elsewhere.
3. Standards of living are lower in the west than the east of Ireland. Young people leave the west for better lifestyles in the east.
4. Many industrial estates and business parks offer high-income jobs in the Leinster region.
5. Many young people attend third-level colleges and remain in the Dublin region, as they become accustomed to the higher lifestyle.

Effects of migration on the west of Ireland

Loss of young population

exam focus

Identify one effect of migration on a donor region and be able to write about it in detail.

1. As young people leave the west, the services (e.g. schools, recreational centres and hospitals) close. The region becomes unattractive to live in, so even more people leave the area.
2. Many people between the ages of 18 and 30 migrate from the area, so marriage rates and birth rates are low.
3. Farms are left in the care of older people who often lack the energy to work them fully. Many farms become neglected or abandoned when the older people die.
4. Industry is reluctant to set up in an area of low population and out-migration, as the labour force is limited.
5. Community services and facilities decline as the population falls. This in turn reduces the attraction of the area for the young people.

Effects of migration on Dublin

Expansion of Dublin

exam focus

Identify one effect of migration on a receiver region and be able to write about it in detail.

1. The population of Dublin has increased. Large suburbs and dormitory towns have developed around the city to create a greater Dublin with a population of 1.3 million.
2. Greater Dublin has expanded rapidly. Its commuter hinterland now reaches the Midlands to the west and Dundalk to Arklow in the east.
3. The cost of housing has risen massively, so many people are unable to purchase their own home.
4. Young educated people from the west of Ireland help to develop the city's economy, e.g. bringing new skills and differing social backgrounds.
5. Overcrowding may be the result in parts of the city. Great demand for accommodation raises prices and this may lead to overcrowding.

Post-1950 migration trends

Focus on any **two** positive and negative consequences of migration.

SAMPLE EXAM QUESTION

Question: Examine one positive and one negative potential consequence of human migration. (2009, 30 marks)

Ireland was overpopulated during the 1950s because it was unable to provide sufficient jobs for its working population and so they had to emigrate to Britain, Australia and America.

Positive effects of in-migration

Cultural effects

- Foreign nationals make Ireland more outward-looking and cosmopolitan.
- People from China, Nigeria, the Balkans, India and the Philippines added a cultural diversity to an isolated, island nation.

Ireland's influx of refugees created a new and increased market for rental accommodation, housing and consumer goods. They played a major and vital role in the creation of the Irish Celtic Tiger economy.

Employment

- Many job vacancies are filled by people who are willing to work for lower wages, adding to the competitive nature of the job market.
- Foreign nationals bring new skills and ideas to the Irish workplace.

Negative effects of in-migration

Repatriation of guest workers

- When foreign nationals are employed nowadays, it is generally on a fixed contract basis.
- New migrants become used to a higher living standard than they were accustomed to at home.
- When their contract expires they must return to the prospect of unemployment or lower wages at home.
- Political pressure is often put on governments to allow such people to stay, especially if some of their children were born in the host country.

Refugees

A high proportion of immigrants into some countries are refugees from wars or persecution. They occur generally in large numbers and the cost of coping with their needs can be a severe financial burden on the host country.

Migration policies in the European Union and Ireland

Migration policy in the EU

- The EU allows for the free movement of workers among all EU countries.
- Its policy states, 'The mobility of workers must be one of the ways by which the worker is guaranteed the possibility of improving his living and working conditions and social advancement.'
- Migrant workers are entitled to remain in a country after working there. In principle this applies to refugees and EU citizens.
- The country that first accepts a refugee must take responsibility for awarding refugee status to that person.

> **key point**
>
> Changes in EU treaties, improvements in transport over the past 40 years and the reduced cost of travel have created a mobile workforce throughout the European Economic Area.

Ireland's immigration policy

The main components of Ireland's immigration policy include:

- Nationals from the European Economic Area (EEA) do not need a visa to live and work in Ireland. The EEA consists of the EU states plus Norway, Iceland and Liechtenstein. For all others, a visa is essential.
- Those who need a visa must apply for a work permit before they enter the state.
- Persons who claim asylum are given full-board accommodation while their claim is being processed.
- Those who do not require a visa include:
  1. Persons who have permission to remain in Ireland, such as people with special skills and foreign full-time students.

2. Persons who have refugee status.

3. Persons who have been granted permission to remain on humanitarian grounds.

4. Persons who are claiming refugee status while their claim is being processed.

Ethnic, racial and religious issues created by migration

Race refers to biological inheritance: to DNA or the genes passed from parents to children. There is no such thing as a 'pure' race.

Ethnicity refers to minority groups with a particular self-identity, such as Cubans in America or Chinese in Ireland.

Minority groups may be defined by:

- place of birth
- language, e.g. Hispanics in an English-speaking country
- religion, e.g. Muslims in a Christian country.

Racial division

Apartheid in South Africa

For many decades, black South Africans were forcibly relocated into townships where they lost their entitlement to citizenship of South Africa

- Apartheid was racial separation of blacks from whites as a principle of society enforced by law.

- Under British law and after independence, segregation of blacks from whites was practised.
- In 1948 racial discrimination was justified and enforced by law.
- Nelson Mandela was imprisoned for protesting against this unjust law.
- Blacks were forced to live in poverty in 'homelands', the most deprived, almost uninhabitable regions of South Africa.
- All homelands people lost their right to citizenship of South Africa.
- Non-whites could not buy land.
- Apartheid ended in 1994.

Ethnic cleansing

International migration often happens as a result of ethnic differences.

- This term was first used in the war that occurred during the break-up of Yugoslavia.
- It is a policy where ethnic groups are either slaughtered or expelled by force, threat or terror from the country in which they live.
- The deliberate attempt to eliminate the Muslim people from Bosnia–Herzegovina led to ethnic cleansing, e.g. the massacre in Srebrenica.

Religious conflict in India

(See pages 153–154.)

Rural-to-urban migration

Impacts of rural-to-urban migration in developing regions

Rapid urban growth
Why did cities grow in developing countries?

- The growth of cities in developing countries resulted from population growth and rural-to-urban migration before industrialisation occurred.
- So the cities came first; then industry developed later, over a period of only 60 years.
- Cities grew mainly because of rural 'push' forces, such as poverty and hunger.
- People moved to cities with the hope of employment and the prospect of access to schools, health services, a safe water supply and other services.

Rapid urban growth and urban problems in developing countries are just some consequences of rural-to-urban migration.

Urban problems
Dense population

- There is an exceptionally high rate of population growth in cities, as most migrants are young adults of childbearing age.
- This young population accounts for over 60 per cent of urban population growth.
- Many cities have grown so large they are now called **megacities**.

- Squatter settlements, called **shanties**, or **bustees** in India and **favelas** in Brazil, have grown on the outskirts of cities.
- Males are the most likely to migrate to cities. This leaves an unbalanced male-to-female ratio in rural regions.

Congestion

Congestion on urban streets is a constant problem in India

Developing world cities have chronic traffic congestion. This is especially true in the cities of India, where cars, motor bikes, buses, carts, elephants and cows may all compete for space. Dust, exhaust fumes and the unrelenting heat all combine to create a difficult living and working environment.

Case study: Bustees in Kolkata and Mumbai

Child labour is common in India

- Over 60 per cent of Kolkata's population lives in bustees and over 500,000 homeless people live and sleep on the streets.
- Permanent slum dwellers are well protected by law in Kolkata.
- Pavement dwellers have no such rights. Many live under bridges, along canals or on land destined for other uses, such as roads.
- One in three people in Kolkata lives in a bustee.
- Open sewers are common and disease is widespread.
- Warm monsoon weather creates ideal conditions for malarial disease.

- Gender bias restricts young girls' educational chances.
- Employment chances are poor without education.
- Child labour is common.
- Population densities are four times higher than that of New York.
- 77 per cent of all families have only one room in which to live.

exam focus

Use your study of India in regional geography to develop your answer.

Questions 12A, 2006; 12C, 2007; 11C, 2008.

23 Settlement

Site, situation and functions of Ireland's settlements

Prehistoric settlements

Ireland's first settlements

- The earliest Irish settlers were hunter-gatherers and belonged to the Middle Stone Age or Mesolithic Period.
- They came to Ireland about **9,000 years ago** (7000 BC).
- They lived close to rivers or lakes where fresh water supplies were available.

- Many settled temporarily on coastal sites where shells and animal and fish bones were dumped in heaps called **middens**.
- Middens appear on Ordnance Survey maps in a linear pattern near present high-tide levels along the coast.

Ireland's first farming settlements

- The first farmers belonged to the Neolithic or Young Stone Age and the Bronze Age.
- They buried their dead in stone tombs called **megaliths**, cairns, passage graves, wedges or dolmens.
- Their tombs form a dispersed pattern:
  - across the Burren in Co. Clare
  - in the drumlin lands of Sligo to Dundalk
  - in West Cork, where the people mined for copper.
- They chose upland areas and raised, dry or hilly lowland sites because the gritty soil was easier to till than the heavy clays of lowland areas.
- The Young Stone Age settlers came about **7,000 years ago** (**5000 BC**).
- The Bronze Age settlers came about **4,000 years ago** (**2000–650 BC**).
- Their works include **megaliths, stone circles, cairns, cist graves, standing stones, wedges, fulachta fiadh.**

Celtic settlements

- These farmers belonged to the Iron Age (650 BC to AD 250).
- They introduced iron working to Ireland.
- They built their ring forts in a dispersed pattern throughout farming lowlands.
- They divided the country into **tuaths**.
- They built **(Lis, Dun) hill forts, (Lis, Dun) ring forts, crannógs, cahers or cashels (stone forts) and promontory forts**, which were built on cliff edges for protection against attack.
- Elevated sites were generally chosen for the more important larger settlements.

Small monastery settlements

- Individual missionaries chose isolated sites in glaciated river valleys for their settlements.
- These sites are listed on maps as **ch**, printed in red. Local place names that include the word 'kill' often suggest such settlements.
- These settlements were near streams or lakes for a fresh water supply.

The historic development of Irish towns

Large early Christian settlements

1. These were sited:
   - at what were then route centres, e.g. Clonmacnoise, Co. Offaly
   - on fertile plains, e.g. Kells, Co. Meath.
2. They were centres of religion and education for people from Ireland, Britain and the European continent. At the centre was the monastery with its churches, round tower, monks' dwellings and graveyard.
3. The words Manister, Monaster, Kil, Cill or Ceall on Ordnance Survey maps all suggest that the town developed as a monastic centre.

Some Irish towns, such as Kildare, began as early Christian settlements

Norman settlements

Many Irish towns began as Norman defence settlements

1. The Normans came to Ireland in 1169 and spread west and north, capturing the best farmland and building castles and towns to protect this captured land.
2. They built:
   - beside existing thriving monastery settlements, or
   - on new sites that were easily defended.
3. They chose:
   - bridging points inland and lowest bridging points on coastal estuaries, and
   - river loops, islands and elevated sites.
4. Unplanned towns developed around the castles, which were enclosed within high, defensive walls with guarded gateways for protection.
5. Abbeys, priories and friaries were generally built outside the town's walls.
6. Abbeys provided services such as education, accommodation for travellers, alms for the poor and hospitals for the sick.
7. Norman towns were market centres, where fairs and markets were held at regular intervals.
8. **Cas, castle, motte, town wall, gate, town gate, abbey, friary, priory, grange, castle land:** all these indicate Norman origins and are printed in red on Ordnance Survey maps.

Planned plantation towns

- Planned towns were built as part of the plantation of Laois–Offaly, Munster or Ulster.
- All have parallel or evenly wide streets.
- Centrally placed Protestant churches introduced the new faith.
- The towns had central diamonds or squares where markets and fairs could be held.

Canal towns

Canals brought new business to rural towns and created an economic revival

- These towns include Newry, Mullingar, Tullamore and Athy.
- Rivers in the Midlands and east were widened and deepened.
- Canals were built during the eighteenth and nineteenth centuries to carry bulky goods from our largest cities and ports to inland towns.
- Canal barges carried people.
- Large grain stores and mills, warehouses and hotels were built alongside canals for easy access for barges.
- Mills for grain and flour, and for wool and linen were built in many towns on canal routes.

Railway towns

- Railways were first built in the nineteenth century.
- Hotels were built near railway stations to cater for long-distance travellers.
- Towns expanded as a consequence of this new business.
- Railway towns prospered at the expense of canal towns. Trains were quicker and cheaper than canal transport.

Seaside towns

- Seaside towns developed as railways were built to join them to nearby cities.
- Army camps were built for summer training of part-time military volunteers at seaside locations. This encouraged the development of golf courses nearby.
- Hotels developed near seaside beaches to cater for visitors.

18th- and 19th-century expansion

1. Most urban rebuilding and redevelopment took place during the eighteenth and nineteenth centuries.
2. This period of urban growth was called the **Georgian period**.
3. Wide streets formed a mesh with blocks of buildings in between, creating a grid pattern.
4. They formed the Georgian suburbs at the edge of the old, often unplanned, medieval towns.

New towns

- Towns such as Shannon New Town in Co. Clare, and Tallaght and Blanchardstown in Dublin, were built to cater for the many migrants who came from rural and inner-city regions.
- Shannon was a well-planned town with local services and an industrial estate to cater for workers' needs.

Rural settlement patterns

There are three categories of rural settlement pattern: dispersed, clustered and ribbon.

Dispersed or scattered pattern

- This is created by widely spaced homes.
- Dispersed or scattered housing is usually associated with farmhouses with outbuildings or sheds nearby. The pattern developed when farms were enclosed after commonage-type farming was abandoned.
- Farm buildings are widely scattered where farms are large, such as in the rich farmlands of Counties Meath, Westmeath, Tipperary, Limerick and Clare.
- In more western regions, many farmhouses are located at the end of long passageways or on roadside sites.

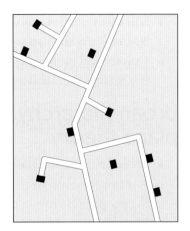

Scattered or dispersed housing is common in rural regions

Clustered settlement

- This pattern is created by groups of houses.
- Dwellings that are grouped together are generally farm dwellings of the eighteenth, nineteenth and twentieth centuries. In isolated cases they may be remnants of the **clochán** system of the west of Ireland.
- Farmhouses were built in clusters in Counties Kilkenny and Waterford as part of the division of land in the eighteenth and nineteenth centuries.
- Some clusters were built at road junctions where shops and a post office, and maybe a filling station, have developed over time.

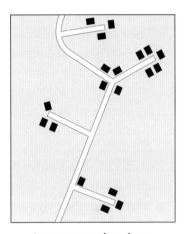

In some rural regions, buildings, especially farmhouses, are arranged in a cluster

Ribbon settlement

- This is a recent pattern development. It is generally composed of individual, one-off houses that developed in a line along a roadway.
- Local planning authorities were lenient as regards planning permission, and there were no overall planning controls for such housing from the 1960s until 2000.
- The presence of telephone cables, electricity lines and piped local authority or private water schemes also encouraged this kind of development.
- Landowners could increase their income from sales of individual roadside sites.

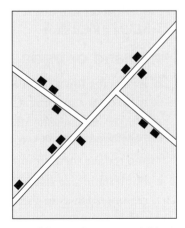

Buildings along a roadside form a linear or ribbon settlement pattern

- Suburban arterial routes (main roads) were the preferred choice for filling stations, bed and breakfast accommodation and buildings for local people.
- County and national development plans no longer encourage ribbon development. It is **unsustainable development**.

Urban hierarchy, hinterland and central place theory

- Settlements can be classified according to size, function and population density.
- A major function of all settlements is to provide services for their inhabitants and the people who live in their **hinterlands** (surrounding areas).
- **Central Place Theory** means that the arrangement of towns is determined by the hinterlands that they serve.

Three basic concepts of central place theory

1. The **range of goods and services** is divided into three categories: high-order, medium-order and low-order goods.

2. **Frequency of demand** refers to the level of demand for goods and services, e.g. daily needs, weekly needs, monthly needs or annual needs.

3. **Threshold** refers to a certain threshold, or minimum number of people, required by each shop/service to be viable, for example, the threshold for a supermarket will be greater than that for a local shop.

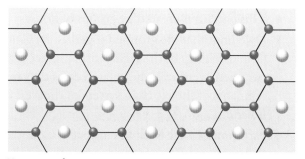

Hexagonal areas
This produces no competition and leaves no area unserved, so it is the best model.

- ● first-order (lowest) settlement, e.g. village
- ◒ second-order settlement, e.g. town

Model of hexagonal areas

Hinterland or trade area

- Every city, town or village has its own hinterland or area from where people travel to do their shopping. Cities have large hinterlands and villages have small ones.
- Hinterlands may be affected by physical features such as unbridged rivers, mountains or high upland, bogland or areas liable to flooding, which may distort and reduce their almost ideal circular shape.
- Hinterland size also varies according to density of population. Villages in isolated regions, such as in the west of Ireland, may have large hinterlands to remain as viable communities; whereas in high-density lowlands a number of villages may each be viable in a similar-sized region.

How modern changes affect the number of functions

- Modern transport, such as cars, allows people to travel further and buy in bulk. This affects the range of services that are viable in rural villages.
- Deep freezes and convenience foods reduce the need to make daily trips to local shops.
- Larger settlements can be more competitive and, by charging lower prices, can attract more customers.
- Villages may no longer have sufficient populations to support their traditional functions, leading to the closure of many of these service outlets.

Some criticisms of central place theory

- It was designed to work on a featureless plain that does not really exist in nature.
- Modern transport systems have undermined the original concept, as they favour some centres more than others.
- Population is not evenly dispersed.
- Settlements compete with each other to enlarge their hinterlands.

Questions 11B, SEC Sample Exam Paper 2006; 12C, 2006; 1B, 2007; 11C, 12B, 2008; 10C, 2009.

24 Land Use

aims You need to understand changing land use patterns and associated planning problems.

Planning strategies in rural areas: Sustainable development

This involves environmentally friendly planning that seeks an acceptable quality of life for present and future generations. It is the careful management of economic activities so that local environments and people's activities are interdependent.

Planners try to promote orderly development to:

- ensure the land is used for the common good (the good of everybody)
- meet the needs of society for housing, food and materials, employment and leisure
- support policies concerned with regional development, social integration, urban renewal and the maintenance of strong rural communities
- balance competing needs and protect the environment as much as possible.

Careful planning can help to achieve these objectives in a number of ways:

- controlling the development of transport, natural resources and the efficient use of energy
- the careful location of industry, houses and business/shops/services
- controlling the shape, size and structure of settlements
- effectively using already-developed areas
- protecting and supporting our natural environment and wildlife habitats, including areas and features of outstanding beauty
- accommodating new developments in an environmentally sustainable and sensitive manner
- strengthening villages and towns, both socially and economically, in order to improve their potential as growth centres.

The role of County councils

County councils are legally obliged to:

1. determine a policy for proper planning and development

2. implement the National Development Plan by:
- controlling planning and enforcing planning decisions
- creating sustainable development in rural areas that respects nature, natural systems, natural habitats and species and protects the environment
- making good-quality decisions and encouraging public participation, openness and proper enforcement
- being responsive to change and reviewing development through compulsory five-year reviews.

Environmental issues

Urban-generated housing in rural areas is regarded by the National Development Plan as being unsustainable because these houses:
- are isolated and away from central services
- are serviced by septic tanks that may pollute ground water
- create suburban development.

Some people disagree because they believe that new rural housing has the advantages of:
- a healthier rural environment than cities for family life
- sustaining rural community life and support services.

Environmental Impact Assessment (EIA)

This involves compulsory environmental impact assessments for:
- major developments such as new roads, and large forestry projects that exceed 70 hectares
- the location of waste material disposal sites
- projects that do not reach acceptable levels of agreement or standards, if it is believed that the project would affect the local environment negatively.

Strategic Environmental Assessment (SEA) examines the policies, plans and programmes of environmental impact assessment.

Changing urban land use patterns

Land use zones and land values in cities of the developed world

- A city's land uses may be divided into concentric zones. The oldest is at the centre and the youngest is at the city's edge.
- The oldest parts at the centre are often the present-day commercial downtown districts.
- The city centre is surrounded by a band of old housing with some old light industrial sites that may now be derelict sites or renewed structures.

- These old housing regions may house ghetto communities.
- A band of newer housing or pockets of high-income housing may surround the old housing.
- The newest housing is in the suburbs, on housing estates.
- Heavy manufacturing is now located in industrial estates on major routes.
- Many office services and wholesale outlets are located in business parks.
- Shopping complexes and hospitals create growth centres in certain locations on city boundaries.
- Some wholesale and light manufacturing land uses form wedges or sectors along major routes, increasing with distance from the centre.

Central Business District (CBD)

- This is the heart of the city, with department stores and specialist shops.
- It has the highest land values and tallest buildings.
- There are multi-storey buildings, offices and apartment blocks.
- Financial and commercial land uses are the most common.

Industrial zones

- The first industries in urban centres were located close to the city centres, because the towns were small. Almost all of these are now closed and their sites are taken by new apartments, shopping or office complexes.
- New industries are located in industrial estates on the outskirts of towns and cities and on main routes.
- Heavy industries are located close to water routes for easy import and export of goods.
- Business, wholesale and science parks are also located on the edge of cities or towns.

New suburban downtowns

- A new type of growth area involves suburban downtowns in large urban regions.
- Offices, hotels, department stores, industrial parks, entertainment facilities and car parking are grouped together to create a growth centre.

Land use zones in developing world cities

Central Business District

This will have:

- the business, employment and entertainment centres
- a central square or plaza with government buildings
- a spine of commercial land use surrounded by high-class residential housing radiating out from the core or centre
- sectors of the best housing around the core
- sectors of modest housing and derelict sites surrounding the high-class housing
- shanty towns surrounding everything for many miles.

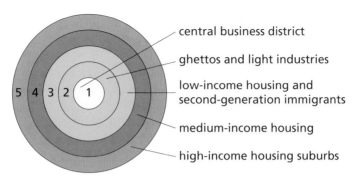

central business district

ghettos and light industries

low-income housing and
second-generation immigrants

medium-income housing

high-income housing suburbs

5 4 3 2 1

Burgess's Concentric Zone Theory

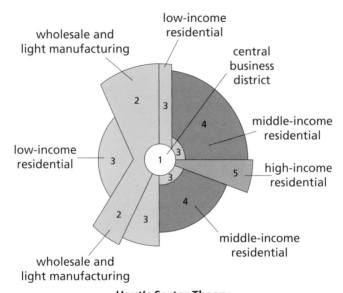

low-income
residential

wholesale and
light manufacturing

central
business
district

middle-income
residential

low-income
residential

high-income
residential

middle-income
residential

wholesale and
light manufacturing

Hoyt's Sector Theory

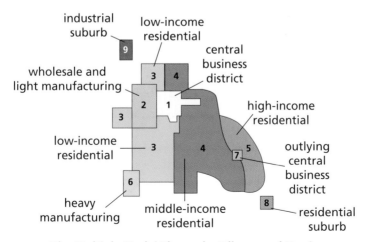

industrial
suburb

low-income
residential

central
business
district

wholesale and
light manufacturing

high-income
residential

low-income
residential

outlying
central
business
district

heavy
manufacturing

middle-income
residential

residential
suburb

The Multiple Nuclei Theory by Ullman and Harris

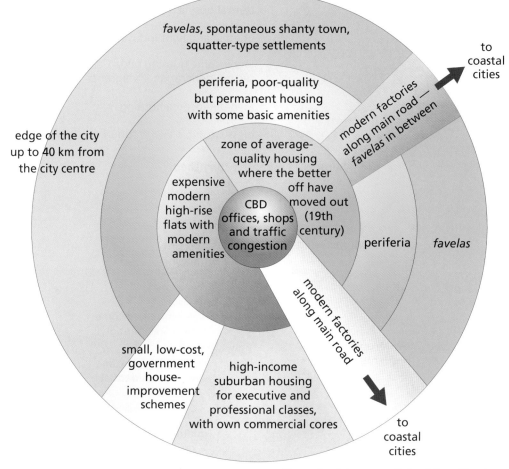

favelas, spontaneous shanty town, squatter-type settlements

to coastal cities

periferia, poor-quality but permanent housing with some basic amenities

modern factories along main road — favelas in between

edge of the city up to 40 km from the city centre

zone of average-quality housing where the better off have moved out (19th century)

expensive modern high-rise flats with modern amenities

CBD offices, shops and traffic congestion

periferia   favelas

modern factories along main road

small, low-cost, government house-improvement schemes

high-income suburban housing for executive and professional classes, with own commercial cores

to coastal cities

(the colonial powers linked the cities to the coast for export of primary goods)

The functional zones of developing world cities

Questions 11C, 2006; 12B, 2007; 12B, 2008; 12C, 2009.

25 Urban Problems

You need to know about the urban problems of developed and developing world cities.

Urban problems of developing world cities

key point

Developing world cities are expanding so rapidly they have individual populations greater than many countries, and alarming social problems.

Bustees in India have many social and environmental problems

Revise the sections on Rapid Urban Growth, Urban Problems, and the case study on Bustees in Kolkata and Mumbai in Chapter 22 (pages 206–207).

Urban problems of developed world cities

For a question asking about two problems in an urban centre, the marking scheme is likely to be:

- two problems identified – 2 marks
- named urban centre/region – 2 marks
- examination – 12 × SRPs (6 × SRPs per problem)
- both problems must be tied to same region chosen.

key point

Developed world cities have created problems such as residential segregation, urban sprawl, pollution and waste disposal. Other problems include urban decay, traffic congestion, and loss of green belts.

Residential areas and segregation within cities

- Certain environments attract a particular type of housing. Local authorities provide subsidised housing, either in flat complexes in inner-city areas or in semi-detached or terraced housing estates.

key point

People with different incomes, cultural or racial backgrounds tend to cluster in separate parts of a city.

- Many housing estates, such as those that were built in the 1960s and 1970s, are now no-go areas where lawlessness is rampant.
- Residential groups sometimes interact with developers and planners to produce areas with compatible neighbours with whom they have most in common and live together for support.

Ghettos

- A **ghetto** is an area of a city that is settled by a minority racial, religious or national group with certain characteristics that distinguish them from the urban population as a whole.
- The term ghetto originally referred to sections of European cities where Jews settled or were forced to live.
- A ghetto today refers to areas where black and other minority groups live, e.g. Chinatown and Harlem in New York.
- A ghetto is a product of discrimination by society against a certain group of less well-off people.
- Cities that experience high immigration tend to be structured in a series of concentric zones of neighbourhoods of different ethnic groups.

Urban sprawl

key point

Urban sprawl is the expansion of urban regions out into the countryside.

- Urban sprawl is a twentieth-century phenomenon. Until the 1960s, urban sprawl was mostly confined to advanced developed societies, such as the USA, Britain and the Netherlands.

- Since the 1960s most urban expansion has occurred in developing countries where shanty town development has swallowed up vast expanses of rural land.

- As cities expand they force surrounding rural areas and some inner-city areas to change their land use function from green areas to built-up, urban land uses.

- Suburban housing estates expand into the countryside, occupying vast tracts of once productive agricultural land.

- Urban traffic congestion increases as vehicles use new feeder roads and streets access arterial routes that lead into the city. This is especially severe during morning and evening rush hour.

- Neighbouring villages and towns are eventually absorbed into the larger urban regions, making them into conurbations. This has happened to create the Greater Dublin region.

- In Ireland, the corruption of planning officials, TDs and county councillors caused land to be re-zoned, leading to loss of green belts and uncontrolled planning. This has led to the growth of one of the poorest planned capital city regions in Europe.

- When a cluster of large cities expand and join, they create a vast urban environment called a **megalopolis.**

- The Randstad is a megalopolis in the Netherlands that has endangered its Greenheart, an open green region of farmland with scattered small towns and villages.

- **Green belts** are open spaces of rural land use, parks or woodlands within towns or between towns. Green belts are designed to be permanent features to:
  1. prevent the development of vast urban regions
  2. prevent continuous urban environments
  3. provide recreation areas within urban centres.

- Local communities, as well as local government, should develop strategies together to protect and manage these areas successfully.

Atmospheric pollution

- Industry, people's homes and their cars produce vast quantities of greenhouse gases that trap the heat that rises through the atmosphere.

- This build-up is causing the atmosphere to overheat. That in turn is causing melting of the Arctic and Antarctic ice sheets and a rise in sea levels.

- The United States, which has 5 per cent of the world's population, produces 25 per cent of greenhouse gases. About 82 per cent of these gases are from fossil fuels used to generate electricity and run cars.
- Smog is a combination of smoke and fog that hangs over a densely built-up area under calm atmospheric conditions. Because there is no wind to blow it away, the fumes from chimneys and car exhausts build up in the air.
- Smog may conceal a range of dangerous chemicals, such as sulphur dioxide and nitrous oxides, as well as a variety of gases from industrial plants.
- Old people, young children and those who already have lung disease are the most vulnerable to respiratory complaints from smog.

Urban waste

The careful disposal of urban waste involves many environmental practices

- Almost 30 per cent of urban sewage waste in Ireland goes untreated into inland rivers and lakes and into coastal waters.
- Over €1 billion was invested in waste water treatment between 2000 and 2006. Additional funds were allocated for further treatment from 2006 to 2010.

Other urban problems include urban decay and traffic congestion.

- In 2000, sewage received no treatment in 36 per cent of urban areas.
- Primary and secondary treatment plants have been developed in many urban areas over the past decade. This was necessary as ground water and many lakes had high nutrient levels as well as pathogens (disease-carrying bacteria) caused by urban waste water disposal.
- However, waste water from some towns is still untreated and most towns and cities lack secondary and tertiary treatment facilities.

Solutions to urban problems

Improvements created by planning and renewal

- Old buildings and derelict sites have been renewed, creating a vibrant, young city area that attracts shoppers and nightlife.
- New streets create easier traffic flows.
- Parking zones and multi-storey car parks.
- The restoration of old buildings with architectural character.
- Pedestrianised streets and new pedestrian crossing places.
- Disc parking that contributes to improved traffic flow and revenue.
- Ring roads and bypasses.
- Tunnels under river estuaries and channels, e.g. the Jack Lynch Tunnel in Cork and the Dublin Port Tunnel.

The Dublin transport strategy

This plan involved:

- a vision statement to create a plan and vision for the future
- an integrated public transport system that everyone can reach within a 10-minute walk at most
- quality bus corridors
- a light rail system in Dublin
- cycle routes
- a National Roads Authority that has responsibility for the development and manage-ment of our roads. This includes PPPs (public–private partnerships) and toll charges.
- PPPs may involve toll charges on new developments over a 30-year period to recoup costs and maintenance charges for investors and obtain best value for money for the taxpayer.

The Luas has reduced street traffic in Dublin and cut down CO_2 emissions

Questions on urban growth: 11B, 2006; 11C, 2007; 12C, 2008; 11B, 2009.

SECTION 3
Options

Higher level students must
study **one** of the following options:
Global Interdependence pages 228–254
OR
Geoecology pages 255–279
OR
Culture and Identity pages 280–300

NB: Study only ONE of these options.

Option 1: Global Interdependence

You must write your answer in **paragraphs** or you may lose cohesion marks.

MARKING SCHEME

Choose three or four headings/aspects for your answer. The marking scheme will be as follows:

Number of aspects:

3 aspects − 27 + 27 + 26 marks

4 aspects − 20 marks each

Identifying heading/aspect − 4 marks

Discussion − 8 × SRPs *or* 6 × SRPs

Overall coherence − 7/6 marks graded or 4 marks graded

Select scheme according to number of headings/aspects discussed

Allow credit for up to 2 examples from SRPs.

26 Models of Development

The meaning of development

In the past, development referred to:
- the state of a country's economy, which was judged solely by the GNP of an individual, or
- the average wealth produced for an individual by the country in one year.

Today it is felt that real development must include sustainable economic, medical, spiritual and cultural aspects of a society.

Development, according to Abraham Maslow, includes a number of human needs that must eventually be reached before a society can be defined as developed. They include:
- basic needs, such as clean water, balanced diet, access to good healthcare
- security, such as personal protection from violence by any individual, groups or the state
- being valued by society, loved by family and friends
- self-respect, through secure employment, with adequate income
- personal growth through development of a person's talents.

The last few needs can be achieved only when basic needs are fulfilled: so there is a 'ladder' of human needs.

Third World images in First World Countries

- The underdeveloped countries contain two-thirds of the world's population, but they receive only one-tenth of news time on Irish news bulletins.
- Most news from Third World regions focuses on wars, famines and disasters.
- Local people are stereotyped as inactive, helpless victims, rather than creative and willing participants.
- TV often focuses on trivial news items when larger, more important issues need to be aired.
- Few news programmes examine the real causes of underdevelopment, such as unfair prices or unfair trading practices.

- Few local people are interviewed on programmes that concern their countries.
- Images from NGO agencies appeal to people for charity. These images may have a reduced effect over time. They also tend to reinforce a stereotyped image of Third World people.

Examining world models and labels

The poorest regions of the world are referred to in a number of ways.

The Three-World Model

Until the 1980s the world was split into three divisions:

- the **First World** – the rich regions such as Western Europe, North America, Australia and Japan.
- the **Second World** – the communist countries of the USSR and Eastern Europe, such as Poland and Hungary. These people enjoyed adequate living standards.
- the **Third World** – the 75 per cent majority of the world's people who were poor.

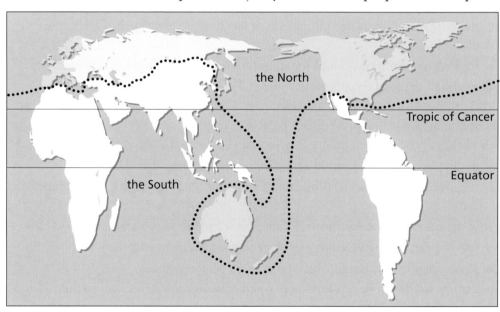

This map is called Peter's Projection. It shows the correct sizes but not the correct shapes of continents. How does this view of the world differ from that presented by most maps of the world that are used in Ireland?

Objections to the Three-World Model:

1. It was felt that this model created a three-tiered society with the rich countries at the top.
2. The Second World no longer exists, owing to the fall of the communist system in the former USSR.
3. The term Third World suggested a third-rate world. However, geographers use the term to suggest the lack of real political power enjoyed by these nations.

The Two-World Model

The Brandt Report in 1980 suggested the following division:

- **the North** – the rich and powerful countries. This includes the First and Second Worlds. However, not all of the countries are located in the northern hemisphere: for example, Australia is not.
- **the South** – the poor countries of the Third World. However, there are great differences in stages of development among these countries.

Other suggested models

- **Developed** countries – those where industry and services are well developed and people have a good living standard economically.
- **Quickly developing** countries – those where industrial development is quickly being established and is leading to improved living standards.
- **Slowly developing** countries – those that are still without any real industrial development and remain the poorest regions of the world.

Question 15, 2007.

27 The Impact of the Global Economy

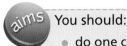
Modernisation and free trade

This model of development is designed to create a world economy (**globalisation**) where all barriers to trade are removed and private enterprise (**capitalism**) is unrestricted by governments or people.

Impact of multinational corporations (MNCs)

Multinational corporations are also called Transnational Corporations (TNCs). Multinationals:

- provide large sums for investment
- provide large numbers of jobs
- provide branch plants for manufacturing and research
- increase exports
- increase imports for manufacturing
- create global trading networks.

But they also:

- cause job losses when local firms close as they are unable to compete with large companies
- create jobs in one region at the expense of job losses in another
- cause branch plants to close because of decisions in another country
- work on the principle of profits first.

The power of some multinationals can undermine the rights of workers to form trade unions, or can undermine the government by threatening to withdraw all investment. Many multinationals are wealthier than some countries.

Multinationals return millions of the profits they make in foreign countries back to their home country.

Study either Wyeth Pharmaceuticals and Healthcare (p. 169–171) or one of your own choice.

Deforestation, global warming and desertification

key point

We live in an interdependent, global economy. Actions taken in one area have an impact on other areas.

Sample question and answer

Examine the impact of any two of the following environmental issues:

Deforestation, global warming, desertification. These are all either a cause or an effect of processes elsewhere.

Deforestation in the amazon basin

Deforestation leads to increased levels of carbon dioxide in the atmosphere and to soil erosion

- Most of the Amazon Basin in Brazil is covered by forests called **selvas**.
- The region contains one-third of all the tropical forests on earth.
- Until the 1960s, this region was lightly populated with native American Indian tribes, who lived as hunter-gatherers in the forests.

Why have the forest's resources been exploited?

- These selvas are viewed as a rich source of tropical wood.
- They are also seen as a wilderness region to be conquered to create profit.
- They have vast mineral deposits of iron ore, bauxite, gold, silver and tin, timber and oil.
- Most of the rich east coast farmland is owned by landlords.
- The Amazon Basin was seen as a way to give land to the poor, hungry, landless peasants without causing conflict with the powerful landowners.

- Large beef cattle ranches aided by government funds focus on producing low-cost meat for American fast food outlets.
- The World Bank supported large projects like that which was responsible for large-scale deforestation of the selvas in the state of Rondonia in Brazil.

The effects of deforestation

- Forest peoples are being forced from their natural environment by the cutting down of the forests.
- These tribes traditionally lived by hunting, fishing and subsistence.
- Constant contact by 'outsiders' is eroding their culture and bringing deadly diseases, such as measles, that their immune systems are unable to withstand.
- Traditional social life has been shattered. Many of the survivors are forced to live in squalid roadside conditions.
- One-quarter of all medicines owe their origins to rainforest plants, even though only one-tenth of these species have been studied.
- Selvas thrive in a very sensitive, balanced ecosystem. Deforestation upsets this balance and leads to a series of knock-on effects.
- Soils that are exposed to the heavy tropical rain are quickly washed away.
- **Global warming**: trees naturally absorb carbon dioxide from the atmosphere. When trees are cut down, less oxygen is reproduced.
- The amount of carbon dioxide increases and the balance of the atmosphere changes.
- **Desertification**: As a consequence of global warming, some desert regions such as the Sahara in North Africa are expanding.

Global warming

The earth's atmosphere is gradually getting warmer. Glaciers are melting in mountainous regions such as the Alps and the Andes. 1999 was the warmest year of the twentieth century.

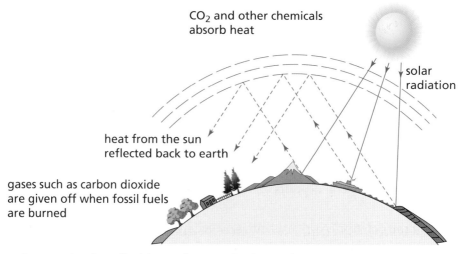

CO$_2$ and other chemicals absorb heat

solar radiation

heat from the sun reflected back to earth

gases such as carbon dioxide are given off when fossil fuels are burned

Increased carbon dioxide, methane and other gases are trapping excess heat and causing a rise in global temperatures

How the greenhouse effect works

1. The sun heats the earth's surface.
2. The earth's surface radiates this heat back into the atmosphere as long-wave radiation.
3. The normal amounts of greenhouse gases (e.g. carbon dioxide and methane) in the atmosphere trap some of this heat.
4. Increased greenhouse gases as a consequence of people's activities are trapping excess long-wave radiation and causing the atmosphere to overheat.
5. Some greenhouse gases are essential for humans to live on earth. But too much of them may cause drastic changes in climate that could lead to severe human and ecological consequences.

Some causes of global warming

- When fossil fuels such as coal, wood and oil are burned they release carbon dioxide into the air. Carbon dioxide traps heat and prevents it escaping into outer space.
- Increased industrialisation, intensive farming and vehicle usage all use vast amounts of fossil fuels.
- A greatly increased use of fertiliser, huge herds of cattle and large areas of paddy rice release extra methane gas.
- The use of chlorofluorocarbons (CFCs) in aerosols, fridges, foams and solvents causes about 14 per cent of global warming.
- America's population produces 25 per cent of the global emissions of carbon dioxide.
- India, with 16 per cent of the world's population, produces only 3 per cent of total carbon dioxide emissions.
- Deforestation is reducing the amount of forest cover worldwide.
- Deforestation reduces the amount of carbon dioxide that can be absorbed from the air, and so adds to global warming.
- In 1973 the world's population was 3.5 billion. Today it is 6 billion.
- This huge increase has led to a corresponding rise in the amount of fossil fuels that are burned.

Consequences of global warming

Negative effects

- Serious tropical diseases, such as malaria, could spread to temperate countries such as Ireland.
- There may be a higher risk of skin cancers among pale-skinned people such as the Irish.
- Trends in world tourism could be dramatically altered.
- Mediterranean regions may suffer a decline in tourism, as temperatures may be too high.
- Winter holiday resorts, for example ski resorts like Zermatt in Switzerland, could have much-reduced snowfalls, which would wipe out their tourist industry.

- If trends continue, predictions indicate that sea levels will rise by 0.2–1.4m.
- Temperatures may rise by as much as 3°C over the next 100 years.
- This means that there would be greater extremes of weather, with freak storms and droughts, causing local starvation and the mass extinction of plants and animals.
- Millions of people would be forced to migrate as their lands become swamped by the rising oceans, e.g. Bangladesh.
- In Europe the polderlands of the Netherlands and much of the Wexford coast may be submerged, unless it is protected by higher dykes.

Desertification in North Africa

The Sahel in Africa has suffered from extreme desertification over past decades

Causes of desertification

- Desertification threatens the lives of hundreds of millions of people in sub-Saharan Africa.
- The Sahel region stretches for almost six thousand kilometres, east to west, across Africa.
- Until recent times, 70 per cent of the Sudan was covered with tropical forest vegetation or savannah woodland. Many of the trees were cut down as the demand for cash crops increased to meet national debts.
- Throughout the 1960s, countries in the Sahel became part of a global economy.
- They began producing goods such as cash crops for a global market.
- Because of this, the area devoted to agricultural crops such as groundnuts increased.
- Farmers became dependent on cash crops for their livelihoods.
- When the rains failed, the soils were left exposed to the winds, which caused erosion of the soil.

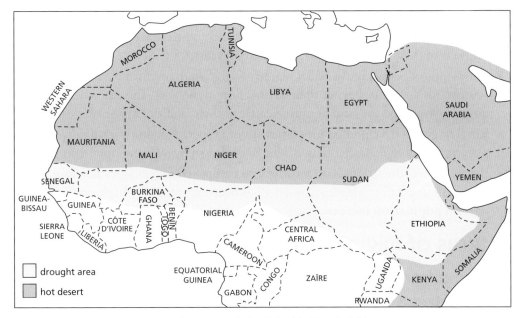

Drought areas of the Sahel in North Africa

- This deforestation, in association with global warming (the greenhouse effect), has led to desertification. Climate change is brought about by the interaction between the forest and the atmosphere.

Consequences of desertification

- When trees are absent, so are clouds. With no clouds, the land becomes dried up by the equatorial sun. When rain does fall, the full force of the rain reaches the ground, and **sheet erosion** occurs. Nutrients and topsoil are washed into rivers and estuaries, creating problems of silting.
- Crops have failed, farm animals have died and people have been left without adequate means of survival.
- Many children in the Sahel region have died of diseases associated with malnutrition, such as kwashiorkor.
- Many people have migrated southwards, causing overpopulation and further over-cropping and over-grazing of land.
- Many have migrated to cities, e.g. Niamey in Niger. This has increased the demand for wood as fuel, which in turn has led to more deforestation.

The impact of social and political decisions

Rural-to-urban migration in the Third World

- Rural unemployment caused by increased migration has led to urban migration in Third World regions. Small landowners cannot compete with agribusiness companies so they sell their farms.

- More than two-thirds of all the world's city dwellers now live in developing countries. Cities such as Mexico City, Sao Paulo and Kolkata have all added millions to their populations over the past 30 years.
- Thousands of people in the Sahel region of sub-Saharan Africa have migrated southwards as a consequence of desertification in the area. These people were farmers who tilled the land or grazed cattle in their traditional homelands.
- Rural migrants have poured into cities out of desperation due to civil unrest, poverty and hunger, rather than having been drawn by jobs and opportunities.
- Because these migrations have mostly been composed of teenagers and young adults, an important additional impact has been exceptionally **high rates of natural population increase** (high birth rates with low death rates).

Patterns of migration movement

Rural-to-urban movements

- Most migrants are searching for employment, better education and health services.
- Many are fleeing ecological disasters, such as desertification in the Sahel.
- Millions flee from civil unrest such as civil wars, as in Sudan in 2004–2005.

Between Third World countries

- This accounts for 80 per cent of all international migrations.
- It results from a number of causes, such as employment-seeking, ecological disasters, war and persecution.

From Third World countries to the developed world

- This occurs from Central and South America to the USA.
- There is also migration from Africa, the Middle East and China to the EU and the USA.
- Poverty and lack of employment at home cause these migrations.

From Eastern Europe to Western Europe

Up to 2 million people migrated from Eastern to Western Europe between 2001 and 2006. This was because of:

- the sense of freedom created by the collapse of the Communist system in Eastern Europe
- poverty or poor living standards, creating a search for a better standard of living
- the persecution of ethnic or cultural groups such as gypsies.

More recently, this trend has slowed, due to a difficult economic climate in the Western countries, such as Ireland and the United Kingdom.

From peripheral regions to core regions

This is fuelled by:

- a search for employment and higher living standards
- a search for better social and cultural centres, from education to nightlife.

Migration to Ireland since the 1990s

- Ireland was an area of out-migration, rather than in-migration, since famine times.
- The 'Celtic Tiger' economy created a need for many workers in all sectors, including:
  - returning Irish emigrants who had worked abroad in the UK, EU or America
  - foreign nationals for work in the service industries
  - refugees, both political and economic, in search of sanctuary and a new life with hope for a better future.

 Questions 14, 2006; 13, 2007; 13, 15, 2008; 14, 2009.

28 Linking Economic Growth with Human Development

aims You need to be able to:

- assess the impact of debt on developing economies
- explain how human development can lead to economic development
- explain how economic development can involve exploitation of people at local and global level
- discuss the role of women in society.

International debt and cycles of poverty

Causes of Third World debt

- The rapid rise of oil prices in 1973 triggered a worldwide recession and caused debt repayments of Third World countries to escalate.
- Profits of oil-producing countries could not be reinvested due to world recession.
- So the banks offered huge loans to Third World countries as development aid.
- Many of these countries were ruled by dictators who invested unwisely in arms or useless development programmes.
- In the 1980s the United States raised their interest rates to attract overseas funds.
- This set in motion a spiral of increased rates throughout the developed world; so debts went out of control and poor countries could not repay even the interest.
- The IMF (International Monetary Fund) was set up by the banks of developed countries to restructure loans so Third World countries could repay their debts by:
  1. increasing cash crops
  2. reducing spending at home on services such as education
  3. stopping subsidising the price of foodstuffs, so essential foods became very expensive
  4. introducing wage control to reduce inflation – but this made living even more difficult

5. devaluing national currencies to make exports cheaper, but that made imports more expensive
6. allowing the repatriation of profits of MNCs.

'petro-dollars' or profits of oil-producing states invested as loans

poverty

Third World countries accept loans from international banks some invest in arms or useless programmes

public services and wages cut cost of living rises

interest rates rise dramatically

debts go out of control IMF established

move money borrowed to pay debts

The circulation of petrodollars

Some solutions to international debt

- By 2000 the world's richest countries agreed to cancel about 30 per cent of total Third World debt, and 100 per cent of some individual countries' debt.
- Debt of the poorest African countries was cleared by the G8 countries in 2005.
- A large percentage of profits of multinational corporations in a Third World country should be reinvested in new industries or services in that country.
- Debt repayments should be reduced further to a level that allows these countries to develop their economy.
- Developing countries that have their debts reduced are required to invest existing repayments to promote the development of self-reliance programmes throughout their country.

Types and advantages of aid

Who benefits from aid?

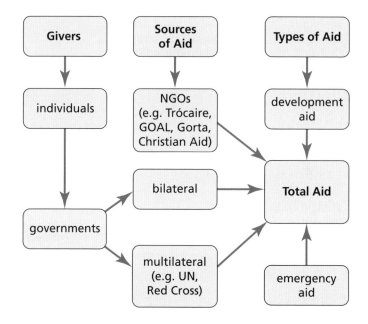

International aid to the South

Aid sources and who benefits

1. **Non-governmental organisations (NGOs)**
   Voluntary organisations such as Trócaire, Concern and Gorta provide both emergency and development aid.

2. **Bilateral**
   This is direct aid from one government to another. Generally this type of aid is used to improve agriculture, education, health services, etc.

3. **Multilateral**
   International institutions such as the Red Cross, the United Nations and the World Bank provide both emergency and development aid.

Emergency aid

Countless lives have been saved from famine and disease as a consequence of natural disasters such as earthquakes, famines and flooding by the provision of:

- food, clothing and shelter
- emergency personnel
- medical aid.

Advantages of emergency aid

Emergency aid is essential to save lives in crisis situations

- The supply of food, fresh water, medicines and shelter has saved countless lives.
- Modern transport systems have made the delivery of emergency aid much easier and more effective than in the past.
- Emergency aid does not disadvantage local food producers.

Development aid

Development programmes in the LDCs (least developed countries), such as Zambia, Ethiopia and Lesotho, include projects such as clean water supplies, farm livestock improvement, adult literacy.

Advantages of development aid

- Vital infrastructure such as water supply pipes and wells, sanitation and new roads can give an initial boost to an emerging economy.
- Farm improvement schemes and education programmes help people to cater for their own future long-term needs.
- Health clinics develop skills of local people to cater for their communities' basic needs.
- Development aid is called 'appropriate aid' because it serves the needs of local communities.

Human development

- People who feel the need to help are given the opportunity to act as volunteers.
- APSO (Agency for Personal Services Overseas) recruits people to work on aid programmes.

- Development education provides workshops, seminars and resource packs to inform the Irish people and people of other countries of the dangers of xenophobia.

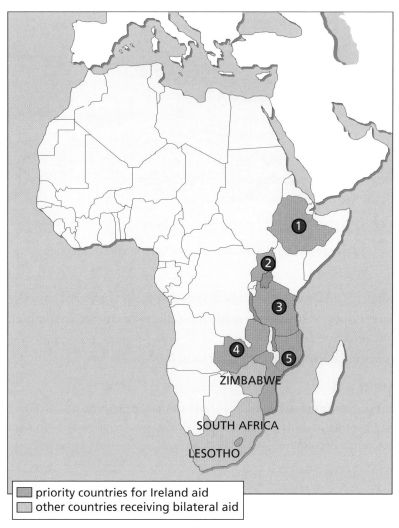

ZIMBABWE

SOUTH AFRICA

LESOTHO

priority countries for Ireland aid
other countries receiving bilateral aid

Sub-Saharan African countries that receive Irish and bilateral aid.
Activity: identify the countries 1–5 that receive Irish bilateral aid.

Disadvantages of aid

- Tied aid may benefit the donor more than the receiver.
- Aid may cause the receiver to become dependent on the donor country. Military aid could be used by a government against an opponent who may be justified in their opposition to certain government programmes.
- Much tied aid is given to better-off Third World countries that may serve the political or economic needs of donor countries.

- Some powerful countries use aid as a means of political control over weaker countries. For example, the US government requested the use of Turkish airports as bases from which to bomb Iraq. When the Turkish government refused this request, the US immediately withdrew millions of dollars of aid from Turkey.
- Battles were fought in developing countries because governments and opposition groups were supported by the United States or Russian aid. Their Cold War was fought on others' soil.
- Aid has been used to encourage global free trade, which exposes the markets of poor countries to the products of rich countries.
- Loans may be given in the form of aid. Some of these loans are given on standard commercial terms, and may create crippling debt over long periods.
- The United Nations agreed that developed countries should set aside 0.7 per cent of their GNP as aid. Few countries have achieved this, with only Denmark, Norway, the Netherlands and Sweden having fulfilled the agreement. United States' aid, for example, is just 0.1 per cent of GNP.

The role of NGOs

What are NGOs?

- NGOs are non-governmental, private agencies that provide aid to developing countries. They include such agencies as Trócaire, Concern, Goal, Afri and Oxfam.
- They provide the following types of aid: emergency relief, development aid, empowerment aid, and education awareness.

Advantages of NGOs

- Their independent status allows agencies such as Trócaire to work independently for justice in places such as South Africa, which was under apartheid policies up to the 1980s.
- Because NGOs are relatively small organisations they do not get involved in mega-projects such as dam construction. They are mostly involved with community-based 'appropriate aid' projects that get local support.

Disadvantages of NGOs

- Competition between NGOs can lead to the agencies adopting 'starving baby' images that may distort the First World's view of the Third World.
- The scale of funds at the disposal of NGOs is relatively small when compared to national government funding. Nevertheless, the funds of the leading Irish agencies Trócaire and Concern help reduce poverty.
- Some NGOs use 'child sponsorship' schemes where individual children in the Third World are sponsored by individuals in the First World. However, this could make such Third World children feel personally in debt to these sponsors and so may reduce their sense of individuality.

Human exploitation

World trade and global exploitation

- It is believed by some people that Third World poverty has increased as a result of global trading.
- The richest 20 per cent of the world's people control 84 per cent of global trade.
- The poorest 20 per cent control less than 1 per cent of global trade.
- Multinational corporations such as Volkswagen have turnovers of twice the GNP of Bangladesh.
- The turnover of Nestlé Corporation is 20 times greater than the entire GNP of Nicaragua.

Reasons for lack of control of global trading by Third World countries

Reliance on a single commodity or raw material

- Third World countries were colonies that supplied commodities such as coffee, tea and cotton for factories in rich countries.
- Prices for these commodities from developed countries are controlled by powerful multinational corporations, such as Chiquita and Nestlé.
- Some Third World countries are totally reliant on a single commodity for export, so if the price for that commodity falls it is a disaster for that country.

Unfair trading

- The prices of goods from developed countries to Third World countries have risen hugely, but the prices of goods from Third World countries to developed ones have fallen.
- So they have had to sell more and more to buy the same amount of goods.
- In 1972 Uganda sold 6 tons of cotton to buy one truck.
- Today it must sell 35 tons of cotton to buy a similar truck.

Fluctuating prices

- Because prices of commodities vary greatly from year to year, Third World countries are unable to make long-term plans for development. Sometimes this is due to poor advice from the World Trade Organisation (WTO).
- As more commodities are grown for sale to pay debts, there can be a glut of some commodities in a particular year. This causes a fall in prices.

Fair trade is one way of increasing the earnings of commodity growers

Case study: Coffee

- Coffee is the world's second most important commodity after oil.
- Some countries, such as Burundi and Ethiopia, depend on coffee for most of their income. A bad harvest or a sudden drop in price can bring bankruptcy to such countries. For example, in 1989 the price of coffee fell by one-third in a single week.
- The price of coffee was regulated in the past. But rich, coffee-consuming countries and the World Trade Organisation ended this practice.

Cheap labour

- Many manufactured products, such as clothing and footwear, are now produced in Third World countries. New technology and multinationals (or TNCs, transnational corporations) have been responsible for this trend, creating globalisation.
- New technology has reduced the need for highly paid, skilled labour.
- Multinationals have brought welcome work for Third World countries, but they gain their profits from poorly paid and badly treated workers.
- Most of the profits of TNCs return to where they have their headquarters.
- For example, the legal minimum wage in Indonesia is $1.27 per hour: but 12,000 factories pay less than 40 per cent of the minimum wage.
- Female workers make up 80 per cent of the workforce.
- A normal working week is 50 hours, with no payment for overtime.

Gender roles

- Certain societies, such as Muslim societies, allow daughters to inherit only half as much as sons. Women cannot file for divorce against their husbands.

> **Tradition, injustice and poverty are three factors that have seriously affected the role of women in society.**

- The Taliban regime in Afghanistan forces women to cover their entire bodies, even their faces. They cannot attend schools or work outside the home.
- China's 'one child per family' policy led to the deaths of many infant girls, as there was a preference for sons to carry on the family name. It also led to selective abortion of many unborn baby girls.
- In many poor countries boys are given preference over girls for facilities such as education.
- Girls can be forced into arranged marriages with distant cousins many times their own age.
- Women must play many roles, as wives, mothers and subsistence farmers, sowing and reaping the crops.
- Women in transnational corporations must work for less pay than men.

Ways of changing gender roles

Self-help
Organised groups of women can challenge their position, assert their social rights and improve their income.

Breaking the cycle of poverty

Education
- Lack of education creates cycles of poverty.
- Improved school facilities can include necessary skills learned in apprentice-type programmes.
- Adult education programmes can help mothers to learn and pass on their new knowledge and desire for learning to their daughters.
- Social education for men may help them to encourage women into education and economic services.

Workplace reform
- Strong trade unions are needed to work for women's rights in places where they are exploited.
- Laws need to be introduced that force equal pay for equal work. In Ireland, the Employment Equality Act was introduced in 1997.

- Additional facilities, such as crèches and maternity leave, encourage mothers to work outside the home.

Aid for women

- Better-designed aid packages would help to facilitate the economic empowerment of women.
- Banking structures should be rethought so that poor women can take out loans to invest in small economic projects. The Grameen Bank in Bangladesh loans money to poor women to buy seeds, cattle, farm machines and even land.

Questions 15, 2006; 14, 2007; 14, 2008; 13, 2009.

29 Sustainable Development – The Way Forward

You need to be able to:

- examine the idea of sustainable development as a model for the future
- discuss the development of fair trade and its impact
- explain how sustainable development involves justice for minorities
- explain how self help can lead to sustainable development.

The sustainable use of resources

The Kyoto protocol

The Kyoto Conference held in Japan in 1997 set a target of an overall reduction of 5 per cent in the production of greenhouse gases by 2012. This was agreed by all participating countries, including all those of the developed world.

key point

Using resources sustainably means meeting the needs of the present without endangering the requirements of future generations.

However, since then:

- the USA and Japan demanded the right to buy 'pollution quotas'
- in 2001 the USA abandoned its Kyoto commitments.

Ireland agreed to keep its 2012 emissions to 13 per cent above its 1990 levels, but by 2000 Ireland's emissions had exceeded 20 per cent. However, Ireland intends to do the following:

- phase out coal burning at Moneypoint or change it to natural gas supply
- source more energy from wind power
- reduce carbon emissions from vehicles, with higher taxes on fuel to reduce consumption
- introduce energy-efficiency certificates for houses for sale that were built before 1991
- initiate a grant-based tree-planting programme to reduce carbon emissions.

The sustainable use of forests

Sustainable use of forests means:

- conserving some forest regions
- managed use of other forests
- afforestation programmes.

Forestry in Scandinavia

- Over 200,000 hectares of forest are harvested each year.
- Seventy per cent is reforested manually. Natural regeneration occurs in the remaining area.

- Disease in forests is carefully controlled.
- Improved land drainage helps trees grow faster.
- Careful use of fertiliser increases yields.

The sustainable use of fish stocks (See page 184)

Fair trade

The meaning of fair trade

key point

- All producers should be enabled
to earn an adequate living by
prices for produce, such as coffee,
being index-linked to the prices
charged by developed countries
for manufactured goods such as
coffee products.

> Globalised trade is driven by the aim of
> achieving constantly greater profits for
> multinational corporations.
>
> This policy increases inequalities between
> rich and poor regions.
>
> Globalised trade is not aimed at improving
> levels of human development.

- Fair wages and safe working
environments should be provided for workers.
- Goods sold should be economically and ecologically sustainable.
- Third World countries should gain a reasonable degree of control over their own
country's economy.
- Small-scale producers should be able to contribute to a country's exports.

The unfair existing global trading system

- The prices of Third World commodities fluctuate widely on the world market. This
policy is encouraged by wealthy nations to their own benefit.
- The products of most multinationals are made in poor countries by people who
work in poor working environments, such as sweat shops, for minimum wages.
- Some products, such as tropical hardwoods, are produced by destroying tropical
forests.
- Trade barriers are created against some poor countries for political or other reasons.
- Multinationals (transnational corporations) have increased their control of world
trade. Seventy per cent of global trade in wheat is now controlled by six
multinationals.
- Changes by the International Monetary Fund (IMF) have reduced the control of
governments over the activities of multinational companies.

Fairtrade Mark Ireland

- The Fairtrade Mark Ireland and other Fairtrade labelling organisations have been
established to promote fairer trading practices of quality products.
- The Fairtrade Mark is a guarantee to consumers that the producers have been paid
a fair price for their produce and that the producers work in safe and decent
working conditions.

The Fairtrade system in practice

- The first world importers deal directly with the producers to eliminate middlemen.
- The producers are offered a guaranteed minimum price that is higher than the international market price.
- Some money is paid in advance to the producers and an additional premium is given for some local community projects.
- The producers must guarantee to provide a safe working environment and an eco-friendly production system.
- The Fairtrade Labelling Organisation International (FLO) certifies that the production process of the coffee has met its standards.
- The consumers are willing to pay about two cents extra per cup for this Fairtrade product.

How has Ireland and Europe responded to Fairtrade produce?

- Sales of Fairtrade certified products in Ireland in 2009 were €33 million. Sales in the UK topped £800 million. Fairtrade products can now be found in over 3000 independent Fairtrade shops and over 6,700 supermarkets all over Europe.

How has Fairtrade affected some producers?

- In the Volta Rivers Estate in Ghana workers are now paid twice the national minimum wage and own 25 per cent of the company's shares.
- Toilets and showers are installed on the estate and water is piped to the workers' village.

How does Fairtrade produce affect the consumer?

- Fairtrade systems produce healthier foods.
- A more eco-friendly production system uses fewer chemicals than other growers.
- Banana crops are sprayed only 10 times annually, compared to 40 sprayings on other plantations.
- Chemicals such as paraquat are no longer used on Fairtrade crops. Some 20 per cent of male banana workers in Costa Rica were left sterile in recent years after handling toxic chemicals.

Justice and minority groups

Bonded labour

- Bonded labour is the most common form of slavery in the world today.
- About 20 million people are in bonded labour.
- About 4 million people are in bonded labour in Pakistan.
- Bonded labour exists in several Third World countries.

key point

The level of development of any society can be measured by the degree of justice with which that society treats its weakest members.

- Bonded labour begins when a person borrows money from an unscrupulous moneylender. In return the borrower agrees (bonds) to work for the moneylender until the loan is paid.
- Wages paid by the moneylender are low and insufficient to meet the interest, so the loan continues to increase.
- The bonded labourer/borrower is persuaded/forced to work indefinitely and without wages for the lender.
- Other family members may be forced to work against the loan and this can continue for generations, so that some family members are born into slavery.

In 1991 the Pakistani government banned the practice of bonded labour. But:

- moneylending landlords are people of influence and few are charged with the crime
- the Pakistani government denies that bonded labour is common in Pakistan
- they state that there are only 7,000 people in bonded labour. Human rights groups claim that over 4 million Pakistani people are in bonded labour
- there are no work-related government schemes for people who are freed from bonded labour.

The campaign for an end to bonded labour

- High Court rulings have helped free over 12,000 bonded labourers.
- The Rugmark label is an indication that no illegal child labour was involved in manufacturing.

Self-help development in Third World and peripheral regions

- It is increasingly important that people-centred development is undertaken by self-help development schemes in which responsibility rests with members of each scheme.
- Such groups can link up with and gain financial and other support from larger, well-established development bodies. These include:
  - NGOs such as Trócaire, Oxfam and Christian Aid
  - women's movements that work for basic salaries and the abolition of discrimination against women
  - cultural movements that help strengthen local cultures to counteract influences from westernised globalisation.

Case study: Self-reliance in Kerala, India

Regional government initiatives in Kerala have achieved the following results:

- The people of Kerala in southern India live on average more than 10 years longer than other Indians.
- They enjoy better health, education and transport services.
- There are fewer inequalities between males and females and between castes.

These results have been achieved through land reform and financial security.

- Over 1 million people were given direct access to land.
- Local co-operative credit was arranged to buy livestock and inexpensive hand tools.
- Community-based schemes provided clean, fresh water and primary healthcare to reduce disease and death rates.
- As people became more financially secure they had fewer children. Local family-planning campaigns helped reduce birth rates.

Case study: Self-help project in eastern Ethiopia: The eastern highlands project

Activities

- *Crop production:* farmers are provided with plentiful supplies of seeds and trained in crop-production techniques.
- *Livestock production:* farmers are assisted in animal breeding, poultry rearing, bee-keeping and the production of animal feed.
- *Soil and water conservation and afforestation:* seed nurseries are established and trees and grasses planted in gullies to reduce erosion.

Aims of project:

- to increase foodstuffs and farm income in a sustainable way
- to improve basic services
- to restore local natural resources.

- *Education:* primary schools are being established in the area. Adult classes are conducted in environmental awareness, HIV awareness and family planning.
- *Public health:* the project supports the staffing and training of clinical staff, who focus on community vaccination programmes, health education and child nutrition.
- *Women's programme:* helps women to generate an income by learning skills such as needlework, dressmaking and market gardening.
- *Water supply:* wells are bored for small irrigation systems and domestic water supplies.

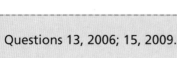

Questions 13, 2006; 15, 2009.

Option 2: Geoecology

MARKING SCHEME

Choose three or four headings/aspects for your answer. The marking scheme will be as follows:

Number of aspects:

3 aspects − 27 + 27 + 26 marks

4 aspects − 20 marks each

Identifying heading/aspect − 4 marks

Discussion − 8 × SRPs or 6 × SRPs

Overall coherence − 7/6 marks graded or 4 marks graded

Select scheme according to number of headings/aspects discussed

Allow credit for up to 2 examples from SRPs.

30 The Development of Soils

 aims You need to understand that soils develop from the weathering of rocks and from redeposited weathered material.

The scientific study of soils is known as **pedology**. Soil is the surface layer of loose material that covers much of the earth's land surface. It contains both organic and inorganic matter. It is part of the natural environment that links the relationship between bedrock, climate and vegetation.

Soil composition

All soils contain mineral particles, humus, water, air and living organisms such as bacteria.

Mineral matter

- A soil gets its mineral content from its parent material. The parent material can be bedrock that has been broken down by physical and chemical action, glacial deposits, river deposits or wind-blown deposits.
- Mineral content refers to minerals such as calcium, phosphorus, potassium, potash and other compounds.
- These are the foods that plants need in order to grow.
- The parent material determines the soil colour, depth, texture and pH value.

Organic matter

- Organic matter is also referred to as **humus**.
- Humus forms from decayed plants, and to a lesser degree from animal life through the action of bacteria and other micro-organisms.
- Humus also improves the texture of a soil.
- Humus binds soil particles together, which increases the soil's ability to hold moisture.
- Plant roots help to bind soil particles together.

Climate

- The distribution of the various soils coincides with the distribution of the world's climate.
- So climate influences the type of vegetation that grows in a region.
- The greater the amount of vegetation that grows in a region, the greater the humus content of the soil.

- Climate influences the rate at which weathering of the soil and decay of its plant matter occur.
- Heavy rainfall causes **leaching** of the soil's minerals.
- **Weathering** is the first state of soil formation.

Slope and water movement

- Steep slopes encourage the removal of fine particles by rainwater.
- Gentle and flat slopes encourage the accumulation of fine particles.
- When rainfall is greater than evaporation, water moves from the surface layer to lower layers and carries down nutrients with it. This process is called **leaching**.
- The downward movement of water may create a hard pan that can prevent drainage and lead to waterlogging.

Air

- Air is vital in the soil for **oxidation**, which converts parts of the organic matter into oxygen.
- Air is also vital for the bacteria present in the soil, which require oxygen and are therefore said to be **aerobic**.

Soil characteristics

Texture

- Texture refers to the proportions of sand, silt and clay particles that make up the soil.
- Texture determines the soil's ability to:
  1. retain and transmit moisture
  2. retain nutrients
  3. allow roots to penetrate it.
- **Sandy soils** consist of 70 per cent or more sand particles by weight and have few nutrients. They feel gritty to rub.
- **Clay soils** consist of 50 per cent clay particles by weight. Clay soils are rich in nutrients, but are likely to become waterlogged. They feel sticky or plastic when wet.
- **Silty soils** are intermediate between sandy and clay soils. Silty soils have a smooth, soap-like feel.
- **Loam soils** are ideal for agriculture. They contain a mixture of particles of many different sizes. Loamy soils are well aerated, with some moisture and plant food.

Colour

- Humus-rich soils are dark brown or black in colour.
- Brown soils of temperate forest lands, such as Europe, get their colour from decayed leaves and plant particles.

- Organic matter, such as leaves, in rainforest soils decays rapidly owing to the high humidity of the forest floor.
- Dark soils absorb more sunlight and so are warmer than light-coloured soils.
- Warm soils aid germination of seeds and have a long growing season.
- Soil texture can be determined by examining a soil sample. This can be done by mixing a soil sample with water in a jar.

Soil structure

- Soil structure refers to the shape of the soil grains or particles.
- In undisturbed soils, the clustering of particles forms different shapes known as **peds**.
- The shape and alignment of the peds, together with their size, determine the size and number of pore spaces through which air, water and organisms can pass.
- Soils with a **crumb structure** give the highest agricultural yield because it provides the best balance between air, water and nutrients.

Water content

- Water moves downwards by **percolation** and upwards by **capillary attraction**.
- Water in the soil becomes a weak solution of many mineral compounds.
- The chemical processes that take place in a soil do so mainly in solution.
- Water content varies between soils, from almost nil in arid climates to waterlogging in wet clay soils.
- Constant percolation of water downwards in mid to high latitudes, owing to high rainfall, causes leaching.
- **Leaching** is a process whereby minerals are drawn downwards from the upper horizon at the surface, to lower horizons. Leaching creates **podzol** soils.

Organic content

- Organic matter includes humus, and is formed mostly from decaying plants and animals.
- Humus gives the soil a dark colour.
- The highest amounts of organic matter are found in the **chernozems** or **black earths** of the North American prairies, Russian steppes and Argentinian pampas.
- Fallen leaves and decaying grasses and roots are the main sources of organic matter.
- Soil organisms, such as bacteria and fungi, break down the organic matter.
- Where soil organisms are present and active they will mix the plant litter into the A horizon, where it decomposes into humus.

pH value

- A soil's **pH** measures its acidity or alkalinity.
- A soil with a low pH value is said to be **acidic**. This happens when minerals such as calcium, magnesium and potassium are leached by heavy rain.
- A very low pH, or acid soil, slows down decomposition and may even prevent decay, as in the creation of peat.
- A high pH means an **alkaline** soil. This indicates it has a high calcium (lime), magnesium and potassium content.

Questions 17, 2007; 16, 2009.

31 Factors that Affect Soil Characteristics

aims You need to know:
- the factors that affect soil characteristics
- how people interfere with these processes.

Factors that affect soil formation

Parent material

- If the soil is composed of unconsolidated deposits such as boulder clay, soil formation will occur more rapidly than if it were bedrock.
- Soils inherit their characteristics from parent material.
- Soil from limestone areas will contain calcium and other minerals and will become alkaline.
- Soils from sandstone regions will be free-draining and sandy and will heat up quickly in spring.
- Soils from clay regions will have poor drainage and may become waterlogged.

Climate

Effects of temperature and precipitation include:
- constant heat and moisture encourage constant growth
- soils in hot, wet regions tend to have lots of vegetative cover, such as rainforest or monsoon forest
- decomposition occurs rapidly
- chemical weathering occurs rapidly, creating deep-red soils
- heavy rainfall causes leaching
- long spells of drought, such as may occur in grassland regions, tend to increase the amount of minerals, such as calcium, by evaporation.

Topography

- Deep soils develop on level surfaces.
- Where slopes are steep, thin soils develop, owing to erosion by run-off and gravity.
- Gently sloping ground helps drainage.
- High ground is exposed and is cold.
- Soils on high ground are generally thin, with few minerals.
- South-facing slopes are generally warmer and encourage growth early in the season.

Living organisms

- Plant roots help to bring soil particles together, which is especially important on steep slopes.
- Plant roots absorb moisture and nutrients.
- Worms, beetles and other insects help to aerate the soil.
- Insects, fungi and bacteria break down plant matter.

Time

- Soils develop over long periods, often thousands of years.
- Soils can also be eroded away in short spells, only years or even months. Example: wind erosion in the Dust Bowl of North America.
- Soils may develop quickly or slowly, depending on the parent material.

Water-retention properties

- Water in the soil is essential for plant growth.
- When water is absent plants wither and die unless they are adapted to drought conditions, as desert plants are.
- Water-retention rates are determined by soil structure and texture.
- Clay soils can hold more water than sandy soils.
- Too many clay particles lead to waterlogging.

Processes that influence soil formation

SAMPLE EXAM QUESTION AND ANSWER

Question:

Examine two of the natural processes which influence soil formation.

Marking scheme:

Number of aspects:

3 aspects − 27 + 27 + 26 marks

4 aspects − 20 marks each

Identifying aspect − 4 marks

Discussion − 8 × SRPs *or* 6 × SRPs

Overall coherence − 7/6 marks graded or 4 marks graded

Answer:

Aspect 1 – Leaching

Leaching is a process whereby soluble minerals are dissolved by percolating ground water and are washed down to lower horizons in the soil where they are deposited. Leaching is widespread in the wet climate of the West of Ireland and at the Equator in latosol soils.

Tropical latosols (equatorial soils) are exposed to torrential downpours daily. Iron compounds in the soil are oxidised and turn the soil a red colour. These red soils are called laterites. Laterisation is a form of extreme leaching. The high temperatures of the tropics contribute to leaching/laterisation by speeding up the chemical reactions of water on rocks, such as the oxidation of minerals such as iron.

Latosols are very poor in nutrients due to the leaching process. Nutrients are mainly confined to the surface where there is decomposing leaf litter and dead plant matter.

The chemical weathering of rainforest soil creates many important mineral deposits through a process called 'secondary enrichment'. This occurs because chemical weathering and percolating water together concentrate the small amounts of metals that are widely scattered throughout the soils into economically valuable concentrations.

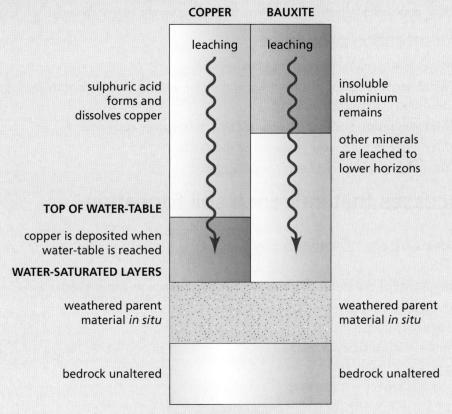

Soil profile of leached mineral-bearing laterite

For example, bauxite, the principal ore from which aluminium is made, is formed due to leaching. When aluminium-rich soils are subjected to the intense and prolonged weathering of the tropics, most of the common elements, including calcium, sodium and silicon, are removed by leaching. Because aluminium is extremely insoluble, it becomes concentrated at the surface as bauxite.

Secondary enrichment of iron ore may also occur when soluble iron compounds are washed down through leaching and deposited in lower horizons to form a concentrate of iron ore, such as magnetite.

Aspect 2 – Podzolisation

Podzolisation is an extreme form of leaching by acidic ground water. It occurs in cool areas of heavy rainfall such as on many of Ireland's uplands and highlands. It also occurs in boreal regions of coniferous forest or moorland vegetation. Groundwater is generally acidic but becomes more acidic when it percolates through decayed or dead vegetation. Acid rain also increases podzolisation.

Podzol soils form under coniferous forests because pine needles are slow to compose and form acid soils. Regions of coniferous forest such as bogs in the West of Ireland and mountain regions such as the Scandinavian highlands may create acid soils due to the rotting of the granite rocks that form them. The acidic ground water dissolves all soil minerals except silica in the form of quartz. Quartz is a very weather-resistant mineral.

Podzol soils have a very distinctive soil profile. The A horizon has a bleached or very pale colour due to the presence of these quartz crystals and because it has been drained of coloured minerals.

The B horizon below is enriched with the dissolved minerals and is darker in colour. The B horizon may also contain a layer of reddish iron oxide (rust). This rust acts as a cementing agent and forms an impermeable layer through which percolating ground water cannot pass. This layer is called the hard pan.

The stony C horizon sits directly on the bedrock.

Aspect 3 – Salinisation

Hot dry regions experience the reverse process to leaching. Evaporation and capillary attraction cause salts in ground water to rise through the soil and build up in the upper layers. Salt is deposited on the surface as a hard white crust. If the salt concentration becomes too high, plants are poisoned and die. The roughing of the surface soil helps reduce the effect of capillary attraction and evaporation.

Salinisation is a problem for farmers who have to wash the salt away or break up the crust before their crops can be sown.

Irrigation is a process where reservoir or well water is sprayed on surface soil to water plants in dry regions. The evaporation of this water causes a salt deposit to build up over time and may lead to soil poisoning if it is not carefully managed. This effect can be reduced by growing crops that need less water. Irrigation salinisation in Australia is estimated to cost the farming community €307 million each year. Southern California is also a hot dry region that is intensely irrigated and has salinisation problems.

Calcification results in calcium being built up close to the surface of the soil. This helps make the soil very fertile. Chernozem soils, or 'black earth' soils of the steppes of Russia and the Ukraine are grasslands where calcification occurs naturally. Chernozems are also found in the prairies of North America.

Classification of soils

World soil maps do not always show the soils as they exist in reality; instead they show the zonal soil most likely to occur in a region.

There are three basic soil groups: **zonal**, **intrazonal** and **azonal**.

Zonal soils

Zonal soils are classified according to the climate zone in which they occur. They are mature soils with distinctive profiles and clear horizons. They include the following.

Tundra soils

- These are soils in Arctic regions. *Examples:* northern Canada, Scandinavia, Russia.
- Vegetation consists of lichens, shrubs and mosses.
- They have a shallow, brown to dark-grey A horizon.
- The subsoil is permanently frozen (**permafrost**).

Latosols

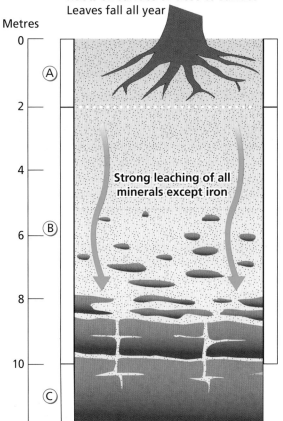

Tropical regions
High rainfall and temperatures
Bacteria alive throughout the year
Roots on surface or close to surface
Leaves fall all year

Metres

Neutral due to humus

Strong leaching of all minerals except iron

Acid soil
Iron exposed to oxygen forms from oxide (bright red colour)

Rapid weathering and leaching cause a layer of iron oxides to build up. This is called laterisation.

Latosol soil profile

- These are soils of hot, humid regions in the tropics. *Examples:* India, Indonesia, Brazil.
- High rainfall has leached out most minerals except for iron and aluminium oxides.
- Iron oxides in the B horizons tint the soil a red colour, forming laterite.
- Chemical weathering is dominant and plant matter is broken down quickly.
- They are generally soils of a tropical region such as rainforest or monsoon forest.

Podzols

- These soils occur in the coniferous forest belt in northern latitudes.
- Pine needles form the ground cover beneath the forest canopy.
- Percolating rainwater leaches out surface minerals that are redeposited to form a hard pan, which creates waterlogging.
- They are acidic and need large amounts of lime and fertiliser to make them fertile.

Chernozems (Black earths)

- These are found in temperate grassland regions. *Examples:* the steppes of Russia and the Ukraine, the pampas of Argentina, the prairies of North America.
- Because rainfall is low, the A horizon is black owing to a high humus content and little leaching.

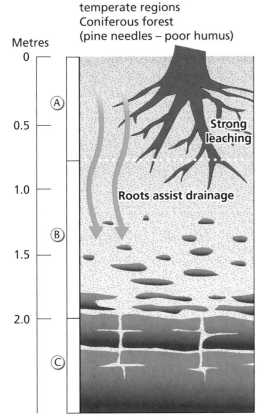

Podzol soil profile

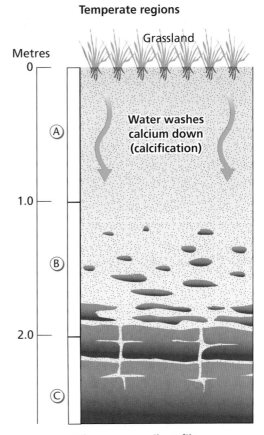

Chernozem soil profile

- Calcium deposits are deposited in the B horizon.
- They are neutral soils with a crumb structure and are very fertile.

Desert soils

- These occur in hot, dry regions of arid and semi-arid regions in temperate and tropical areas. *Examples:* the Atacama in Peru and Chile, and the Californian and Nevada deserts.
- Humus is limited, owing to the almost complete absence of vegetation.
- Intense sunshine creates salt deposits from evaporation of ground moisture. This process is called **salinisation**.

Intrazonal soils

Intrazonal soils are individual soils that develop within regions of zonal soils where local factors such as parent material or drainage may have a more dominant effect than climate.

Identify some plant characteristics in this photograph that help desert plants survive long periods of drought

Peat soils

- Peat soils are black and the surface material consists of partially decayed vegetation. The remaining soil consists of dead plant matter.
- They form in regions of cold that have persistent rainfall.
- They support only acid-loving plants such as rhododendron and heathers.

There are two types of peat soil in Ireland:

Blanket peat

- ○ Blanket peat covers hill and mountain tops inland and along the counties of the west coast.
- ○ Acid groundwater prevents decay of plant matter.
- ○ It is shallow: only about two metres deep.

Raised peat
- ○ Raised peat developed in shallow lakes.
- ○ These may be 10 metres or more in depth and have been exploited commercially.

Gley soils
- These form in waterlogged regions because of the presence of impermeable soils such as shales or clay.
- They have a blue-grey colour owing to lack of oxygen, and that prevents decay.
- They are found in the Cavan–Dundalk drumlin landscape, in Antrim–Derry coastal regions and in South Clare.

Rendzinas
- These form in limestone and chalk regions and their surface cover consists of grasses.
- The A horizon is black or dark brown. There is no B horizon.
- The surface soil sits directly on the bedrock.
- This kind of soil is suited to beef cattle rearing, as in the Burren or karst regions.

Terra rossas
- These are mature, limestone-based soils.
- Iron minerals in the soil have been oxidised, creating a red soil.
- Terra rossa soils are found in the Mezzogiorno in southern Italy and in the coffee-growing regions of Brazil.

Azonal soils
- Azonal soils are soils with an immature profile that have not had time to develop fully.
- The parent material may be weathered rock or debris that may have been transported from some other location by ice.
- Their location is not confined to any specific climatic zone.

Lithosols
- These are stony, shallow soils formed from the weathering of the bedrock.
- Erosion and sometimes mass movement may prevent the development of a soil profile.
- They are common on upland slopes.

Regosols
- These are derived from volcanic deposits, sand deposits or alluvial deposits.
- The A horizon is light in colour.
- There is no B horizon.
- The C horizon consists of silt or sand or a mixture of both.
- These soils form alluvial deposits on river floodplains, such as the Tigris–Euphrates rivers in Iraq and the Indus and Ganges flood plains in India and Pakistan.

Human interference with soil characteristics

Overcropping and overgrazing

Irish example: the Burren in Co. Clare (see page 278).

Case study: Causes of desertification in the Sahel

What is meant by desertification?

It refers to the reduction in vegetation cover, thereby exposing the soil to erosion by wind, rain or both, so making a region unable to provide for its natural wildlife or human populations.

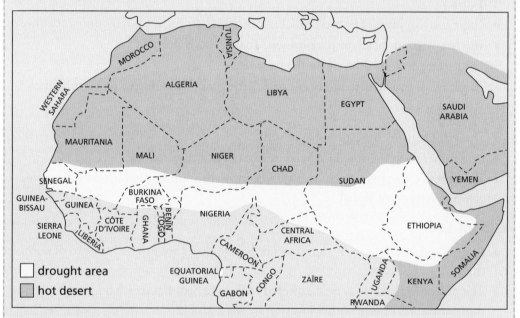

Drought areas of North Africa

Climate influence

- Rainfall has reduced by at least 30 per cent over the past 10 years.
- Rain has arrived late during the wet season, so affecting wildlife.
- There have been many years of drought with below-average rainfall over the past 40 years.
- Higher world temperatures are taking effect owing to global warming and increased evaporation levels.

Changing agricultural practices

- Cattle ownership indicated status or wealth, leading to increased herd numbers.
- Overgrazing was caused by increased cattle numbers in tropical grassland regions that bordered deserts or semi-desert areas.
- Increased water supply from wells led to local overgrazing and damage to the land by increased cattle numbers.

- Reduced nomadic tradition due to more intensive use of land led to overcropping and overgrazing. Land had no time to recover.
- Increased tillage for cash crops such as groundnuts on marginal land replaced grazing, so the fallow year practice was abandoned.
- Overcropping led to reduced yields and finally the soil became sterile.
- Reduced yields led to increased tillage area.
- Trees and bushes, such as acacia, were cut down for firewood. This led to increased wind effect and soil erosion.
- Lack of ground cover led to reduced evaporation and so less rainfall.

Soil conservation

- **Contour ploughing**: soil is ploughed across the slope rather than up and down the slope. Each drill ridge acts as a dam for down-slope water movement. Contour ploughing reduces erosion by 50 per cent.
- **Terracing** is best on very steep slopes that are used for tillage crops or vines.

Crop rotation

Some crops, such as nitrogen-fixing alfalfa grasses, replace the mineral content used by previous crops.

New farming methods

- **Strip-cropping** involves planting crops that mature at different times in widely spaced rows. Exposure of large regions of soil is prevented, so reducing the effects of wind erosion.
- Crops of different heights are also used for the same purpose.
- **Shelter belts**, such as rows of trees or shrubs, are planted to reduce wind speed.
- **New animal breeds** were introduced into the Sahel. These included smaller, better-quality herds that fattened more quickly or produced more milk.
- Goats and sheep were introduced to areas of poor scrub that would otherwise go unfarmed.

Questions 16, 2006; 16, 2007; 16, 17, 2008; 17, 2009.

32 Biomes

aims You need to study one major biome.

exam focus

Study **Temperate Deciduous Biome** (pages 270–272) **AND EITHER** Equatorial Forest Biome (pages 272–275) **OR** Desert Biome (275–277).

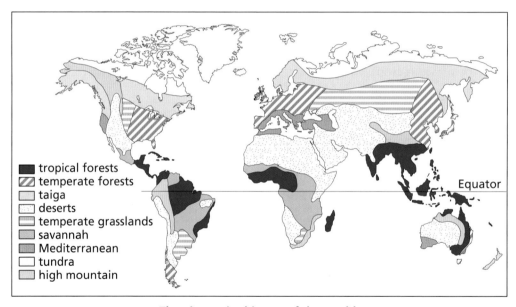

tropical forests
temperate forests
taiga
deserts
temperate grasslands
savannah
Mediterranean
tundra
high mountain

Equator

The nine major biomes of the world

Temperate deciduous biome in Europe

An Irish and European example: Brown earths – An Irish soil profile

- **Brown earths** are found in temperate regions of deciduous forest.
- Because there is little leaching there are no distinct horizons. However, the A horizon is a little darker than others.
- They have a crumb structure and are naturally very fertile.
- Many earthworms and living organisms are found in them.

Location

Found on the western side of continents, between 40° and 60° north and south of the Equator.

Climate – Influencing factors

- Close to mild, moist ocean conditions.
- Affected by warm, moist south-westerly winds.
- Average winter temperatures 4–6°C.
- Average summer temperatures 15–16°C.
- Moisture throughout the year, with a winter maximum of 1,000–1,500 mm.

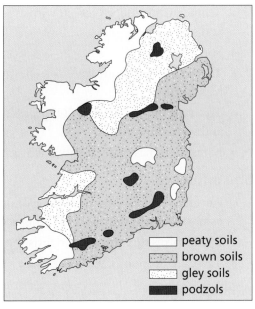

peaty soils
brown soils
gley soils
podzols

Ireland's most common soil types

Natural vegetation

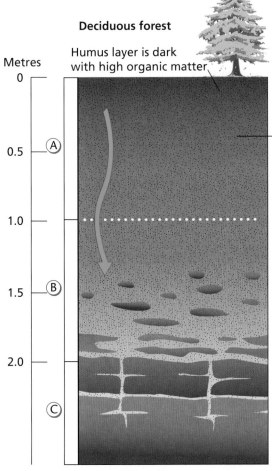

Deciduous forest

Humus layer is dark with high organic matter

Metres

(A) 0.5

1.0

(B) 1.5

2.0

(C)

Rich in mineral matter called **topsoil**. Many living organisms

- Soil is brown, well aerated
- Soil originally developed under deciduous forest cover (before agricultural practices) and influenced by **glacial deposits**

Brown earth profile

- Temperate deciduous forest, with ash, oak, elm, beech, chestnut, hazel, hawthorn and sycamore.
- Some layering.
- Tallest: oaks; second layer: ash, chestnut, elm and beech; third layer; hazel and hawthorn.
- Tree type influenced by soil type, as local soils vary depending on slope, bedrock and soil composition.
- Forest floor has many plants, such as ferns, mosses, brambles, orchids.

Soil influence

- Autumn leaf fall allows recycling of nutrients, humus is created by bacteria, and osmosis absorbs nutrients into the trees, creating new leaves.
- Earthworms mix this plant debris throughout the A horizon.
- These are deep soils, with some tree roots reaching and breaking up the bedrock.

Animal life

Grey and red squirrel, badger, fox, rodents, wild boar, wolf, rabbit, hare. Many of these have become extinct in some regions as a result of human interference.

Human interference

- Most woodland has been cut down to make way for agriculture.
- Grazing animals keeps landscape open (without trees).
- Oaks were cut down for large wooden galleons during colonisation.
- Farming has added many nutrients by means of artificial fertilisers.

Case study: Burren in Co. Clare

- Woodland cover was cut down for farming.
- Soil was tilled by early farmers and exposed to strong westerly winds.
- Soil was eroded, leaving bare, rocky, limestone landscape called karst.

Equatorial forest biome

SAMPLE EXAM QUESTION AND ANSWER

Question: Describe and explain the main characteristics of one biome that you have studied.   (80 marks; 2008, 2006)

Answer:

1. Climate

This region extends right across the globe between latitudes 5° north and south of the Equator, so it has an equatorial climate. The angle of the noonday sun varies only from 90 degrees, when the sun is directly overhead at the Equator, to

66 degrees, when it is directly over the Tropic of Cancer (on 21 June) or the Tropic of Capricorn (on 22 December). So sunlight hits the earth directly, not at an angle. Average temperature each month is about 27°C and the annual range is only 2°C. The temperature rarely gets higher than 35°C or drops below 24°C. This is due to consistent cloud cover that blankets the equatorial skies over the forest. In reality rainforests can feel much hotter than this due to the intense humidity of the region.

Relative humidity at ground level may often reach as much as 88 per cent. Transpiration from the trees generates high levels of water vapour and the high temperatures increase the ability of the air to hold this moisture. Rainfall amount varies as the sun travels from the Tropic of Cancer to the Tropic of Capricorn. This gives a slight dry-season effect at the edges of the forest zone. Rainfall totals vary but it is always in excess of 2500 mm in each of the forest zones across the globe. Parts of Sumatra gets 4,500 mm annually. Rain falls in short heavy downpours, with strong winds that often shake the canopy. The forest floor becomes temporarily flooded but quickly filters through the soil cover. The largest and most famous rainforest is in the Amazon Basin that includes parts of Ecuador, Venezuela, Peru, Bolivia and Brazil. Other regions include the Congo Basin, Indonesia and northern Australia.

2. Soil

The latosol is the zonal soil associated with tropical rainforests. Latosols are poor in nutrients due to leaching by the heavy rains over thousands of years. The soil has a red colour due the oxidation of iron compounds.

The rainforest has a very short nutrient cycle. Nutrients are mainly found in the living plants and the layers of the decomposing leaf litter on the surface (the O horizon). The high humidity and the various decomposers such as insects, bacteria and fungi quickly convert this dead plant and animal life into humus. Plant roots absorb these nutrients the moment they are released. Ninety-nine per cent of nutrients are held in the root mats of the forest floor.

Only 5–8 per cent of sunlight reaches the forest floor, so the soil and undergrowth are deprived of this source of energy.

The chemical weathering of rainforest soil creates many important mineral deposits through a process called 'secondary enrichment'. This occurs because chemical weathering and percolating water concentrate the small amounts of metals that are widely scattered throughout the soils into economically valuable concentrations.

For example, Bauxite, the principal ore from which aluminium is made, is formed due to leaching. When aluminium-rich soils are subjected to the intense and prolonged weathering of the tropics, most of the common elements, including calcium, sodium and silicon, are removed by leaching. Because aluminium is extremely insoluble, it becomes concentrated at the surface as bauxite.

Secondary enrichment of iron ore may also occur when soluble iron compounds are washed down through leaching and deposited in lower horizons to form a concentrate of iron ore, such as haematite.

3. Plant life (flora)

Identify the buttress roots on these emergers

There are four distinct layers of vegetation in a rainforest: the emergents; the canopy; the understorey; and the forest floor.

Emergers

The emergers are the tallest trees (up to 80 metres high). They are spaced far apart with umbrella-shaped branches that stand well above the canopy. Because these trees are exposed to drying winds, they tend to have small, pointed leaves. These giant trees have straight smooth trunks with few branches. Their root system is very shallow but they have large buttress roots that spread out as much as nine metres to support such tall trees in the wet soils. Many of these trees are tropical hardwoods, such as teak.

The canopy

The canopy is the main forest cover of tree tops that form a layer below the emergers. The canopy is found about 20–40 metres above the ground. There may be an upper and lower canopy in some regions. Some plants of the canopy include thick lianas and epiphytes, like mosses, lichens and flowering orchids. Plants such as the orchids get their inorganic nutrients from the air and from rainfall and they live perched on branch joints. Unlike plants in the temperate deciduous biome, some of these plants have drip tips to shed water quickly. Some waxy jug-like leaves allow plants to gather as much water as possible during downpours and then discard it before it stagnates and breeds bacteria.

Some leaves are able to turn with the sun so they always absorb the maximum amount of sunlight.

The understorey

The understorey is a dark environment that is under the canopy. Most of the understorey of a rainforest has so little light that plant growth is limited. There are short, leafy, mostly non-flowering shrubs, small trees, ferns and vines or lianas that have adapted to filtered light and poor soil.

The forest floor

The forest floor gets so little light that few plants grow here. Dense vegetation grows in clearings when large trees fall. Plants such as lianas cling to the tiny branches of young plants. As the trees grow so too do the lianas as they hang from forest branches for support.

Only the most vigorous plants in the clearings survive to reach the sunlight.

4. Fauna (animal life)

Camouflage is one very effective way in which animals adapt to their environment. One of the most effective ways to adapt and be safe is to look like a leaf. Moths and other insects may look like dead or living leaves and are difficult to see amid the surrounding foliage. The rainforest floor is littered with dead leaves: insects are abundant here and may be in danger from predators, so they adapt their camouflage to their surroundings. There are many varieties of stick insect that look like a twig. Tree frogs also use camouflage.

Animals also use colour to warn predators that they are poisonous. For many this is just a bluff but some, such as the poison arrow frog and some snakes, are poisonous. Bright colours generally indicate danger.

Tree trunk environment

There are many environments within rainforests and each environment has its own population of insects and animal life. For example, woodpeckers drill holes in dead tree trunks because the wood is soft and easy to penetrate. They use these holes to make their nests. Living trees are also used by some woodpeckers. Tree sap seeps from these tree-wounds and acts as an irritant to snakes that try to seek out the woodpeckers' nests. Other animals, such as some monkeys or birds, use these holes once they become unoccupied.

Some birds feed on insects going up a tree while other birds feed on them as they come down, depending on the location of insects in the bark.

Pollination

Plants use nectar in their flowers to attract insects to aid pollination. Other plants, such as kapok, have fluffy tops attached to their seeds for dispersal by the wind. Kapok is an emerger so it needs its seeds to be carried far away to ensure its survival.

Desert biome

A desert region is an area characterised by little or no rainfall, where vegetation is sparse or absent.

Small local areas may have lush vegetation if water is available close to the surface. Such areas are called **oases**.

Desert characteristics

- Deserts may be either hot or cold, with less than 250 mm of precipitation annually.
- Desert surfaces are generally boulders, gravels, bare rock or sand.
- All deserts have their own characteristic fauna and flora.
- Desert moisture is unpredictable in distribution and amount.

- Rainfall may occur in sudden downpours in localised areas, creating flash floods.
- Coastal mists may affect coastal deserts where there are cold currents offshore.
- Hot deserts lie between 15° and 30° north and south of the Equator.
- They are affected by the trade winds, which create high-pressure zones.
- Compression of the descending air causes it to heat and retain its moisture.
- Clear blue skies and sunny weather dominate.
- Some hot deserts result from the rain-shadow effect, for example the Atacama and the Kalahari. Here coastal mountains create rain on the windward side and are sufficiently high so that winds are dry as they descend on the rain-shadow side, creating drought.
- Temperate deserts lie between 30° and 40° north and south of the Equator.
- Some deserts are also affected by rain-shadow and cold ocean currents, for example the Patagonian Desert in Argentina.

Case study: North American deserts

- The North American deserts include four regions: the Chihuahua Desert, the Sonora Desert, the Mojave Desert and the Great Basin.
- They lie between the Rocky Mountains and the Sierra Nevada mountains.
- The Mojave, Sonora and Chihuahua are hot deserts.
- The Great Basin is colder because it is more elevated than the others.

Climatic characteristics

- All suffer extremely long drought periods.
- Localised summer downpours create flash floods.
- Temperature in winter is about 8°C, while summer temperatures average 30°C.
- Diurnal range can be as great as 30°C, owing to lack of cloud cover.

Soils

- Soils are aridsols.
- Soil texture varies from fine sand to gravel and stony.
- Some regions have deep soil deposits from continuous deposition of surface streams.
- Soils are poorly developed, owing to the absence of moisture for break-up of minerals and the lack of plant matter.
- Intense evaporation creates alkaline soils with calcium, sodium and gypsum minerals.
- Calcification is the dominant process.
- Salinisation is also common, creating salt deposits in saltpans.

Vegetation

- Some plants have adapted well to the short downpours. These are **ephemerals** that complete their life cycle in two to three weeks.

- Ephemerals open their seed pods during the downpours as a physical reaction to the water. They sprout quickly, flower, pollinate and die within a short time.
- Some plants, such as the giant saguaro, store water. It has the following characteristics:
  1. needle leaves to break the wind, creating a cooling effect for the plant
  2. vertical grooves to direct water to its base, where its roots absorb it quickly
  3. waxy bark to prevent evaporation.
- Cacti are common in American deserts.

Fauna

- Desert regions have few animals owing to the lack of water supply. Those that do live in these hot, dry regions have adapted to their surroundings.
- Nocturnal or early-morning animals include the rattlesnake and the elf owl.
- The tarantula, the desert tortoise and kangaroo rat burrow into the sand to avoid the hot sunshine.
- Some animals, such as the rabbit, are dormant during the hot summer.
- Reptiles produce uric acid instead of urine, so wasting little water.
- The roadrunner, a desert bird, runs instead of flying to reduce energy loss.

Questions 17, 2006; 18, 2007; 18, 2008.

33 How People's Activities have Altered Biomes

 aims You need to understand how people's activities have interfered with biomes.

Early settlement and the clearing of forest cover

- Farming, more than any other activity, has led to deforestation on a world scale.
- The knowledge of farming spread from the Middle East to Europe. It was first practised in the Middle East about 10,000 years ago.
- It reached Ireland about 6,000 years ago.
- It led to deforestation on a large scale in some regions when trees were cut down to create tillage and grow crops.

Deforestation in the Burren, Co. Clare

- The Burren had a gritty soil cover after glacial times about 10,000 years ago.
- Early farmers cut down the trees so they could till the crumbly soil.
- Over-exposure to coastal winds and rain led to erosion and loss of soil.
- Today most of the Burren is a barren, rocky landscape.

The felling of tropical forests

- Large regions of tropical forest have been cut down over the past four decades.
- In Brazil this deforestation was carried out for hardwood timber supplies, such as teak and mahogany.
- Large ranches were also created in the cleared forest land to supply fast food chains with meat.
- Soil erosion is common where deforestation has occurred.
- Plantation agriculture and wood demand in India have led to large loss of forest land.
- Native tribes lose their homeland and their way of life as they are forced from their lands.
- Big industrial projects such as hydroelectric dams lead to large-scale deforestation. Valleys are also flooded behind dams. *Example:* the Tucurui project in Brazil.

Intensive agricultural and industrial activities

- Most agricultural lowlands that are intensively farmed were once covered by deciduous woodland.
- Such regions include Western Europe and America. Most American houses are timber-framed. This means that large quantities of wood are needed for construction.
- California's redwoods were cleared by lumber companies and miners.
- Over 500 square kilometres of natural habitat are lost to development in California each year. This includes semi-desert land around Los Angeles.
- Las Vegas has become a large, sprawling, urban region that was built in a desert environment.

Questions 18, 2006; 16, 2008; 18, 2009.

Option 3: Culture and Identity

exam focus

You must write your answer in **paragraphs** or you may lose cohesion marks.

MARKING SCHEME

Choose three or four headings/aspects for your answer. The marking scheme will be as follows:

Number of aspects:

3 aspects — 27 + 27 + 26 marks

4 aspects — 20 marks each

Identifying heading/aspect — 4 marks

Discussion — 8 × SRPs *or* 6 × SRPs

Overall coherence — 7/6 marks graded or 4 marks graded

Select scheme according to number of headings/aspects discussed

Allow credit for up to 2 examples from SRPs.

34 Populations: Physical and Cultural Factors

aims You need to:
- learn examples of racial conflict
- understand the impact of migration on racial patterns.

Racial groups

- A person's race or racial group cannot be changed.
- Race is a biological inheritance.
- Race refers to physical characteristics such as skin colour, height, hair type, physique and shape of head.
- These characteristics are passed through genes from parents to offspring.

Ethnic groups

- **Ethnic** refers to a minority group with a collective self-identity within a larger host population, such as Italians or Irish in New York, or Chinese in Ireland.
- The Aborigines of Australia, who were cut off on the once-isolated island continent, are an ethnic group.
- The Kalahari Bush people, who were isolated in the Kalahari semi-desert region of southern Africa, are another such group.

Skin colour and race

- In the past, racial groups were classified by skin colour: white, yellow, red, brown and black.
- Scientists today believe that dark- and light-coloured skins developed because of humans' adaptation to their environments.
- Skin colour is a result of the presence of melanin-producing cells in our bodies.
- We all have the same number of melanin-producing cells.
- In dark-skinned people these cells produce 43 times more melanin per cell than in light-skinned people.

- Melanin is necessary to combat the effects of ultraviolet light by absorbing dangerous rays, and so it protects us against cancer.
- The greater the amount of sunlight, the greater the need for melanin to protect against skin cancer.
- Dark skin was also needed to protect against the effects of strong sunlight on the production of folic acid.
- Groups further away from the Equator needed some ultraviolet light to create vitamin E, so humans developed genes for creating light-coloured skin.
- Therefore different skin colours developed at different latitudes, so that people could live healthy lives in those places.

Race and genetic make-up

- Any person's race accounts for only 1.5 per cent of his or her genetic make-up.

There are five recognised ethnic or racial groups:

Caucasians

Europeans and people of European ancestry; brown-skinned people, such as Arabs and people of the Indian subcontinent.

Northern, Central and East Asians
Chinese, Inuit, Samis and American Indians (Amerindians).

Africans and black people of African descent (such as African-Americans).

Black Australian Aborigines

The Bush people of the Kalahari

The impact of Europe on world migration and racial patterns

The colonisation of the Americas

- Emigration to the Americas was a 'release valve' for many overpopulated European regions.
- The European-settled lands of North America, Australia and New Zealand, parts of South America and South Africa provided:
  1. cheap food supplies for Europe's growing population
  2. raw materials for its industries.

- The effects of European colonisation on the Native American people were catastrophic.
- The native people of what is now the USA declined from 5 million in 1500 to 60,000 in 1800.
- These native people were devastated by epidemics of infectious diseases such as smallpox and measles.
- Over 12 million Africans were transported to the Americas as slaves.

Multi-racial societies

Case study: France

- Like Great Britain, France is a former colonial power.
- About 14 million French citizens, nearly one-quarter of the total population, have at least one immigrant parent or grandparent.
- A large share of the post-war immigrants and their offspring come from former French colonies in North Africa, sub-Saharan Africa, and from countries in South-East Asia.

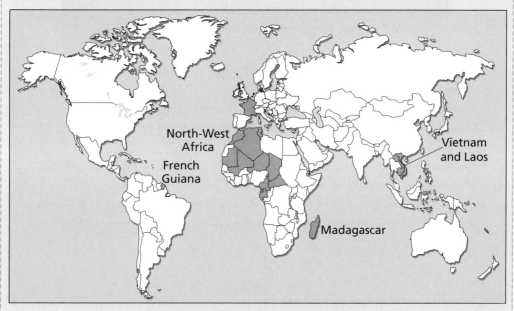

The extent of the former French Empire

- Immigrants also came from colonies in the Caribbean.
- This population is concentrated in the suburbs and urban centres such as Marseilles and Lyon.
- Most immigrants live in ghetto-like communities.
- Large past migrations and high birth rates among immigrants have made Islam the second-largest religion in France.
- Many immigrants, especially those from Algeria and Morocco, came to France as 'guest workers' in the 1960s and 1970s.

Racial mixing

Case study: Brazil

Brazil's soccer team show evidence of a varied ancestry

- Brazil has a population of 167 million people. About 80 million of them are people of black African descent.
- These are descendants of the slaves who were brought to Brazil by the Portuguese to work their sugar and cotton plantations along the north-east coast.
- Of the 80 million black people, about 67 million have combined European, African and Amerindian ancestries.
- The remainder, forming 55 per cent of the population, are mainly of European origin, the descendants of immigrants from Portugal, Italy, Germany and Eastern Europe.
- The Japanese population numbers about 1.3 million.
- Ethnic mixing is so great that hardly any group is unaffected.
- Only about 275,000 Amerindians survive. In the hunger for land and minerals, many have been forced from their forest homelands.
- Few black people are involved in politics and even fewer have positions of power within government, even though they form almost half of Brazil's population.

Case study: The United States of America

- America is a multi-racial society where racial mixing has been slow to occur.
- The African-American group is the only group to have involuntarily emigrated to the USA.
- Only 44 per cent of black people agree that race relations in the USA will eventually improve.
- Racial mixing has increased, especially among the young population. For example, 70 per cent of Italians born after 1970 have mixed ancestry from outside their ethnic group.
- Roughly 99 per cent of African-American women and 97 per cent of African-American men marry within their ethnic group.
- Many black people live in ghetto communities; and ghettos have come to symbolise the place of the poor within cities.
- Some people believe that with no work, no income and no property the only way to achieve a masculine identity is through crime and gang membership.

Racial conflict

Racial conflict in the United States

- The African-American group is the only ethnic group that emigrated to the United States involuntarily.
- Slavery was introduced into the southern states to create cheap labour for cotton and tobacco planters.
- At the end of World War II, Americans showed increasing concern over racial discrimination.
- In the 1950s, the emergence of the Civil Rights Movement resulted in a revival of Ku Klux Klan organisations. The most important of these was the White Knights of the Ku Klux Klan, led by Robert Shelton.
- In the South, especially in the states of Alabama and Mississippi, violence against blacks by whites was rarely fully investigated. Lynching was still used as a method of terrorising the local black population.
- A civil court action by a mother against the Klan over the lynching of her son was successful. She was awarded $7 million and the Klan had to sell all its assets to pay the fine.
- Most civil rights demonstrations stressed non-violence. But the demonstrations sometimes caused tension that resulted in violence.
- Martin Luther King, the black leader of the Civil Rights Movement, who was a Nobel Peace Prize winner, was assassinated.

Racial conflict in India

Racial conflict in India may be looked at under two headings:

1. the caste system
2. northern and southern Indians.

The caste system

The caste system is a form of racial discrimination

- The **caste system** usually refers to the groups of society into which the people of India are divided by religious customs.
- In general it means a **hereditary division** of any society into classes on the basis of **occupation, colour, wealth or religion**.
- India has four castes, the highest-ranking group being the **Brahmins**. People who do not belong to any of these four groups become outcasts or **untouchables**.
- With the introduction of British systems to India, the castes became **rigid social divisions**. No one could rise to a higher caste than the one into which they were born.
- India today has become more flexible in the customs of its caste system. Urban people are less strict about the system than rural people.
- In cities, different castes of people intermarry and mingle with each other.
- In rural areas there is still discrimination based on castes and against the untouchables.
- Most of the degrading jobs are still done by the Dalits or untouchables, while the Brahmins remain at the top of the hierarchy: many Brahmins are doctors, engineers and lawyers.

Northern and Southern Indians

- The people of India belong to all the major racial groups. However, **Caucasians make up 90 per cent of the population.**
- The British promoted religious, ethnic and cultural divisions among their colonized peoples to keep them under their control.
- The British promoted the idea that India is a land of two races – the lighter-skinned Aryans, in the northern half of the country; and the darker-skinned Dravidians, in the southern half.
- European thinkers of that time believed in a racial theory of mankind that was based on colour alone. They saw themselves as belonging to a superior 'white' or Caucasian race.

Questions 20, 2006; 21, 2007.

35 Language and Religion as Cultural Indicators

aims You need to know that language and religion are indicators of ethnic origin.

Language as a cultural indicator

- **Cultural regions** is the general term for areas where some portion of the population shares some degree of cultural identity.
- The culture's language is clearly evident in the place names of such regions, e.g. Gaeltacht.
- The choice of language on signs is another visible symbol of culture in the landscape.

The major language families

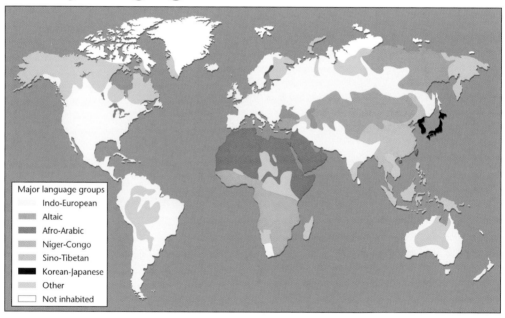

Major language groups
- Indo-European
- Altaic
- Afro-Arabic
- Niger-Congo
- Sino-Tibetan
- Korean-Japanese
- Other
- Not inhabited

The major languages of the world.

The Indo–European family

- About half the world's population speaks languages from this family.
- It began in the region now called Turkey; its speakers migrated to various regions and the language changed along the way.

The Sino–Tibetan family

- The second most widely spoken language, with over 1 billion speakers.
- Includes Chinese, Thai, Burmese and Tibetan.

Arabic–Semitic family

- Includes Arabic and Hebrew.
- Mostly spoken in north and north-east Africa, the Middle East and the Arabian peninsula.
- The spread of the Muslim faith across Africa brought Arabic to this region.

The Ural and Altaic family

Includes Finnish, Hungarian and Turkish, as well as the languages spoken in the Asian part of Russia.

Niger–Congo family

- This language family is also called Bantu.
- The region where these languages are spoken stretches from the Sudan in the north to South Africa in the south.
- It includes Swahili, which developed as a pidgin language from contact with Arabic traders along the east African coastline.

Japanese and Korean family

Limited to Japan, North Korea and South Korea.

Dravidian family

Spoken in southern India and Sri Lanka. Includes Tamil.

Gaeltacht regions

In 1925 Gaeltacht regions in Ireland were divided into two categories:
- **Fior Gaeltacht** regions, where 80 per cent or more of the population spoke Irish
- **Breac Gaeltacht** regions, where 25–79 per cent of the population spoke Irish.

At this time Gaeltacht regions covered substantial areas of the West. Today, however, Gaeltacht regions have reduced in size and number and are confined to scattered regions along the west and south coasts. They have a total population of about 86,000 people.

Initiatives for the survival of the Irish language

- Festivals that promote the language through art exhibitions and music.
- An audio-visual industry that promotes Irish culture within the Gaeltacht and throughout Ireland. These influences include:
  - Raidió na Gaeltachta
  - the TV station TG4
  - local radio stations
  - Irish-language schools (na Gaelscoileanna)
  - summer colleges in the Gaeltacht areas.

Supports for minority languages

- Article 22 of the European Charter of Fundamental Rights states that the EU respects cultural, religious and linguistic diversity.
- The **European Bureau of Lesser-used Languages (EBLUL)** works on behalf of those in the EU who speak minority languages. It creates and supports policies that support these languages.
- The EU gives financial aid to EBLUL.
- International conferences are held to identify ways to improve the situations of these minority languages. These are organised by the **Foundation for Endangered Languages (FEL)**.

Religion as a cultural indicator

Religion creates landscapes by the construction of religious buildings: there are churches in Christian regions, mosques with their minaret towers are found in Muslim areas, there are no bars in Muslim areas.

Personal indicators:

- Sikh men wear turbans and have long beards
- Muslim women wear chadors
- there are differing attitudes, for example towards women, to birth control, to materialism.

The world's major religions

Judaism

- There are only about 14 million Jewish people in the world.
- The religion's origins are traced back to Abraham, who migrated from Mesopotamia, now called Iraq, to Palestine with his followers.
- Isaac, who was Abraham's true heir, became the ancestor of the Israelite people.

Christianity

- Christianity is the largest religious group: over 33 per cent of the world's population are Christians.
- Christianity has its origins in Judaism.
- Christians believe that Jesus Christ was the messiah prophesied in the Old Testament.
- Christianity spread rapidly through the work of St Paul and other missionaries.
- The Romans persecuted the Christians for many years until the Emperor Constantine granted them freedom of religion.
- The Edict of Milan in AD 313 granted religious freedom to Christians in the Roman Empire.
- The rulers of Spain and Portugal were Christian and were they helped the Christian faith spread to Latin America.
- The British and French, also colonial powers, spread Christianity to the USA, Canada and Australia.

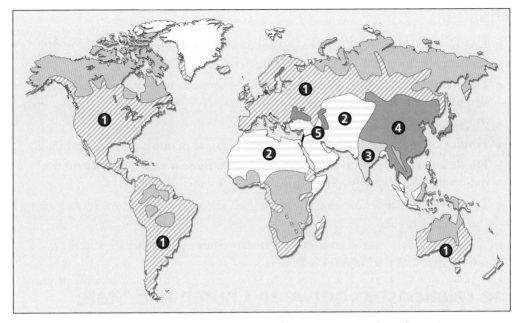

Identify the main religions in each of the regions numbered 1 to 5

- The Jesuits carried Christianity to China.
- Christianity had spread throughout Russia before the Russian Revolution.

Islam

Muslims always face Mecca during prayer

- Islam is the name given to the religion preached by the Prophet Mohammed in the seventh century.
- Mohammed was an Arab who was born in Mecca in about AD 570.
- He preached that there was only one god, Allah.
- Those who believe in Islam are called Muslims.
- Islam has its origins in Judaism and Christianity.
- Mohammed believed that Christ was a prophet of Islam.

Hinduism

- Hinduism is mostly confined to the Indian subcontinent and South-East Asia.
- It is not promoted through missionary activities.
- Hinduism traces its origin to tribes of Indo-European migrants who brought their language, Indo-European, with them.
- The sacred texts of Hinduism are the Vedas.
- Hindus are monotheists, which means they believe in one high god, Brahman.
- Hinduism is divided into three sects, each with its own view of the nature and name of the high god: Vishnu, Shiva or Shakti.
- Educated Hindus believe that the three gods are merely different ways of looking at the same high god.
- The Ganges is the sacred river of the Hindus. They believe that its waters are immaculate and nothing can pollute it.

The relationship between Church and State

The Irish Constitution

The Irish Constitution was introduced in 1937. It:

- recognised the special position of the Catholic Church in Ireland
- guaranteed freedom of conscience and the free profession and practice of all religions.

The power of the Catholic Church was used to influence government decisions such as the withdrawal of the 'Mother and Child' scheme.

Case study: Northern Ireland

- Sixty-two per cent of Church of Ireland members and almost all Presbyterians lived in the same nine Ulster counties.
- Political control was predominantly in the hands of Presbyterians.
- The Plantation of Ulster gave rise to the large Presbyterian population and the spread of Calvinism.
- The Orange Order represented the wealthy landowners, industrialists and the Presbyterian community.
- Social segregation of Catholic communities from Protestant communities led to ghettos in city regions.
- Gerrymandering was common. This was the arrangement of voting so that only those who held property were entitled to vote for local councils, and those who had many properties had many votes.
- There was widespread corruption and discrimination against Catholics.
- Civil rights marches were organised by the Catholic communities to demand equal treatment with Protestants.

Religious conflict

Case study: Religious conflict in Northern Ireland

Discrimination in Northern Ireland caused conflict between Catholics and Protestants during the Troubles

- Between 1966 and 2000, over 3,600 people were killed and 36,000 wounded as the conflict spread into mainland Britain and the Republic of Ireland.
- This period is known as 'The Troubles'.
- Since 1997, a ceasefire has held among the main paramilitary groups, such as the IRA, the UDA and the UFF.
- The **Good Friday Agreement** was signed on 10 April 1998.
- The Former US Senator, George Mitchell, was chairman of the all-party talks that led to the agreement.
- Tension has existed between the two faiths since the reign of **Henry VIII** (1509–47), when the Protestant faith was introduced to Ireland.
- The **Treaty of 1921** recognised this religious division by dividing the country into the predominantly Protestant Northern Ireland and the predominantly Catholic Republic of Ireland.
- The Good Friday Agreement created a 108-member assembly and a 14-member executive body in which both Catholic and Protestant members sit together in government.

Questions 19, 2006; 19, 2007; 19, 21, 2008; 19, 20, 21, 2009.

36 Nationality and Nation States

key point

NATIONALITY

Nation state refers to a country that occupies a specific area of land, and this area is occupied by a national group who share a common culture.

The concept of nation state combines three elements:

- **nation** (or ethnicity)
- **state**: the type of government or regime in power
- **territory**: the area defined on the ground that is controlled by the state.

Nations

- A nation is a group of people who feel bound together through personal ties and who possess a unity and solidarity that has grown by:
  - following a common way of life
  - sharing common experiences
  - possessing common cultural traits
  - inheriting a common tradition.
- **Nationalism** is the cause through which such groups claim their right to be a sovereign power within a particular area of land.
- Nations rarely consist of just one ethnic group.
- The factors that create and maintain national feeling include:
  - ethnic group or race
  - language
  - religion
  - a common enemy.
- A state boundary sometimes coincides with a physical natural barrier, such as a mountain range (e.g. the Pyrenees) or a river (e.g. the Rhine between France and Germany).
- A **frontier** is a zone or area which separates one ethnic group or nation from another, for example the border between Northern Ireland and the Irish Republic.

Everyday expressions of Irish culture and identity

Drama

There are many plays based on Irish culture and folklore.
The Playboy of the Western World and *The Field* are just two of many such Irish dramas that have been performed in the Abbey Theatre in Dublin and at other venues throughout the country.

Sport

- The Gaelic Athletic Association has promoted Gaelic games and has the biggest membership of all sports organisations in Ireland.
- Every parish has its own GAA club.
- Its most important events are the two All-Ireland Finals that are held in September each year.

Music and dance

- Traditional Irish music and dance are popular expressions of Irish culture.
- Feis Ceoil competitions are held regularly.
- The designs on female costumes for Irish dancing are based on Celtic patterns.

Festivals

- St Patrick's Day parades are held on 17 March every year in all our major towns. The largest parade is held in New York, where a large population of Irish people and people of Irish descent live.
- The Twelfth of July festival celebrates the identity of the Unionist community in Northern Ireland.
- Many small towns have special events that celebrate other interests of Irish people, such as the Wexford Opera and Arts Festival.

Summer schools

Summer schools promote learning and interaction among students, poets, writers, politicians and university lecturers in an informal setting.

Festivals and sports in Europe

- The 'Running of the Bulls' is an annual event in Pamplona, in the Basque region of Spain.
- The Munich Beer and Music festival is the largest festival in the world – over 6 million visitors visit each year.
- Ice-skating and skiing are popular sports in snow-covered upland regions such as the French, Austrian and Swiss Alps, and include cross-country skiing, especially in Scandinavia.
- The Tour de France is the most famous of all French sporting events.

Nationality and nation states: Issues relating to physical and political boundaries

Water supplies

- The probability of conflicts over water supplies is great, especially in times of water shortages.
- The rivers that flow through some nations do not rise in those nations. For example, the river Indus in Pakistan rises in India. India takes some water from the river before it flows into Pakistan. If too much is taken, less flows through Pakistan, much of which is desert and relies heavily on this source for its water supply.

Offshore boundaries

- The water, the seabed and their resources – such as oil and gas – within **200 nautical miles** of a country's seashore belong to that country.
- This area is called the country's **Exclusive Economic Zone**.
- Territorial seas extend up to **12 nautical miles** offshore. States must allow the innocent passage of foreign ships through these waters.
- Where states adjoin each other, lines halfway between the nearest shorelines of each state must be decided.

Political boundaries

The political boundaries of a state define its ability to enforce its laws.

Political boundaries and ethnic divisions

Political boundaries often divide an individual ethnic group into two or more divisions.

- The **Basque region** is divided into two parts. The larger part is in Spain; the smaller part lies in France. They are separated by the Pyrenees mountain range that forms the boundary between France and Spain.
- The border area separates the nationalist people in Northern Ireland from their southern cultural neighbours in the Republic of Ireland.

Cultural groups within nation states

Basques in France and Spain see pages 140–142.

Nationalists in Northern Ireland

- People who live in Northern Ireland and wish to be part of a united Ireland are called nationalists.
- Since partition in 1921, nationalists have lived under British rule and have suffered discrimination.
- Nationalists are Irish in their traditions and customs and most are Catholic.

- Nationalist feelings developed as a consequence of the British occupation of the island of Ireland and the oppressive treatment of the Catholic minority for over 70 years.
- The separation by fear of Protestant and Catholic communities has led to the development of ghettos in Derry and Belfast.
- Demands for civil rights and equal treatment with Protestant citizens led to civil rights marches in the 1960s and 1970s. Thirteen civilians were shot dead by the British forces during a civil rights march on 'Bloody Sunday' in January 1972.
- A minority of extreme nationalists support the IRA, an illegal paramilitary organisation.

The IRA and the British Government

- As a consequence of Bloody Sunday the IRA intensified its campaign of violence in British cities and army barracks.
- Internment without trial of IRA sympathisers intensified the campaign further.
- Ten IRA prisoners died in prison to highlight their claim for political rather than criminal status.
- Efforts by SDLP leader John Hume and Sinn Féin leader Gerry Adams led to a ceasefire that continues to this day.

Cultural groups without nationality

Basques in France and Spain

See pages 140–142.

OR

Sikhs in India

- The Sikhs form a cultural group that belongs to a religion founded by **Guru Nanak** about 500 years ago.
- Guru Nanak tried to unite Muslims and Hindus of all castes into a single faith.
- Most people in the Punjab region are Sikhs and followers of Guru Nanak.
- Their holiest shrine is the **Golden Temple in Amritsar.**
- Many Sikhs earned positions of trust in the defence forces during British colonial rule. This gave them a sense of middle-class status when independence came in 1947.
- All Sikhs wear five symbols, called the K symbols: Kesh, Kangha, Karra, Kachha, Kirpaan.
- Sikh male adults wear a dastar, or turban, and have long beards. Sikh women cover their heads with a long scarf, called a chunni.
- Sikhs who follow all these traditions are called Khalsa. People who follow only some of these conditions are called Sahajdharis.

- This symbol of distinct identity, defined by dress code, is called bana.
- Many Sikhs seek full independence from India.
- To satisfy some of their demands the Indian government made the Punjab a separate, Panjabi-speaking state where the Sikhs are the majority rulers.
- Many Sikhs want full independence, in a state they would call Khalistan.

SAMPLE EXAM QUESTION AND ANSWER

Question:

Conflicts exist between political structures and cultural groups. Discuss this statement with reference to examples you have studied. (2009)

Marking scheme:

Number of aspects:

3 aspects − 27 + 27 + 26 marks

4 aspects − 20 marks each

Identifying aspect − 4 marks

Examination − 8 × SRPs or 6 × SRPs

Overall coherence − 7/6 marks graded or 4 marks graded
Select scheme according to number of aspects discussed
Allow credit for up to 2 examples from SRPs (different examples and in different aspects).

If you use three headings you must give eight SRPs.

If you use four headings you need to give six SRPs.

ALWAYS use three or four headings.

For example, you could write about: the political–religious divide in India (see page 152); nationalists in Northern Ireland (see pages 294–295); and the Basque conflict with the Spanish government (see pages 139–141).

Questions 21, 2006; 20, 2007; 20, 2008; 19, 20, 2009.